EMBEDDING FORMATIVE ASSESSMENT:

Practical Techniques for K–12 Classrooms

DYLAN WILIAM
SIOBHÁN LEAHY

Learning Sciences International

1400 Centrepark Blvd, Suite 1000
West Palm Beach, FL 33401
717-845-6300

email: pub@learningsciences.com
learningsciences.com

Printed in the United States of America

20 19 18 17 16 15   3 4 5

Publisher's Cataloging-in-Publication Data
Wiliam, Dylan.
    Embedding formative assessment / Dylan Wiliam [and] Siobhán Leahy.
      pages   cm
    ISBN: 978-1-941112-29-8 (pbk.)
    1. Effective teaching—Handbooks, manuals, etc.   2. Educational tests and measurements.
3. Academic achievement.   I. Leahy, Siobhán.   II. Title.
LB1025.3.W47 2015
    371'.26—dc23

                                                    [2014957216]

EMBEDDING FORMATIVE ASSESSMENT

For our mothers, Iona and Heather

Table of Contents

Chapter 4
Strategy 2: Engineering Effective Discussion, Tasks, and Activities That Elicit Evidence of Learning

Chapter 5
Strategy 3: Providing Feedback That Moves Learning Forward

Chapter 6
Strategy 4: Activating Students as Learning Resources for One Another

Techniques: Tips, Cautions, and Enhancements

Acknowledgments

W. James Popham
Emeritus Professor
University of California, Los Angeles

Susan M. Brookhart
Consultant, Brookhart Enterprises LLC
Helena, Montana

Damian Cooper
Education Consultant
Mississauga, Canada

Francis (Skip) Fennell
Professor of Education & Graduate and Professional Studies
Project Director, Elementary Mathematics Specialists and Teacher Leaders Project
McDaniel College, Westminster, Maryland

Margaret Heritage
Senior Scientist
WestEd
San Francisco, California

Beth D. Sattes
Educational Consultant, Enthused Learning
Charleston, West Virginia

Jackie A. Walsh
Education Consultant and Author
Montgomery, Alabama

About the Authors

Dylan Wiliam, PhD, is a leading authority on the use of assessment to improve education. He has helped successfully implement classroom formative assessment in thousands of schools all over the world, including the United States, Canada, Singapore, Sweden, Australia, and the United Kingdom. A two-part BBC series, *The Classroom Experiment*, tracked Dr. Wiliam's work at one British middle school, showing how formative assessment strategies empower students, significantly increase engagement, and shift classroom responsibility from teachers to their students so that students become agents of and collaborators in their own learning.

Dylan Wiliam is a professor emeritus of educational assessment at University College London. After a first degree in mathematics and physics, and one year teaching in a private school, he taught in urban schools for seven years, during which time he earned further degrees in mathematics and mathematics education.

From 1996 to 2001, Wiliam was the dean and head of the School of Education at King's College London, and from 2001 to 2003, he served as assistant principal of the College. In 2003, he moved to the United States as senior research director at the Educational Testing Service in Princeton, New Jersey. In 2006, he returned to the United Kingdom as deputy director (provost) of the Institute of Education, University of London. In 2010, he stepped down as deputy director to spend more time on research and teaching.

Over the past fifteen years, Wiliam's work has focused on the profound impacts of embedding classroom formative assessment on student learning. In 1998 he coauthored, with Paul Black, a major review of the research evidence on formative assessment, together with a guide to the research for policy makers and practitioners, entitled *Inside the Black Box*. This booklet and subsequent booklets on formative assessment for practical application in the classroom and to individual subject areas are available from LSI. He is the author of *Embedded Formative Assessment* and coauthor, with Siobhán Leahy, of the *Embedding Formative Assessment Professional Development Pack* (now available in North America). Dr. Wiliam's *Leadership for Teacher Learning* is also forthcoming from Learning Sciences International in summer 2015.

 *Siobhán Leahy, MS,* was a principal of three secondary schools for seventeen years. She has extensive practical experience in using teacher learning communities to embed classroom formative assessment and has worked with educators in the United States, the United Kingdom, and Australia on how to support teachers in developing their classroom practice. She is coauthor and developer, with Dylan Wiliam, of the *Embedding Formative Assessment Professional Development Pack.* She received her master of science from South Bank University, London, and her bachelor of science in management sciences from the University of Warwick, in the United Kingdom.

Introduction

We wrote this handbook to support individual teachers who want to improve their classroom practice by using formative assessment techniques. Previously we had designed a pack for schools to support their teachers by introducing formative assessment through *teacher learning communities* (two years of monthly meetings), but we realized that there must be many teachers who would like to develop their practice on their own or with a small group of colleagues. This book is for you.

Embedded Formative Assessment, published by Solution Tree in 2011, summarizes several strands of research evidence that show classroom formative assessment is a powerful lever for changing practice. Indeed, as far as we know right now, there is nothing else that has a greater effect. Although *Embedded Formative Assessment* contains a number of practical classroom-tested techniques for implementing formative assessment, much of the book deals with an analysis of research studies on feedback and other aspects of formative assessment, in particular exploring what the research does—and, just as importantly, does not—show. In other words, *Embedded Formative Assessment* is concerned with making the case for formative assessment—both in terms of the "why" and the "what"—as well as providing suggestions for how to get started.

This book is more focused on the practicalities of implementing, and sustaining, the development of formative assessment in classrooms. You may have read *Embedded Formative Assessment* and would like a few more ideas about practical techniques that you can use in your classroom to develop your practice of formative assessment. On the other hand, you may not have read *Embedded Formative Assessment* but are convinced by the research on formative assessment, and just want to "cut to the chase." If you need a review of formative assessment, there is a summary in this book.

Another difference is that in *Embedded Formative Assessment* the practical techniques are presented in a list at the end of each chapter, with no attempt to relate the techniques to each other. Here, we try to group similar techniques together, drawing out their similarities, which should make it easier for you to see how to modify and adapt them for your classroom.

As well as providing practical ideas for classroom formative assessment, this book makes suggestions for how you can work with others to gain support for the difficult work of changing practice. If you have a group of teachers already keen to work together on these ideas, we suggest that you use the *Embedding Formative Assessment Professional Development Pack* (Wiliam & Leahy, 2014), which provides everything a building needs for two years of professional development focused on classroom formative assessment, with teachers working collaboratively in teacher learning communities. However, if you are on your own, or there are only two or three others who want to work on these ideas in your school, this book provides some practical ideas for how you can get the best support from your colleagues. We have placed this discussion of your own professional learning before the chapters on the five key strategies of formative assessment because it is valuable to think about the challenges involved in changing your classroom practice before you decide which specific techniques you will use.

We hope that this book gives you the structure to take small steps, engage your students in their own learning, and increase their achievement. You might find it useful to use highlighters or page flags/self-adhesive notes to traffic light the techniques as you read about them. For example, use green for "I already use this technique," yellow/orange for "I will try to use this technique," and pink for "I will not use this technique." We encourage you to write all over this book in whatever way will be of most use to you. We also provide a sample letter to parents that you might want to send home (with an administrator's approval) to let parents know when you are changing your classroom practice.

Before you start you might want to complete a sheet with the formative assessment techniques you already use in your classroom (provided at the end of this introduction), and also ask your students to complete the **student reflections on learning survey** and/or the **student feedback to teacher survey** (both at the end of this book) so that you have a baseline to compare your classroom practices in, say, six months' time.

At several points in the book, we include quotations from students who participated in a reality TV show entitled *The Classroom Experiment*. This was the result of a project in which Dylan persuaded some seventh-grade teachers to try out a few of the techniques we describe in the book. A TV crew followed the students around every day for fifteen weeks, and the resulting 120 hours of video were edited down to two one-hour episodes shown on consecutive evenings during prime time on network TV in the United Kingdom (Barry & Wiliam, 2010; Thomas & Wiliam, 2010). While a venture like this would not qualify as formal research, we think that the voices of the students make such important points about their learning that they are worth including.

This book contains the following:

- An introduction to the five strategies of formative assessment, for those who either have not read Dylan's book or want to remind themselves about this.
- A section on the professional learning that teachers need in order to increase learning outcomes for students.

- Each of the five strategies, containing research background, techniques, and other suggestions, presented as individual chapters:
    - Strategy 1: Clarifying, sharing, and understanding learning intentions
    - Strategy 2: Engineering effective discussions, tasks, and activities that elicit evidence of learning
    - Strategy 3: Providing feedback that moves learners forward
    - Strategy 4: Activating students as learning resources for one another
    - Strategy 5: Activating students as owners of their own learning
- Consistent end-of-chapter structure:
    - A recap
    - A reflection checklist
    - An action planning form
    - A peer observation form
- Reproducibles you might want to use more than once:
    - Reflection checklist for each of the five strategies
    - Action planning form
    - Peer observation form
    - Student survey
    - Student feedback to teacher survey
    - Learning log
    - Student reflections on learning survey
    - Example of a letter to parents
- Conclusion
- Appendix on effect sizes
- References

We advise you to note here the techniques that you regularly use. You can then compare this with the techniques that you are regularly using once you have read this book and trialed many of the techniques.

THE TECHNIQUES I REGULARLY USE

Clarifying, sharing, and understanding learning intentions and success criteria:

Engineering effective discussion, tasks, and activities that elicit evidence of learning:

Providing feedback that moves learning forward:

Activating students as learning resources for one another:

Activating students as owners of their own learning:

Other techniques:

Chapter 1

WHY FORMATIVE ASSESSMENT SHOULD BE A PRIORITY FOR EVERY TEACHER

The term *formative assessment* has been around for almost fifty years, but as yet, there is little consensus as to what it means. Some people suggest using *assessment for learning* instead (Broadfoot et al., 1999), but that merely moves the burden of definition—a little like stamping on a bulge in a carpet only to find that it reappears somewhere else. Others have tried to make sure that *formative assessment* is used only to describe educational practices of which they approve—essentially trying to make *formative assessment* synonymous with *good assessment*.

We think that particular boat has sailed. People do, and will continue to, use the term formative assessment in whatever way suits them. Those who want to sell tests may well describe their tests as formative assessments, and those who advocate regular monitoring of student progress through common assessments will describe these assessments as formative. That is why we think there is little value in trying to define formative assessment in a restrictive way that includes a usage with which people may disagree. People aren't going to change the way they use terms because others disagree with them.

What we do think is valuable, however, is to understand the differences in the way that people use the term formative assessment so that we stop worrying about whether an assessment is formative and instead think about whether it will help our students learn more.

That said, there is one issue we think should not be a matter of debate, and that is whether formative assessment is a process or a "thing." Many people talk about formative assessment in the plural (i.e., formative assessments), and we think that this doesn't make any sense, because the same assessment can be used formatively or summatively. For example, a teacher sets some practice tests for a class preparing for a state test. If the teacher scores the test, it provides information about which students have learned the material being tested and which have not. If all that happens is the scores get recorded in a grade book, the test is functioning summatively.

That the test is serving only a summative function is not necessarily a bad thing. There is now a substantial body of research that shows regular testing increases student achievement by improving students' abilities to retrieve things from memory (P. C. Brown, Roediger, & McDaniel, 2014) and reducing anxiety (see, for example, Agarwal, D'Antonio, Roediger, McDermott, & McDaniel, 2014).

If the teacher stopped there, while the activity would be valuable, we do not think it would make sense to call this process formative. Students would learn more as a result of the practice testing, but the results of the assessment would not "form" the future direction of their learning (indeed, the benefits of practice testing occur even if the test is never graded).

However, the test scores might also indicate to the teacher which students need additional support, allowing her to help the students who need it most. By helping the teacher make a smarter decision about the allocation of her time, the test results would form the direction of the students' learning. Even better, if the teacher were able to see that the errors a student made on the test indicated a specific misunderstanding, the assessment might help the teacher provide more specific feedback to the student. For example, the teacher might notice that a student doing multi-digit subtractions consistently subtracted the smaller digit from the larger, irrespective of whether it was in the minuend (the number being subtracted from) or the subtrahend (the number being subtracted):

$$
\begin{array}{r}
9\ \ 2\ \ 1 \\
-\ 5\ \ 7\ \ 3 \\
\hline
4\ \ 5\ \ 2
\end{array}
$$

This would give the teacher a clear plan of action about what to suggest to the student in order for him to improve his work. In other words, the same assessment can serve both a summative purpose (telling the teacher how good the student is at arithmetic) and formative one (telling the teacher what to do next).

This is why we think that it does not make sense to talk about formative assessment in the plural. Any assessment can function formatively or summatively. Some assessments are better suited to serve a formative function, and others are better suited to serve a summative function, but the important point is that the formative/summative distinction makes most sense when it is applied to the evidence an assessment generates, and the use to which it is put, rather than the assessment itself.

As noted earlier, there are many different approaches to defining formative assessment and assessment for learning (for a reasonably comprehensive review, see Wiliam, 2011b). However, there appear to be four main points of difference in the various definitions that various authors propose:

1. The amount of time that elapses between the collection of the evidence and the impact on instruction
2. Whether it is essential that the students from whom evidence was elicited are beneficiaries of the process

3.   Whether students have to be actively engaged in the process

4.   Whether the assessment has to change the intended instructional activities

We discuss each of these briefly in turn here:

1. *Time between evidence collection and use.* Perhaps the most common approach to formative assessment in US schools involves the use of what are sometimes called *common formative assessments* [sic]. The idea is that teachers meet to construct or select assessments that faithfully represent the learning intentions they have adopted for their students, and the assessments are then administered to all the students in a particular grade in the building, and, sometimes, across the whole district. Once the assessments are scored, teachers meet to review their students' performance, check on any students who are not making the expected progress, and decide what steps to take to ensure that all students are making the necessary progress. This process does lead to increased student achievement (Gallimore, Ermeling, Saunders, & Goldenberg, 2009; Saunders, Goldenberg, & Gallimore, 2009), but some authors argue that the length of time between evidence collection and action being taken is far too long.

2. *Do the assessed students benefit?* Some authors argue that to be formative, the students from whom assessment evidence was collected have to be beneficiaries of the process. In other words, if you learn something teaching a period one class that you use to improve the teaching of the same lesson to a period two class, authors would not regard that as formative assessment, because the students from whom the data were collected (the period one class) are not direct beneficiaries of the process.

3. *Do students have to be actively engaged in the process?* Many teachers ask students to complete an "exit pass" toward the end of a lesson, in which the students are asked to respond to a question on a three-by-five-inch index card and hand them in to the teacher as they leave the classroom at the end of the lesson. Some teachers insist that students write their names on the reverse of the exit passes so that the teacher can provide feedback (although it seems to us that if the teacher is going to provide individual feedback on the work, the students may as well have written their responses in a notebook). Other teachers do not require students to write their names on the back of the exit passes, because the focus is on the learning of the whole class. The reason the teacher asks for the exit passes is to help her make a decision about the learning of the students as a group and decide where to begin the next lesson. For some teachers, the fact that students do not get any personal, individual feedback is a problem. For others, the fact that the teacher used and elicited evidence of student achievement to improve instruction is enough. We discuss the use of exit passes in more detail in Chapter 4.

4. *Does the evidence have to change the planned instruction?* Many authors argue that the essence of formative assessment is that the evidence collected must somehow improve the instruction, but there are occasions where the evidence collected does

not change the instruction but merely confirms that the teacher's intended course of action was appropriate. For example, if the exit pass responses confirm that all the students understood the content of the lesson, the teacher would move on. The decision to move on is now based on evidence about the students' understanding rather than a hunch, or students self-reporting that they understood—for example, by showing "thumbs up."

We could fill the rest of this book with a discussion of the relative merits of the different views about what is and what is not formative assessment, but it seems to us that it would not be particularly fruitful. People would still disagree and continue to "talk past" each other by using the term formative assessment in different ways. For this reason, we believe that it is best to cut through all the debate and accept that people will continue to use the term in whatever way suits them, and adopt an inclusive rather than exclusive definition. To this end, we think it is appropriate to adopt the inclusive definition of formative assessment Black and Wiliam (2009) propose, in which they define assessment as being formative:

> to the extent that evidence about student achievement is elicited, interpreted, and used by teachers, learners, or their peers, to make decisions about the next steps in instruction that are likely to be better, or better founded, than the decisions they would have taken in the absence of the evidence that was elicited. (p. 9)

Black and Wiliam draw out a number of consequences of this definition:

1. Anyone—teacher, learner, or peer—can be the agent of formative assessment.

2. The focus of the definition is on decisions. Rather than a focus on data-driven decision making, the emphasis is on decision-driven data collection. This is important because a focus on data-driven decision making emphasizes the collection of data first without any particular view about the claims they might support, so the claims are therefore accorded secondary importance. By starting with the decisions that need to be made, only data that support the particular inferences that are sought need be collected.

3. The definition does not require that the inferences about next steps in instruction are correct. Given the complexity of human learning, it is impossible to guarantee that any specified sequence of instructional activities will have the intended effect. All that is required is that the evidence collected improves the likelihood that the intended learning takes place.

4. The definition does not require that instruction is in fact modified as a result of the interpretation of the evidence. The evidence the assessment elicited may indicate that what the teacher had originally planned to do was, in fact, the best course of action, as we saw with the earlier exit pass

example. This would not be a better decision (since it was the same decision that the teacher was planning to make without the evidence), but it would be a better *founded* decision.

We feel there are two further consequence of this definition that are worth noting. The first is that formative assessment is applicable across the age range. It works equally well with five-year-olds and twenty-five-year-olds (and indeed eighty-five-year-olds!). The second is that formative assessment is curriculum neutral. The way we define formative assessment is completely independent of what students are learning. All formative assessment requires is that you are clear about what you want your students to learn, because if you are not, you don't know what evidence to collect, let alone how to help your learners. This is important because many writers try to use formative assessment to support a particular view of what students should be learning in school. For us, formative assessment arises as a consequence of the fact that students do not always learn what we teach, and we had better find out what they did learn before we try to teach them anything else.

And this is why we are convinced that formative assessment is not just the latest fad in education. For any teacher, examining the relationship between "What did I do as a teacher?" and "What did my students learn?" is always the most powerful focus for reflecting on your practice, for as long as you continue to do the job.

Now that we have defined formative assessment we can look in detail at what kinds of formative assessment have the biggest impact on student learning. In other words, rather than arguing about which particular approaches to classroom assessment deserve the qualifier "formative," we instead ask whether learning is improved, and if so, by how much, and this is where the research evidence comes in.

Over the past thirty years, many reviews of the research on feedback and other aspects of formative assessment have been published, and these are summarized in Table 1.1. You can find a summary of the most important findings in Wiliam (2011b), and many are discussed in the following five chapters. However, the most important takeaway from the research is that the shorter the time interval between eliciting the evidence and using it to improve instruction, the bigger the likely impact on learning. Using formal testing to monitor student achievement and make instructional adjustments on a month-to-month basis—what might be called "long-cycle" formative assessment (Wiliam & Thompson, 2008)—can improve achievement, but the effects are generally small. Getting students more involved in their own assessment so that they understand what they need to do to succeed week to week—that is, "medium-cycle" formative assessment—is also helpful. But the biggest impact happens with "short-cycle" formative assessment, which takes place not every six to ten weeks but every six to ten minutes, or even every six to ten seconds.

Table 1.1: Reviews of Research on Feedback and Other Aspects of Formative Assessment

Study	Focus
Fuchs and Fuchs (1986)	Formative assessment, focusing on students with special educational needs (21 studies)
Natriello (1987)	Formative and summative assessment procedures and their impact on students (91 studies)
Crooks (1988)	Classroom assessment practices and their impact on students (241 studies)
Bangert-Drowns, Kulik, Kulik, and Morgan (1991)	Feedback in "test-like" events such as end-of-chapter quizzes (40 studies)
Dempster (1991, 1992)	Classroom tests and reviews (56 studies) and issues of implementation
Elshout-Mohr (1994)	Feedback in self-directed learning (including studies published only in Dutch)
Kluger and DeNisi (1996)	Feedback in schools, colleges, and workplaces (131 studies)
Black and Wiliam (1998a)	Formative assessment in K–12 education
Nyquist (2003)	Feedback and other aspects of formative assessment with college-age students (187 studies)
Brookhart (2004)	Review of formative assessment and other aspects of classroom assessment
Allal and Lopez (2005)	Review of research studies on formative assessment published only in French
Köller (2005)	Review of research studies on formative assessment published only in German
Brookhart (2007)	Expanded review of formative assessment and other aspects of classroom assessment
Wiliam (2007b)	Review of studies on formative assessment in mathematics education
Hattie and Timperley (2007)	Extended review of research on feedback
Shute (2008)	Review of research specifically focused on intelligent tutoring systems
Andrade and Cizek (2010)	Handbook of research on formative assessment
McMillan (2013)	Handbook of research on classroom assessment

Go to www.learningsciences.com/bookresources to download figures and tables.

Of course the definition of formative assessment we gave earlier provides little guidance about how to implement effective classroom formative assessment, and in particular what it looks like in practice. To address this, Leahy, Lyon, Thompson, and Wiliam (2005) propose that formative assessment could be conceptualized as the result of crossing three processes (where the learner is going, where the learner is right now, and how to get there) with three kinds of agents in the classroom (teacher, peer, learner), as shown in Table 1.2.

The resulting model identifies the five key strategies of formative assessment. The first—clarifying, sharing, and understanding learning intentions and success criteria—deals with the joint responsibility of teachers, the learners themselves, and their peers to break this down into a number of criteria for success. The second strategy deals with the teacher's role in finding out where learners are in their learning, once he is clear about the learning intentions (this sequence is deliberate—until you know what you want your students to learn, you do not know what evidence to collect). The third strategy emphasizes the teacher's role in providing feedback to the students that tells them not only where they are but also what steps they need to take to move their learning forward. The fourth strategy emphasizes the role that peer assessment can play in supporting student learning and also makes clear that the purpose of peer assessment within a formative assessment framework is not to judge the work of a peer so much as to improve it. Finally, the fifth strategy emphasizes that the ultimate goal is always to produce independent learners.

Table 1.2: Five Key Strategies of Formative Assessment (Leahy et al., 2005)

	Where the learner is going	Where the learner is now	How to get there
Teacher	Clarifying, sharing, and understanding learning intentions and success criteria	Engineering effective discussions, tasks, and activities that elicit evidence of learning	Providing feedback that moves learning forward
Peer		Activating students as learning resources for one another	
Learner		Activating students as owners of their own learning	

In the five main chapters of this book, we discuss each of the strategies in more detail. If you are familiar with *Embedded Formative Assessment* (Wiliam, 2011a) the structure will be familiar to you, for the simple reason that what we see as the five key strategies of formative assessment haven't changed. However, as noted in our introduction, while we do cite some research studies in these five chapters, the focus is much more on the practicalities of implementing the strategies in your classroom. In doing so, each chapter follows the same basic pattern. We outline the key ideas behind the strategy and then go into more detail, providing a number of practical techniques that are ready for classroom implementation. While *Embedded Formative Assessment* lists a number of techniques (fifty-three in fact!), these were presented without much explanation. Here, we provide a number of tips for effective implementation and some ideas for how the techniques can be varied or enhanced. We also discuss a number of potential pitfalls in the implementation of these techniques that we have found in our work with teachers over the past few years.

Chapter 2
YOUR PROFESSIONAL LEARNING

INTRODUCTION

In the following chapters, we discuss a number of techniques that you can use to increase student engagement, collect evidence about student achievement, and make your teaching more responsive to the needs of your students. Most of these ideas have been around for many years and are effective in raising achievement. Yet they are not in widespread use. This suggests that actually implementing these techniques is more difficult than it might appear, and therefore we need to think carefully about how to support you in developing your use of formative classroom assessment. That is the focus of this chapter.

CONTENT, THEN PROCESS

In a chapter in an earlier publication (Wiliam, 2007a), Dylan points out that while investment in teacher professional development has been a feature of the educational landscape for many years, evidence that it made any difference to student achievement is depressingly thin. Michael Fullan puts it like this: "Nothing has promised so much and has been so frustratingly wasteful as the thousands of workshops and conferences that led to no significant change in practice when teachers returned to their classrooms" (Fullan & Stiegelbauer, 1991, p. 315).

Part of the reason is that much teacher professional development is focused on what is easy to deliver rather than what makes a difference to student outcomes. Policy makers behave rather like desperate hitters who come up to the plate and try to hit a home run off every pitch. The result is, of course, a lot of strikeouts. What we need instead is "small ball": get walked to first, steal second, get bunted to third, and score on a sacrifice fly.

But in professional development, like in small ball, the details matter. Many people advocate professional learning communities as the answer, but this is to put process before content. Professional learning communities are good ways to achieve some goals, but much less effective for others. For example, if we want to increase teacher subject knowledge, professional learning communities would be a rather inefficient way to do that.

Some form of direct instruction by experts would be more effective. That is why process should come *after* content. First we should decide what kinds of changes in teaching will make the largest impact on student outcomes, and then—and only then—we should work out the best way to secure these changes. In other words, we should determine the content of teacher learning first, and the process should then be chosen to meet that end. If we start with process, we are, in effect, saying something like, "Professional learning communities (or coaching, or whatever else is currently popular) are the answer. Now what was the question again?" Or, as Abraham Maslow put it, "He who is good with a hammer tends to think that everything is a nail."

We call this fundamental principle of teacher professional development "Content, then process." To be successful, teacher professional development needs to concentrate on both content *and* process (Reeves, McCall, & MacGilchrist, 2001; Wilson & Berne, 1999), but the content must come first. In other words, we need to focus on *what* we want teachers to change, and then we have to understand *how* to support teachers in making those changes.

The content element is the focus of the following chapters of this book, and it has two components. First, *evidence*: the research evidence suggests that classroom formative assessment can have a significant impact on how much students learn. Indeed, the evidence suggests that attention to classroom formative assessment can produce greater gains in achievement than any other change in what teachers do. Second, *ideas*: in the following chapters, we share a number of practical techniques that you can use to further develop your practice of formative assessment.

However, knowing what will help you most is only part of the solution, making the previous quotation from Michael Fullan so important. The professional development that he describes is not misguided in its aim. Much of the content of that professional development is entirely appropriate. What is not given enough thought is how to support teachers in making changes to their practice when they return to their classrooms—the *process* of teacher change.

As a result of extensive work with teachers and administrators over ten years, trying to promote and support the development of classroom formative assessment, we conclude that there are five key process components: choice, flexibility, small steps, accountability, and support (Wiliam, 2006a). We discuss each of these in turn below.

CHOICE

It is often assumed that to improve, teachers should work to develop the weakest aspects of their practice, and for some teachers, these aspects may indeed be so weak that they should be the priority for professional development. But for most teachers, the greatest benefits to students are likely to come from teachers becoming even more expert in their strengths. In early work on formative assessment with teachers in England

(P. Black, Harrison, Lee, Marshall, & Wiliam, 2003), one of the teachers, Derek (a pseudonym), was already quite skilled at conducting whole-class discussion sessions, yet he was interested in improving this practice further. A colleague of his at the same school, Philip (also a pseudonym), had a low-key presence in the classroom and was more interested in helping students develop skills of self-assessment and peer assessment. Both Derek and Philip are now extraordinarily skilled practitioners—among the best we have ever seen—but to make Philip work on questioning, or Derek on peer assessment and self-assessment, would be unlikely to benefit their students as much as supporting each teacher to become excellent in his own way.

Furthermore, when teachers themselves make the decision about what it is that they wish to prioritize for their own professional development, they are more likely to "make it work." In traditional top-down models of teacher professional development, teachers are given ideas to try out in their own classrooms but often respond by blaming the professional developer for the failure of new methods in the classroom (e.g., "I tried what you told me to do, and it didn't work"). However, when teachers make the choice about the aspects of practice to develop, they share the responsibility for ensuring effective implementation.

Viewed from this perspective, choice is not a luxury but a necessity. If teachers are to develop their practice in the way that makes the most difference to their students, they need choice, because for the vast majority of teachers, only they know what aspects of their practice are likely to be the most productive to develop. Of course, this choice must be exercised within a framework that provides some assurance the changes are beneficial, which is why the five strategies of formative assessment we discuss in the following chapters are so important. However, within this framework, the choice of what aspects of teachers' practice to prioritize for development must be left to practitioners, who know more about their own classrooms and their own students than anyone else.

FLEXIBILITY

As well as choice of what to prioritize in their development, teachers also need to modify ideas other teachers develop in order to make the ideas work in their own classrooms. Part of the reason for this is differences between teachers in their teaching styles, but it is also important to recognize that there are differences from school to school and class to class. What works in one context may not work in another, because schools differ in their openness to experimentation and appetite for risk. The expectations of the students are also important. Where students are insecure, they may be uncomfortable with changes that make new and unfamiliar demands of them, even when these changes are beneficial (Spradbery, 1976). As a result, teachers may need to modify the way they introduce techniques. The expectations of parents can constrain what is possible, too, at least in the short term.

You therefore need the flexibility to be able to "morph" the classroom formative assessment techniques with which you are presented to fit your own classroom context (Ginsburg, 2001). The danger in this is that a teacher may so modify an idea that it is no longer effective—what Ed Haertel describes as a "lethal mutation" (A. L. Brown & Campione, 1996).

For example, in Strategy 4, we show that collaborative learning can produce significant increases in student achievement but only where it is implemented in a way that emphasizes group goals *and* individual accountability. But we also know that many teachers are reluctant to ensure students are individually accountable for contributing to the work of the group, and do not implement collaborative learning in a way that increases student achievement. What is needed, therefore, is a way of allowing teachers flexibility, while at the same time constraining the use of that flexibility so that modifications to the original ideas do not unduly weaken their effectiveness. This is why it is so important to make the distinction in the following chapters between *strategies* of classroom formative assessment on the one hand and *techniques* that can be used to enact these strategies in classrooms on the other. The key strategies of formative assessment are always smart things for a teacher to do. However, the actual techniques teachers use to enact these in their practice require careful thought. Some techniques work better in certain school subjects, and some work better with certain students. It is also important to note that the teacher's belief in the value of a technique is important.

For example, many teachers are comfortable using ice-pop sticks with fifth graders but think they are a little too childish for eighth graders. Having said that, teachers of advanced placement courses in high schools find ice-pop sticks a useful technique for random questioning because when eighteen-year-olds are asked to answer a question, their first reaction is, "Why me?"; with the ice-pop sticks, the answer is, "It's your unlucky day. Deal with it. Now what's the answer to the question?"

You should be free to adopt whichever of these techniques you wish, therefore providing choice—the first of the five process requirements. By anchoring the techniques to (at least) one of the five key strategies, we provide a means by which you can modify the techniques but still provide a reasonable assurance of fidelity to the original research. Therefore you have a reasonable guarantee that the techniques will be effective in increasing student achievement.

The late Millard Fuller, founder of Habitat for Humanity, pointed out that in matters of environmental awareness, it is generally easier to get people to *act* their way into a new way of *thinking* than get them to *think* their way into a new way of *acting*. Traditional approaches to the dissemination of educational research are, in effect, trying to get teachers to think their way into a new way of acting. In contrast, encouraging teachers to adopt new practices that they then incorporate into their routine teaching is a way of getting them to act their way into a new way of thinking.

This is an important insight because changing what teachers think, if it does not change what they do, does not benefit students. Students benefit only when teachers change what they do in classrooms. For example, if we train quarterbacks by instructing them to read books and watch films, such activities may have some value, but ultimately, the players need to be able to put these ideas into practice—and that is the hardest part. Indeed, we do not think it is too much of an overstatement to say that the reason for the relative ineffectiveness of most professional development over the past quarter century is because it has been based on an incorrect diagnosis. We assume that the "problem" is teachers do not know enough, so we herd them into rooms to hear experts supply the missing knowledge. Then we assume that, with their deficits in knowledge rectified, teachers are more effective.

It hasn't worked because the diagnosis is wrong. Teachers don't lack knowledge. What they lack is support in working out how to integrate these ideas into their daily practice, and this takes time, which is why we have to allow teachers to take small steps.

SMALL STEPS

It is important for schools to improve—and quickly. For that reason, it is hardly surprising that policy makers, politicians, and administrators want to get teachers developing their classroom formative assessment practices as quickly as possible. However, the research evidence shows that teachers are slow to change their classroom practices. Indeed, many people have gone as far as to claim that teachers are resistant to change— that they cling to a set of professional habits, which to a very real extent represent a core part of each teacher's professional identity and this is why they are unwilling to change. If we want to support teachers in developing their practice, we need to understand why changes in practice are so slow. Is it just resistance to change, or something deeper?

It is important to understand the reasons because what we do to support change depends on the reasons for the slowness of previous attempts. If teachers are resistant to change because they are happy with the way things are, and don't want to change, then we could, for example, look for ways of overcoming resistance. This is often the rationale for incentive schemes—the idea is that teachers adopt new ideas if paid to do so. However, the evidence from careful evaluations of incentive schemes shows that they are not particularly successful (see, for example, Springer et al., 2010).

A far more likely reason for the slowness of teacher change is that it is genuinely difficult, because high-level performance in a domain as complex as teaching requires automatizing a large proportion of the things that teachers do. For learning drivers, using the turn indicator, checking the rearview mirror, and steering all at the same time seem impossibly complicated—and undertaken consciously, they are. Experienced drivers practice these activities so many times that they become automatic, and therefore the activities take up little of the available resources for cognitive processing. However, as anyone who tries to change the way he drives discovers, these automatic procedures are extremely hard to change.

It is only by observing novice teachers that one realizes how expert the best teachers are. Expert teachers, with a few commands and a wave of the arms, get students into a classroom, seated, and at work in a matter of seconds, whereas with novice teachers, the same process can have the appearance of herding cats.

These polished routines are the result of hundreds, thousands, and sometimes even hundreds of thousands of repetitions. They are what get teachers through the day—without them, their jobs would be impossible. But as Berliner (1994) mentions, the "automaticity for the repetitive operations that are needed to accomplish their goals" also means that once established, these routines are hard to change.

A few years ago, Dylan was working with teachers in HoHoKus, a K–8 school district in northern New Jersey. One fifth-grade teacher was trying to use "No hands up except to ask a question," but she found this very difficult because every time she asked a question, she would begin the question by asking, "Does anyone . . . ?" or "Has anyone . . . ?" She asked him, "Why am I finding this so hard?" They sat down and figured out that in the twenty-two years she had been teaching, she probably asked half a million questions in her classroom. When you've done something one way half a million times, doing it any other way is going to be very difficult.

Teaching is even more extreme than driving a car in this respect, because every teacher comes to the profession with a series of "scripts" of how classrooms should operate "hardwired" into their minds from their time as a student. These scripts, such as requiring students to raise their hands if they have an answer to a teacher's question, seem natural, but of course they are learned, and get in the way of learning (Wiliam, 2006b).

Moreover, many of the changes in practice associated with implementing formative assessment are not just difficult to change because they are habituated—they also contradict widely distributed and strongly held beliefs about, for example, the value of grades for motivating students. Even when teachers are convinced of the value of approaches such as "comment-only grading," they are often dissuaded from trying them out by more senior colleagues who dismiss innovations as fads advocated by ivory tower academics who don't know what real teaching is.

The consequence of all this is that in implementing any professional development model, we have to accept that teacher learning is slow. In particular, for changes in practice—as opposed to knowledge—to be lasting, it must be integrated into a teacher's existing routines, and this takes time. Many people involved in professional development are familiar with the experience of encouraging teachers to try out new ideas and seeing them enacted when they visit teachers' classrooms, only to learn shortly afterward that the teachers revert to their former practices.

That is why we have to allow anyone who is changing something at which she is already expert to take small steps. The collection of routines that teachers establish to get through the day is their greatest asset, but at the same time a liability, because getting better involves getting a little bit worse, at least for a while. When Tiger Woods wanted to change his golf swing after winning the 1997 Masters golf tournament, he withdrew from competition and practiced his new swing until he was happy with it. But no teacher is going to get three months to practice new techniques in front of a mirror before trying them out in the classroom, which is why changing one's teaching is such a daunting prospect. It involves disrupting the things that get you through the day. No wonder one teacher describes changing her classroom routines as "engine repair, in flight."

Much professional development has been ineffective because the diagnosis is faulty. Teachers don't tend to lack knowledge so much as the ability to translate their intentions into action, and here we have much to learn from Weight Watchers.

Weight Watchers ought to be the least successful organization on the planet, because everyone who wants to lose weight knows what to do: eat less and exercise more. That's it. There is no secret third rule of weight loss that is revealed upon payment of a subscription to Weight Watchers. For example, perhaps if we stir our breakfast cereal counterclockwise, it might turn the dextrose in the sugar into left-handed sugar molecules that our bodies would not absorb. Unfortunately not. It's just eat less and exercise more. But Weight Watchers realizes that it is not in the knowledge-giving business; it is in the habit-changing business. People who want to lose weight know what they need to do. What they need are structures and supports that help them do what they want to do.

In the same way, if we are serious about helping teachers improve their practice, we have to help teachers change their classroom habits. And just in the same way that weight-loss programs need to be focused on weight loss that is sustained, we need to support teachers to make changes in their practice that last.

We have lost count of the number of times that we describe a teaching technique to a group of teachers only for one of them to say, "I used to do that. It was good." Teachers are bombarded with new ideas, which they are encouraged to try out, but before they have time to consolidate these new ideas into their practice, some newer idea comes along. This is why the idea of "sharing good practice" can be so dangerous as a model for teacher professional development. Of course, teachers need new ideas, but most teachers already have more good ideas than they will ever be able to incorporate into their teaching. What teachers need is help creating new habits, and this is a challenge in all areas of human endeavor.

If we are going to help teachers change their classroom habits, we need to recognize that this is going to be very challenging, and will require both support and accountability, which are the subjects of the next two sections.

Accountability

All teachers need to improve their practice; not because they are not good enough, but because they can be better. For that reason, we think it is entirely appropriate to hold teachers accountable for making improvements in their practice. We also believe that in developing their practice, teachers should develop those aspects of their practice that are likely to be of most benefit to their students; in other words, they should be accountable to the evidence about what is likely to benefit students. This is not meant to imply a slavish following of the latest research findings, but that teachers need to be literally accountable—they should accept that they should expect, and be able, to render an account of why they chose to develop one aspect of their practice rather than another.

In our work with teachers, we find it helpful to engage them in detailed planning of what changes they plan to make in their teaching. This process could be called *action planning*, but it is important to note that in our experience, this is best done with a highly structured approach—very different from the tokenistic action planning that occurs at the end of many teacher professional development events.

Of course, there are many different protocols that you could adopt for action planning, but our experience of working with teachers developing their practice of formative assessment suggests that the following features are particularly important:

1. *The action plan should identify a small number of changes that you will make in your teaching.* When teachers try to change more than two or three things in their practice at the same time, the result is often that their classroom routines deteriorate significantly, and they then fall back on those routines with which they feel comfortable or safe. Like the story of the tortoise and the hare, teachers who try to change too many things at the same time end up making less progress than those who make small, gradual, manageable changes.

2. *The plan should be written down.* Writing the plan down makes it more likely that you will think the plan through while writing it down, makes the ideas more concrete, and also creates a record, which means that you are less likely to forget what you planned to do.

3. *The plan should focus on the five key strategies of formative assessment.* As noted earlier, you should prioritize changes that are likely to benefit students, and although there are other changes that might benefit students, the robustness and coherence of the research on the effects of formative assessment suggest that this should be the starting point for all teachers.

4. *The plan should identify what you hope to reduce or give up doing to make time for the changes.* Most teachers are working as hard as they can, so if they treat these changes as an addition to their load, the changes are unlikely ever to be implemented. To make time for these changes, the action

plan must identify something the teacher is currently doing that he will stop doing, or do less of. Asked to make such clear priorities, people often hope that they can make the necessary changes by being more efficient in their use of time, but this is usually hopelessly optimistic. The only way to make time for new things is to reduce, or stop doing entirely, things that you are currently doing, in order to create time for innovation.

Support

The last process element—support—is closely related to accountability. Indeed, some authors describe them as a single feature of effective learning environments for teachers: supportive accountability (Ciofalo & Leahy, 2006). The central idea is the creation of structures that, while making teachers accountable for developing their practice, provide the support for them to do this. Support and accountability can therefore be thought of as two sides of the same coin.

You can see the closeness of the relationship between support and accountability when we consider the process of action planning, which can be thought of both as providing a measure of accountability and providing support for teachers to change their practice. Some teachers find it demeaning, or even insulting, to be asked to put down in writing what they are going to try out in their classroom. But in looking back at the process, teachers have said time and again how useful the idea of committing their plans to paper was, both in terms of making their plans concrete and making a commitment to their peers. Tim, a math teacher at Spruce Central High School, was reflecting, after participating in teacher learning communities (TLCs) for a year, on the experience of making a written commitment to the rest of the group toward the end of each meeting:

> I think specifically what was helpful was the ridiculous [. . .] forms. I thought that was the dumbest thing, but I'm sitting with my friends and on the [. . .] form I write down what I am going to do next month. Well, it turns out to be a sort of "I'm telling my friends I'm going to do this" and I really actually did it and it was because of that. It was because I wrote it down. I was surprised at how strong an incentive that was to actually do something different [. . .] that idea of writing down what you are going to do and then because when they come by the next month you better take out that piece of paper and say "Did I do that?" [. . .]Just the idea of sitting in a group, working out something, and making a commitment [. . .] I was impressed about how that actually made me do stuff. (Lyon, Wylie, & Goe, 2006, p. 20).

Clearly, creating this "supportive accountability" could be done in a number of ways. One way is to assign each teacher a coach, but this is expensive and it is by no means clear that an adequate supply of appropriately skilled coaches are available. For these reasons, between 2003 and 2006 working with colleagues at the Educational Testing Service, we developed and piloted a number of models for supporting teachers (for extended accounts of these early developments, see Thompson & Goe, 2008; Wylie, Lyon, & Goe, 2009; Wylie, Lyon, & Mavronikolas, 2008). What we learned we summarize here.

SUPPORTING FORMATIVE ASSESSMENT WITH TEACHER LEARNING COMMUNITIES

One of our earliest models involves a facilitator meeting every two or three weeks with groups of four to six high school teachers to discuss the changes they were attempting to make in their practice. As a result of this work, it became clear that a two- or three-week cycle did not allow enough time for the teachers involved to plan and implement changes in their practice in time for reporting back at the next meeting. Those who have never been teachers cannot understand this. Surely, they say, a teacher could try out a new idea in two or three weeks. But because they have never been teachers, they do not understand the complexity and fragility of a teacher's working life. Moreover, many of the techniques require careful planning, and don't work with all subject matter. If a teacher wants to try out getting the students to use "traffic lights" to take a self-assessment (see Chapter 7), this needs to be done in a lesson where the learning intention and success criteria can be expressed clearly in language that is understandable to students. If a teacher wants to use the ABCD cards for a hinge question (see Chapter 4), she needs to decide which lesson to try this out in and where in the lesson to check on the students' understanding, and may need to arrange time to meet with another teacher to discuss the design of the question. Four weeks appears to be a minimum period of time for teachers to plan and carry out a new idea in their classroom.

On the other hand, implementation that involved meetings that occurred at intervals of six weeks or more appeared to lose momentum. This led us to adopt a monthly cycle of meetings, and in trying out this model in literally hundreds of schools in dozens of districts over the past ten years, we have not come across any evidence that suggests that intervals between meetings of approximately four weeks is not an optimum, at least in respect to changes in practice related to formative assessment.

Originally we had assumed that schools would be able to find two hours for each of the monthly meetings; while this was clearly possible in some districts, in others it was not, so we looked carefully at ways of reducing the length of the monthly meeting. After experimentation with different lengths of meetings (including meetings as short as sixty minutes), we concluded that seventy-five minutes should be an absolute minimum. In some schools, because of the lack of a single seventy-five-minute slot, teachers tried having two forty-minute slots, but this appeared to be much less successful than a single seventy-five minute slot.

Our experiences with meetings with small numbers of participants also led us to conclude that the minimum number of participants needed for a meeting to be effective is around eight. Meetings with fewer than eight participants often required significant input from the group's leader or facilitator, particularly when occasional absences due to illness and other factors further reduced the size of the group. While such intensive support from the facilitator might provide an effective learning environment for those attending, such a model would unlikely be scalable.

On the other hand, where the group was much larger than twelve (as was often the case in our early work in the Cleveland Municipal School District), there was not enough time to hear back from each member of the group. In interviews, many participants in teacher learning communities told us that it was the fact that they knew they would be required to give their colleagues an account of what they had been doing that made them prioritize working on changing their classroom practice over all the pressing concerns of a teacher's life (Ciofalo & Leahy, 2006). Given that on any day, one or two teachers are likely to be absent for any number of reasons, to ensure that a group has at least eight participants, a group size of ten to twelve is recommended.

As well as design guidelines for the size of group and frequency of meetings, we also explored the extent to which it was necessary for teachers to share particular assignments (e.g., early grades or subject-specialisms in secondary schools). It had been our experience that teachers greatly value meeting in mixed-subject groups, in order to get ideas from teachers of different subjects or different ages. However, we also observed many instances of a teacher rejecting suggestions from other members of the group with a claim that the suggested idea would not work for her own subject-specialism. In order to balance these tensions, we explored models where the teachers do not all come from the same subject-specialism, but, in order to provide some disciplinary support, we ensured that for each teacher in the group, there was at least one other with the same age- or subject-specialism. To date, we do not have any data that suggests that any particular method of constituting a group is better than another, although we are aware that the scope for deep conversations about subject matter is likely to be limited where the group is made up of individuals with different subject-specialisms (Grossman, Wineburg, & Woolworth, 2000). One model that some schools have adopted, which appears to work well, is to begin with mixed or hybrid models, and then, after a year or two, move toward more specialist groupings, making it possible to "deepen the conversation."

One final design feature of the monthly meetings of the teacher learning communities was related to their structure. We were aware that in most approaches to teacher professional development, novelty was often regarded as paramount, in order to keep things "fresh." The disadvantage of such an approach is that participants arrive at the meeting not knowing the roles they are expected to play, so the organization of the teachers' learning, rather than the learning itself, was foregrounded.

On the other hand, we were aware, through the work of Lee Shulman on professional learning in law, medicine, and other professions, that most professions adopt standard ways of organizing the learning of professionals, and these "signature pedagogies" are enduring and widespread.

> Another interesting question about these pedagogies is: why do they persist? Why do they last so long? I think the answer is that even though I can point out the flaws in every one of these signature pedagogies—and each is flawed—by and large, they work. They achieve the ends for which they were "designed," or in a kind of Darwinian sense, they survive the competition with alternative pedagogical means. (Shulman, 2005, p. 15)

For this reason, we realized that there could be considerable benefits of adopting a standard structure for these monthly meetings. The fact that each meeting followed the same structure meant that participants came to the meeting knowing the roles they were to play, both in terms of reporting on their own experiences and providing support to others. We explored a number of possible different models, but the one that follows has worked well in all the different settings in which it was tried.

Introduction (5 minutes)

The meeting facilitator hands out agendas and presents the learning intentions for the meeting.

Starter Activity (5 minutes)

Participants engage in an activity to help them focus on their own learning.

Feedback (25 minutes)

Each teacher gives a brief report on what she committed to try out during the "personal action planning" section at the previous meeting, while the rest of the group listen appreciatively and then offer support to the individual in taking her plan forward.

New Learning About Formative Assessment (25 minutes)

In order to provide an element of novelty into each meeting of the TLC, and provide a steady stream of new ideas, each meeting includes an activity that introduces some new ideas about formative assessment. This might be a task, a video to watch and discuss, or a "book study" in which teachers discuss a book chapter relevant to formative assessment that they have read over the past month.

Personal Action Planning (15 minutes)

The penultimate activity of each session involves the participants planning in detail what they hope to accomplish before the next meeting. This may include trying out new ideas, or it may simply be to consolidate techniques with which they have already experimented. This is also a good time for participants to plan any peer observations that they plan to undertake. It is our experience that if the participants leave the meeting without a definite date and time to observe one another, the peer observation is much less likely to take place (Maher & Wiliam, 2007).

Summary of Learning (5 minutes)

In the last five minutes of the meeting, the group discusses whether they have achieved the learning intentions they set themselves at the beginning of the meeting. If they have not, there is time for the group to decide what to do about it.

These meetings provide both support and accountability. Many teachers have spoken about the usefulness of these meetings for providing advice about how they might move forward when they are "stuck," but they also create a strong measure of accountability for teachers to actually implement their plans.

Chapter 3

STRATEGY 1: CLARIFYING, SHARING, AND UNDERSTANDING LEARNING INTENTIONS AND SUCCESS CRITERIA

OVERVIEW

When we ask teachers about their learning intentions for a particular lesson, it is common for them to reply by saying, "I'm going to have the students do this." In other words, teachers respond in terms of the activities in which they plan to engage their students. This is, of course, entirely understandable. The only way that teachers get students to learn is by engaging them in activities. However, if the teachers select activities without a clear view of the learning that is intended, it is far less likely that the students will learn what they need to learn. By engaging in an activity, students usually learn something, but not all outcomes of learning are equally valuable. By being clear about what it is we want students to learn—in Stephen Covey's words, by "starting with the end in mind" (Covey, 1989)—it is more likely that our students will learn what we need them to learn.

WHY USE THIS STRATEGY

Before we can find out what our learners are learning, before we can give feedback, before we can engage our learners as resources for one another and as owners of their own learning, we have to be clear about where we are going.

GETTING TO UNDERSTAND THE STRATEGY

Ralph Tyler's *Basic Principles of Curriculum and Instruction* was first published in 1949. It is a testament to its influence that more than six decades later, it is still in print. Tyler identifies "four fundamental questions which must be answered in developing any curriculum and plan of instruction":

1. What educational purposes should the school seek to attain?
2. What educational experiences can be provided that are likely to attain these purposes?

3. How can these educational experiences be effectively organized?

4. How can we determine whether these purposes are being attained?

(Tyler, 1949, p. 1)

In many ways, such a formulation, and in particular the idea of starting with the purposes of education, is obvious. As Yogi Berra, the former New York Yankees baseball player, once said, "If you don't know where you are going, you might wind up somewhere else." The fundamental questions are also empowering for students. As one tenth-grade student said,

> Something like English, for every topic we start we get success criteria with different grades on it and we have to highlight the key bits and the things we can include in our essay or coursework to get that grade. (Wiliam & Leahy, 2014)

It is therefore hardly surprising that designing educational experiences backward from the intended outcomes has been extremely influential (see, for example, Wiggins & McTighe, 2000). However, while it seems straightforward to specify aims for our students' learning—so much so that many teachers and schools begin their implementation of formative assessment by working on learning intentions—it is important to understand that developing good learning intentions is not easy, and our work with teachers suggests that this first strategy may actually be the most difficult of the five formative assessment strategies to implement well.

In particular, the apparent straightforwardness of specifying learning intentions and success criteria has led to simplistic and rigid implementation that undermines their effective use. Many frameworks for the evaluation of teaching provide rubrics of teacher behaviors, and it is common to find that to attain the highest level of performance, teachers must, among other things, begin each instructional sequence with a clear statement of the intended learning outcomes. As a result, many districts mandate that every lesson must begin with a learning outcome. The consequences are a predictable "culture of compliance"; teachers post learning outcomes on a board, students copy these into their notebooks, and the lesson then often proceeds without further reference to the learning outcomes, unless, of course, an administrator happens to stop by to observe the lesson. One student, who was asked to describe a learning intention, said, "It's what we copy into our books at the beginning of the lesson, while we're talking to our friends."

Now, of course, it is, in general, a good idea that students know where they are going—we are both embarrassed about how long we spent teaching without telling our students where we were going. After all, it is really rather obvious that if our students know where we are headed, we are more likely to arrive at the correct destination. But there are at least three reasons why starting every single lesson with a learning outcome is likely to be a bad idea.

First, sometimes you don't always know exactly where the lesson is going. If you are teaching high school chemistry students how to balance chemical equations, there is a single, well-defined goal for the whole class. You are trying to get every single student to the same point, so if the student's solution differs from the standard solution, the student is probably heading off in the wrong direction and needs to be brought back on track. However, if you are asking the students to respond to a poem by Emily Dickinson, it is entirely appropriate that some students head off in different directions from others. In such a situation, there isn't a single goal for the whole class but a whole "horizon" of equally acceptable goals. Indeed, it is okay if different students learn different things. Sometimes, of course, it seems as if a student is headed in a completely inappropriate direction, but this can often be the result of the student finding a more creative approach to the task than those envisaged by the teacher.

This illustrates a more general point, which is that sometimes it is appropriate to do things not because they are guaranteed to result in specific learning outcomes but because they are important experiences for students. The national curriculum for students in Scotland explicitly recognizes this by talking about "experiences and outcomes" rather than relying solely on "outcomes." There are some things that we want students to experience not because they necessarily lead to specific learning outcomes but because they are valuable things to do together. It may not be possible to predict with any certainty what the learning outcomes will be, but if your experience is that a particular task in the past resulted in valuable and significant learning for your students, our view is that it is appropriate to use the task.

Second, sometimes telling students where you are going spoils the journey. For example, a teacher might set a class a problem in which the key to solving the problem is realizing that triangles with the same base and same height have the same area even though the base and height of the triangles are not given in the problem, so it is not possible to calculate the area (see Wiliam, 2011a, pp. 56–57). If you tell the students they are doing problems that involve areas of triangles, what could be an interesting and challenging problem is reduced to a rather more routine exercise.

Third, and perhaps most important, starting every lesson with a learning outcome is a recipe for uninspired and uninspiring teaching. Those who mandate starting every lesson with a learning outcome forget one important, and universal, fact about schools: not all children are motivated. If all students were indeed motivated, we could announce any learning outcome, and our students would be delighted. They would come into our classrooms and tell us that they were desperate to learn something, and they would be happy with any learning outcome we choose. Unfortunately, this is not the reality faced by any teachers we know. Our students do not always come into our classrooms desperate to learn. They need to be engaged and enthused, and, again unfortunately, statements of content standards excite very few students. They get excited by ideas, arguments, discussions, and debates. And this is the real skill of good teachers: to find a way to engage students in rigorous content matter by making it come alive.

For example, a teacher begins a ninth-grade science lesson by asking the class, "Why does it take longer to cook potatoes at 400°F in an oven than it does at 212°F in a saucepan of boiling water?" Most of the students know enough about cooking potatoes to realize that the premise of the question is correct—it does indeed take longer to cook potatoes by broiling than by boiling—but none of the students notice the potential paradox. The important point here is that the teacher did have a clear learning intention in mind at the outset, and in fact shared it with the students after the discussion, but the teacher judged that the best way to start the lesson was not with a learning intention but with an engaging question.

So, in general, teachers do need to plan their classroom activities backward from the learning goals, but these cannot always be specified in advance. And it is not always advisable to tell the students at the outset either, because it spoils the journey and there are better ways to engage and motivate students. In the remainder of this chapter, we look at a number of techniques that you can use to develop, clarify, and share learning intentions with your students, and ensure that they understand where they are going.

TECHNIQUES

Keep the Context of Learning Out of the Learning Intention

Before we discuss learning intentions and success criteria, it seems sensible to discuss three assumptions that we believe should drive what teachers do. The first assumption is that your main aim as a teacher is to change your students. Most of the time, we are trying to get our students to be able to do things that they could not do before, although there are also times when we are trying to get them not to do something that they might have done before, like get pregnant or take drugs. But the teacher's main aim is always to change his students. The second assumption is that this change is directed and planned. We are not interested in random changes in what students can do, but we are interested in particular changes in our students that we believe have value. The third assumption is that these changes are more likely to come about if we have a clear plan for what we want our students to learn.

Ralph Tyler's model for the development of curriculum and instruction outlined earlier is sometimes called the "objectives" model for the obvious reason that the model assumes objectives should drive curriculum and instruction; and in some ways, the idea of learning intentions and success criteria is just a modern take on the same idea. Indeed, we could just carry on using the terms *aims* and *objectives*. However, we believe that a change in vocabulary is justified, because people often use *objectives* to mean "behavioral objectives," and one major criticism of Tyler's objectives model is there are many things we want our students to learn that are not easily described in behavioral terms.

In this chapter, we use *learning outcomes* to describe what it is that students can do as a result of engaging in educational activities (literally, the outcomes of the learning process). Of course, as every teacher knows, what students learn as a result of engaging with a particular sequence of educational activities is not easy to predict. Sometimes students learn what we want them to learn, and sometimes they learn something else. We use *learning intentions* to describe the things that we want our students to learn and *success criteria* to describe the criteria that we use to judge whether the learning activities in which we engaged our students were successful. One fourth grader describes being given success criteria thus: "It's like knowing the teacher's secret" (Spendlove, 2009, p. 18).

Elementary school teachers often communicate learning intentions and success criteria to their students as WALT (We are learning to . . .) and WILF (What I'm looking for). Others have used a puppet called Timmy the teaching tiger or Ollie (OLI or "our learning intention") to convey the learning intentions. Such acronyms can be useful in engaging students in the process, but as Shirley Clarke (2001) points out, it is important to ensure that the focus is on what these terms mean, and how they relate to the work, otherwise they just become "gimmicks."

In a later work, Shirley Clarke (2003) shows that devising learning intentions and success criteria is actually very difficult. Or, to be more precise, devising bad learning intentions and success criteria is actually very easy, but devising good ones is a significant challenge—one, like developing good questions (see next chapter), that is so challenging that no teacher ever truly masters it. However, there are some very simple and straightforward things that teachers can do to substantially improve their learning intentions.

Perhaps the most straightforward is to address the fact that, as Shirley Clarke points out, learning intentions are far less useful if they specifically include the context of the learning. She describes an elementary school teacher who tells her students that the learning intention is "To understand the effects of banana production on the banana producers" (Clarke, 2003, p. 23). The reason for this particular activity is almost certainly not to ensure that students come to understand the specific difficulties faced by banana producers. This particular task has more likely been selected because the teacher is using this specific context to illustrate the more general impact of production on producers, and it would be better if the learning intention reflected this. The learning intention would therefore become "to understand the impact of production on producers" with banana production being the context of the learning.

This example illustrates a rather important principle at the heart of teaching, which is that when we teach our students how to do something, we are rarely interested in their ability to do the things we have taught them. That sounds paradoxical but it is, in our experience, true. If we teach our students to add two numbers, such as 278 and 345, we are no longer interested in those two numbers; our students can almost certainly add those two numbers because we have shown them how to do it. We are interested in whether they can use what they learned to add two different numbers. If we teach our students how to punctuate a sentence, we are no longer interested in that particular sentence; we are interested in whether our students can apply what they have learned to a different sentence, or, even better, that they can punctuate when writing a story as opposed to doing a punctuation exercise. Another way of stating this principle is that generalizability is at the heart of good teaching. If the only things our students can do are what we have taught them to do, they can't do very much at all, because those exact circumstances are unlikely ever to arise again. The only useful learning is that which the student can apply beyond the context of the learning.

This might seem straightforward to accomplish, but it turns out our brains aren't very good at disentangling the context of the learning from the learning itself. It has long been known that adults rarely use what they have been taught in school to solve problems in the "real world." For example, Nunes, Carraher, and Schliemann (1993) find that Brazilian market traders, fishermen, building site foremen, carpenters, and farmers are able to solve a variety of mathematical problems more effectively than students with more years of schooling, but they do not use the formal school-taught methods.

Another example comes from the work of Jean Lave (1988), who describes a group of adults in a Weight Watchers class learning to prepare meals:

> In this case they are to fix a serving of cottage cheese, supposing the amount laid out for the meal is three-quarters of the two-thirds cup the program allowed. The problem solver in this example begins the task muttering that he took a calculus course in college. . . . After a pause he suddenly announces that he "got it!" From then on he appears certain he is correct, even before carrying out the procedure. He fills a measuring cup two-thirds full of cottage cheese, dumps it out on the cutting board, pats it into a circle, marks a cross on it, scoops away one quadrant, and serves the rest.

> Therefore, "take three-quarters of two-thirds of a cup of cottage cheese" is not just the problem statement but also the solution to the problem and the procedure for solving it. The setting is part of the calculating process, and the solution is simply the problem statement, enacted with the setting. At no time does the Weight Watcher check his procedure against a paper and pencil algorithm, which would produce $3/_4$ cup $\times$ $2/_3$ cup = $1/_2$ cup. Instead, the coincidence of the problem, setting, and enactment are the means by which checking took place.

As these and many other examples show, our brains do not appear to be very good at transferring knowledge from one context to another. Many people imagine that our brains are somehow like computers that either have particular knowledge or don't, but it turns out our brains don't work like this.

For example, the results of one experiment shows that scuba divers who were taught things at the surface remembered 55 percent more of what they had been taught when they were tested at the surface than when they were tested underwater. But when they had been taught things underwater, they remembered 35 percent more when they were tested underwater than when they were tested at the surface (Godden & Baddeley, 1975).

In another experiment, a group of adults were each given three gin and tonics and then taught a nineteen-item set of instructions for a route on a map. The following day, half of the students were tested on their recall of the instructions sober, and half were tested after three more gin and tonics. The students tested while intoxicated recalled almost 40 percent more of the details than those tested while sober (Lowe, 1980).

Finally, students who were tested in the room in which they were taught something got better scores than if they were tested in a different room (S. M. Smith, Glenberg, & Bjork, 1978).

We see this failure of our brains to transfer from one context to another played out in middle and high schools every day. The science teacher asks the math teacher, "Why can't these students do equations and graphs?" and the math teacher lamely replies, "Well, they can do equations and graphs in the math classroom."

This research has led some to conclude that teaching abstract ideas in the hope that students are able to transfer learning from one context to another is impossible (Lave, 1988, p. 19). However, as Anderson, Reder, and Simon (1996) point out,

> Contrary to Lave's opinion, a large body of empirical research on transfer in psychology . . . demonstrates that there can be either large amounts of transfer, a modest amount of transfer, no transfer at all, or even negative transfer. How much there is and whether transfer is positive depends in reliable ways on the experimental situation and the relation of the material originally learned to the transfer material. (p. 7)

In particular, we know that transfer from one context to another is much more effective when students encounter the same idea in more than one context (Bjork & Richardson-Klavehn, 1989), and this is why the idea of keeping the context of the learning separate from the learning intention is so important. Returning to the example of banana production discussed earlier, the learning intention is "to understand the impact of production on producers"; the context of the learning is banana production; and potential success criteria would describe the extent to which students could apply what they had learned in the context of banana production to a different context, such as sugar production.

Tips

Get Students to Apply What They Have Learned in Other Contexts

Designing learning activities backward from the learning intentions and success criteria that they are intended to engender feels odd at first, but with practice, it becomes natural. To get you started, look at the following list of potential learning intentions. Decide whether each one is really a learning intention or just an activity, and for those you think are learning intentions, decide whether they are context free. Then, for those that relate to your own teaching responsibilities, spend some time thinking about how they might be improved.

We are learning to:

- know ways of controlling floods in Bangladesh
- express ideas, words, thoughts, and feelings through creative work in dance
- recognize triangular numbers
- paint a landscape
- make a plastic key fob
- create a cartoon animal using descriptive phrases and sentences
- complete all ten questions on pages 23 to 25
- use science equipment and kitchen compounds to carry out purposeful experiments
- identify the causes of plantation slavery
- count up to ten in French

As an example, for the first of these, the important observation is that it is unlikely that the teacher chose the topic primarily for the students to understand how to control floods in Bangladesh. It is far more likely the teacher intends that the students understand the factors that affect flooding in general, with Bangladesh as a special case. So the learning intention becomes "Know ways of controlling floods," with Bangladesh being the context of the learning. Possible success criteria might then relate to being able to list different causes of flooding, knowing how each of these might be mitigated, and then applying the knowledge in a different context.

As soon as you begin to think of what you are teaching as special cases of something else, you will begin thinking about the more general category of which this particular example is a special case, and then you can start generating other examples in the same category. Table 3.1 shows examples of some confused learning intentions based on the work of Shirley Clarke (2005) but extended to show how removing the context of the learning from the learning itself makes it easier to identify appropriate success criteria.

Table 3.1: Confused and Clarified Learning Intentions and Success Criteria

Confused learning intention	Clarified learning intention	Context of learning	Potential new context
To be able to write instructions on how to change a bicycle tire	To be able to write instructions	Changing a bicycle tire	Writing instructions on how to make a sandwich
To be able to construct arguments for or against assisted suicide	To be able to construct arguments for or against emotionally charged propositions	Assisted suicide	Constructing arguments for or against abortion
To create a written description of a friend	To be able to create an effective characterization	Describing a friend	Creating an effective characterization of a relative

Mix It Up

The ability of students to apply things in other contexts is increased if their learning activities are varied. Students generally prefer to do one thing at a time, and get frustrated if the activities involve "chopping and changing" between different activities, but they tend to learn more. This was rather powerfully illustrated by a twelve-week experiment that involved sixty-four eight-year-old students who practiced throwing beanbags into buckets in gym class (Kerr & Booth, 1978). Half of the students practiced tossing the beanbags into a bucket three feet away, while for the other half the practice was varied by having the bucket either two feet away or four feet away. At the end of the experiment, all the students were tested on their ability to throw the beanbag into a bucket three feet away. The students who had practiced with buckets placed two and four feet away, and who therefore never practiced throwing a beanbag into a bucket three feet away, actually outscored the students who did nothing but practice throwing beanbags into a bucket three feet away. Of course, this is just a single study, but there is now substantial research evidence that despite their preference to work on one idea or context at a time, students learn more when they are required to vary their practice (for an authoritative yet readable summary, see P. C. Brown et al., 2014).

Go to www.learningsciences.com/bookresources to download figures and tables.

Cautions

Differentiate Success Criteria, Not Learning Intentions

Many districts have adopted "differentiated instruction" as a policy for their class-rooms, although this often appears to be done with little clear idea about what the term actually means. Indeed, most definitions of differentiated instruction are rather vague, in effect saying little more than students are different, and we should recognize this in our teaching. Nevertheless, in many districts, teachers are encouraged to cater to differences in their students by having different learning intentions for different students in their class. This seems to us unfortunate for at least two reasons: first, it assumes that the teacher knows which students are capable of which work, there-fore creating a danger of self-fulfilling prophecies, and, second, it is a lot of work for the teacher. Now, of course, different students will learn different things in a lesson, particularly one where teachers give students independence over their work, so it is unlikely that a single success criterion is appropriate for all students. However, we do think that all the students in the group should have reasonably similar goals. In other words, we think that differentiation should take place in terms of the success criteria rather than the learning intentions.

As a concrete example, consider a lesson on the area of a trapezoid. In a typical middle school classroom in the United States, the teacher explains the rule to students, performs one worked example for the whole class on the board, and then students practice the technique individually, in their seats, while the teacher walks up and down the aisles, providing additional support where needed. In Japan, it is more likely that the teacher shows one way of finding the area of a trapezoid to the class, and then invites students, working in pairs or groups, to see how many conceptually distinct ways they can gener-ate to find the area of a trapezoid. For example, if the teacher introduces the "duplicate and rotate" method:

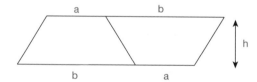

then students might find the "parallel cut and rotate" method:

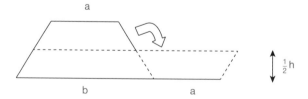

There are exactly thirteen conceptually distinct ways of finding the area of a trapezoid. Many are simple to find, but others are much harder, either because they are not easy to spot, or because the algebraic manipulation required to show that the method still results in the standard formula of $\frac{1}{2}(a + b) \times h$ is much more demanding, such as the method that involves completing the triangle and then using properties of similar triangles to subtract the area of the smaller triangle from that of the larger triangle:

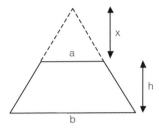

The important point about such a task is that the learning intention is the same for all members of the class—to find as many conceptually distinct ways of calculating the area of a trapezoid given the length of the two parallel sides and distance between them. The differentiation comes as a result of the way that the teacher implements the activity, supports some students, and pushes others to find specific methods, such as the example using similar triangles just described.

Enhancements

Process versus Product Success Criteria

Some authors argue that success criteria are more useful if they address the process by which students are to produce the work than if they merely describe the features of the final product. Clarke (2005) defines *process success criteria* as those which "summarise the key steps or ingredients the student needs in order to fulfil the learning objective—the main things to do, include or focus on. These give a framework for formative assessment to take place" (p. 29).

Process success criteria can be particularly helpful to students if they break the process that students are expected to follow into a number of smaller, more easily managed steps. This idea is nicely encapsulated by Liane Paixao (2014), who wrote and recorded a song that summarizes the benefits of process success criteria from the student's point of view:

Break It Down

You want me to follow you, steady
But I don't think we're really ready
You gimme no clue, came out of the blue
I'm feeling so lost
I cannot pack and go

So, where are you leading me to?
That, you don't say . . .

I gave up on guessing, and then you complain

It feels like a game

I zone out for the day

(You gotta break it)

CHORUS:
Break it down, break it down
Break it down for me
Learning can be so easy
When every step is there
And I can see

Don't go 'round turning my rocks over
Pinpointing all that's error
Without showing how to learn from them
And make it all better
You wait until I fail to tell me
That I really could
I could've done much better
It is water under the bridge
It doesn't matter (You gotta break it)

(Chorus)

BRIDGE:
I gotta learn on my own, guide me
Warn me before a sharp turn, mind me
Life is a slippery slope that we can't cruise on blindly
Gotta learn how to get to where I gotta go (yeah)

Scaffold my learning
and coach me along the way
Empower me so that one day
I can stand on my own

Break it down, break it down . . .

The danger with process success criteria, of course, is that they can be too specific. If the process success criteria lay out, step-by-step, exactly what the student has to do to be successful, little learning is likely to take place. Moreover, students are less likely to generate insightful solutions.

For example, a teacher is instructing a class how to identify the largest fraction from a set. A suitable learning intention is "to identify the largest fraction in a set," and the product success criteria are differentiated to include examples of differing difficulty. One way to do this is to have a criterion relating to those cases where one of the denominators is a common denominator for all the fractions in the set and another criterion where none of the denominators is a common denominator of the set:

Example 1 $\frac{4}{5}$ $\frac{3}{4}$ $\frac{7}{10}$ $\frac{17}{20}$

Example 2 $\frac{4}{5}$ $\frac{3}{4}$ $\frac{7}{10}$ $\frac{5}{8}$

A typical set of process success criteria for such a task would remind the students to first identify the lowest common denominator for the four fractions being compared, convert all the fractions to equivalent fractions with a common denominator, and then compare the fractions. However, if students are not given process success criteria that tell them how to identify the largest fraction, some might convert the fractions to percentages, and others might realize that identifying the largest fraction is equivalent to identifying which fraction needs the smallest amount added to it to make into one whole, which are, in our view, eminently sensible, and perhaps even superior, approaches to solving the problem. The important point here is that while rubrics may identify the most common trajectory of improvement for most students, there will be students who improve in different ways and follow different tracks.

Similar considerations apply to planning frames and writing templates. In the same way that leg braces can be both a support and constraint (think, for example, of the eponymous hero of the movie *Forrest Gump*), process specifications and structures can help weaker students do better work than they might without those supports, but they constrain all students from finding imaginative and creative solutions to tasks they are set. This does not mean that we should not use process success criteria—as noted earlier, they can be an important element in supporting our students' learning—but we do need to make sure our students understand that if they feel confident that they know what they are doing, they can throw the leg braces away. This means that occasionally, perhaps even frequently, our students will fall flat on their faces, but, as will become clear when we discuss eliciting evidence, failures are indications that the work is sufficiently challenging to make it worthwhile. As Thomas Edison once said, when asked about his failure to produce a workable filament for the electric light bulb, "I have not failed. I've just found 10,000 ways that won't work."

To Be Formative, Learning Intentions and Success Criteria Need to Be Generic

The foregoing discussion of process success criteria illustrates a more general point relating to the idea of generalizability in learning that we discussed earlier. The aim of any learning intention or success criterion is not to help the students complete the activity—it is to help them learn. Checklists that provide step-by-step instructions for students to follow do not help students complete tasks on their own. This is because what psychologists call "executive control"—deciding what to do next in a task—is being done by the checklist, not the student. Too often, the result is students who can complete a task when directed but cannot work independently.

This point often gets lost when teachers are devising learning intentions and success criteria. If students are to learn something in doing one task that they can carry over to another task, the same learning intentions and success criteria must apply to more than a single task. Specific learning intentions and success criteria do help different raters agree on whether students have achieved a particular level of attainment, so they are useful for summative assessment. However, where the assessment is intended to function formatively, a degree of generality has to be built into the learning intentions and success criteria (Arter & McTighe, 2001). Of course, if the success criteria are too general, they become so meaningless that they provide little or no guidance for students. The art (and it is an art rather than a science) is to find an appropriate balancing point between these two extremes, and, of course, the location of that balancing point will be different for different students, different for different aspects of the subject matter, and different for students at different stages of expertise.

Be Aware of Strengths and Weaknesses of Analytic and Holistic Learning Intentions and Success Criteria

Similar considerations apply to the debate about whether learning intentions and success criteria should be analytic or holistic. It might be assumed that analytic approaches to describing quality, in which different aspects of quality are identified, might be superior for both summative and formative purposes. Specifying the dimensions of quality that are important increases the likelihood that different raters look at the work in the same way, therefore improving the usefulness of descriptions for summative assessment. Moreover, when the learning intentions and success criteria highlight the important dimensions of quality, students are more likely to pay attention to the aspects of the work that matter, and therefore improve the quality of their work.

These arguments certainly have merit, but it is also important to remember that analytic approaches to describing quality often miss out on the "glue" that holds a piece of work together. Sometimes a piece of work seems to check all the right boxes, but somehow the whole is less than the sum of the parts. And at other times, a piece of work can get all the pieces wrong but somehow cohere as a whole. As with so many aspects of formative assessment, there are no simple answers here, but we hope that the principles we lay out help you resolve—in ways that better meet the learning needs of your students—the various tensions we discussed.

Start With Samples of Work, Rather Than Rubrics, to Communicate Quality

The extraordinary increase in the use of scoring rubrics for all kinds of assessments in the United States in recent years is perfectly understandable. If, as this chapter argues, students do better if they know what they are meant to be doing, laying out the characteristics of different standards of work must surely be helpful. However, it is our view that the use of rubrics has, in many cases, spread to a point where the benefit may well be less than the harm.

Before we point out the shortcomings of rubrics, however, we want to make it clear we are not saying that rubrics cannot be useful in education—indeed, we believe that they have an important role to play—but we think the intelligent use of rubrics requires a deep understanding of their potential shortcomings.

First, rubrics are essentially unidimensional. While most rubrics identify multiple aspects of a piece of work, the improvement in each aspect is almost always along a single dimension. In other words, there is only one way in which that aspect of the work can be improved. This may be appropriate for some kinds of work, but wherever a measure of creativity is involved, a piece of work can be improved in a number of different ways, but only one of these is usually reflected in the rubric. Those using the rubric are therefore channeled into producing improvements only along the dimension identified in the rubric.

Second, rubrics are often more focused on evaluating student achievement than improving. Alfie Kohn suggests that there are three main reasons why we want to assess the quality of our students' efforts: to rank students, induce them to try harder, or provide feedback that helps them improve (Kohn, 2006, p. 14). Proponents of rubrics point out that rubrics can give students feedback to enable them to improve their work, which is certainly true, but the fact that rubrics almost always identify a number of different levels of quality in student responses suggests that the evaluative function is also vital. And it is important to remember that the intent behind the use of rubrics is irrelevant; what matters is what rubrics do to students.

Third, rubrics rarely have the same meanings for students that they do for teachers. The highest level of a rubric for a piece of persuasive writing might require that the essay make an effective argument, but if the student does not know what constitutes an effective argument, the rubric is of limited use.

While rubrics have a role to play, we believe they are best regarded as the *culmination* of a developmental process that begins with examination of samples of students' work. So, before your students do a laboratory report or write a ghost story, spend some time getting them to look at other students' attempts at similar tasks. Many teachers believe that it is wasteful to take time that students could use to generate their own work to look at the work of others, but there are two immediate benefits of getting students to look at samples of student work: first, students are better at spotting mistakes in the work of others than they are in their own work. Assessing one's own work, as well as assessing the work of one's peers in the classroom, is emotionally charged, and the emotional resonances can often interfere with engaging in the demands of the task. However, assessing the work of anonymous others is emotionally neutral, so students are able to focus more effectively on the task. Second, when students notice mistakes in the work of others, they are less likely to make the same mistakes in their own work.

For the youngest students, we recommend starting with just two pieces of work where one is relatively strong and one is relatively weak. For example, the teacher might present a kindergarten class with two photographs of something children have built such as a sandcastle or something made of Lego® bricks and ask them which is better, and why. In general, students seem to find it easier to identify qualities of good work when two pieces of work are contrasted than when they are given a single piece of work, regardless of whether it is strong or weak.

Where the two pieces of work are relatively large— for example, watercolor paintings or drawings— the teacher can display them side by side to the class. For smaller pieces of work, a document camera (sometimes called a visualizer or visual presenter) is very useful. The teacher can then ask students whether one of the two is better than the other, and if they respond that one is better, the teacher can ask which one it is and why. Think-pair-share (see next chapter) is a particularly useful technique here for giving students time to think about their perceptions of quality and begin to develop some vocabulary to put this into words.

As students become more sophisticated in their appreciation of the differences in quality between different pieces of work, you can use samples of work that are much closer in quality, and introduce more gradations of quality by including more examples. The language that students use to describe their perceptions of the differences in quality between different pieces of work will then naturally lend itself to the construction of success criteria for the work. More importantly, the success criteria will be anchored in actual samples of work rather than vague and decontextualized statements that can be interpreted in a number of ways.

Success criteria can be simple checklists of features that need to be present for the work to be regarded as good, such as the following checklist for early writing, which can be accompanied by pictures or diagrams to cue less fluent readers:

❑ All my sentences start with a capital letters.

❑ Every sentence ends with a "stop sign" ("." "?" or "!").

❑ I used finger spacing between words.

❑ I used the word wall to spell my words correctly.

❏ My handwriting is neat.

❏ I read through my work to make sure it sounds right.

Before showing the work to the teacher, students can then be asked to check through the list. Some teachers ask students to use the checklist to complete a self-assessment by choosing an emoticon such as a happy or sad face. Asking students how happy they are with their work does have a role to play, even in pre-K (most adults are surprised how well even four- and five-year-olds are able to evaluate their own work). However, when the students are using a checklist, it probably makes more sense for them to make sure each of the required features is present. After all, we don't want students handing in writing that they know isn't good enough and they know how to improve!

Tips

Remember That Rubrics Are Really Nothing More Than Collections of Success Criteria

Heidi Andrade (2000) defines a rubric as follows:

> An instructional rubric is usually a one- or two-page document that describes varying levels of quality, from excellent to poor, for a specific assignment. It is usually used with a relatively complex assignment, such as a long-term project, an essay, or a research paper. Its purposes are to give students informative feedback about their works in progress and to give detailed evaluations of their final products. (p. 13)

Before we go on, one feature of the definition needs discussion. It is true that rubrics are usually given to students to help them complete a specific assignment. However, as noted above, if the rubric is focused solely on what a student needs to do to complete just that task, it is not much use in helping the students learn. Such a rubric will be useful for summative assessment because it can ensure that students are clear about the requirements of the task so that "If they know it they show it." But to support learning, rubrics must be relevant to multiple tasks, ideally over an extended period of time, so that students can come to understand the deep principles that underpin quality work across a range of settings and tasks. Although we have not conducted a definitive study, it seems to us that most of the rubrics given to students are much better suited to summative functions of assessment rather than guiding student learning in the future.

In North America, rubrics are almost always presented in terms of a rectangular grid, with the vertical dimension used to identify different aspects of the task and the horizontal dimension used to identify different degrees or gradations of quality. Some authors have degrees of quality increasing from left to right, which makes sense given that in English, we read from left to right, and in mathematics and science, graphs are almost always drawn with values on the horizontal axis increasing from left to right. Other authors prefer to have degrees of quality decreasing from left to right so that the rubric headlines high-quality rather than low-quality work. We can see advantages of both and no compelling reason to prefer one over the other. Whichever works best for you and your students is the one to use.

Another issue that needs to be settled in devising a rubric is how the levels of quality are described. Some rubrics simply use numbers (e.g., "1," "2," "3," and "4") while others use labels such as "below basic," "basic," "proficient," and "advanced," or "novice," "apprentice," "practitioner," and "expert." The problem with such labels is that they can send the message to students that once they get to the top level, they are done, which, of course, in learning is never the case—there is always a next level. Some teachers have asked students to choose for themselves how the different levels of achievement are described. One group of students chose a bicycle to represent the lowest level of achievement, a car for the second, and a space rocket for the third. However, perhaps the best idea of this kind we have seen from students, which really highlights the developmental nature of the best rubrics, was a group who chose frogspawn for the lowest level, tadpoles for the second, and a frog for the third.

The rubric format is now so common we often forget that the format makes us do things that may, or may not, be helpful. For example, we have yet to see a rubric that has a blank cell. There is something in every cell because, for some reason, there has to be, and so we contrive entries by using adjectives such as "some" and "many" to create distinctions that allow us to put something in every cell. However, for some aspects of work, there isn't really a continuum of development, but just two levels, equivalent to understanding something and not understanding something. Think of riding a bicycle. At level 1, there would be "Can't do it" and at level 4, "Can do it." There really isn't anything at levels 2 and 3. Children move so quickly from level 1 to level 4, it would be artificial and misleading to put anything between them.

Another problem with the rubric format is it creates the impression that the degrees of quality are somehow equivalent across the different components of the rubric. In other words, giving a 3 to a piece of work on two different components of a rubric sends the message that these two aspects of the work are equally good, and, perhaps more problematically, that if a student gets a 2 on one component of the rubric and a 3 on all the others, the work is somehow weaker on the component that was scored a 2. This may, of course, be the case, but in our experience this is unlikely unless the rubric has been specifically constructed in this way, which makes even greater demands on how the rubric is constructed, and which in turn leads to the problems we discussed in the previous paragraph.

As we said earlier, none of this means that rubrics are not useful; they can be highly effective ways of communicating standards of achievement to our students, not least because the format is extremely simple and compact. But all teachers need to be aware that sometimes we pay a high price for that simplicity and compactness. If it makes sense to arrange your success criteria in the form of a scoring rubric, then by all means do so.

But also consider what you are giving up by using this format, and also consider whether a different format, such as a checklist, might be more effective for your students.

Cautions

Use Examples Where Deep Features Are Not Aligned With Surface Features

When quality has multiple dimensions, care needs to be taken that students are not able to determine which pieces are better by focusing on surface features. For example, if you want to get students to focus on characterization, it might be useful to have one piece of work with deep characterization but poor grammar, spelling, and handwriting, and another piece with good grammar, spelling, and handwriting but weak characterization. Similarly, where pieces of work involve extended pieces of writing, be careful not to fall into the trap of "longest is best." For example: A social studies teacher is sharing learning intentions with an eighth-grade class by giving them a source document, a key question about the document, and four different responses to the question. Students are asked to work in pairs to put the four responses in order of quality. However, because the longer pieces are better, some students are able to generate the correct order of quality by focusing on length. The teacher learns his lesson, and in the future makes sure that sometimes the shortest answer is the best, and the longest answer is the worst.

Be Aware That Sometimes Quality Cannot Be Put Into Words

Perhaps the greatest danger with rubrics is that they are used where quality really cannot be effectively described in words. As Roger Shattuck once said, "Words do not reflect the world, not because there is no world, but because words are not mirrors" (quoted in Burgess, 1992, p. 119). Sometimes the best we can do is help our students develop what Guy Claxton calls a "nose for quality" (Claxton, 1995). If the teachers in a building have a shared sense of quality, and they are able to share this with their students, then even if this understanding cannot be put into words, there is an effective basis for high-quality assessment. When teachers have a shared understanding of quality, even without rubrics, different teachers will give similar ratings to students' work and it is this agreement between teachers that provides a secure basis for summative assessment. And when, in addition, students understand quality, they are better able to guide their own work, which is the key aspect of the first strategy of formative assessment and the focus of this chapter.

Don't Abdicate Responsibility for Quality

Many people describe the process of constructing learning intentions and success criteria with the students as a process of "negotiating" or "co-creating" learning intentions and success criteria with students. We have no problem with the process, nor the terms, but we think it is important that it is clear the teacher is in charge of the process. The teacher is the expert in the subject and the students are novices, so while it is appropriate for the teacher to listen to the students' views, it is essential that the final learning intentions and success criteria, however they are developed, are consistent with the teacher's under-standing of quality in the subject.

Enhancements

Use Rubrics as the Starting Point for a Dialogue Between You and Your Students

One of the advantages of rubrics is that they allow teachers to give really quick feedback to students on their work. For example, a teacher gives her students a rubric for a writing task that identifies six aspects of quality: focus, organization, grammar, effectiveness, length, and completeness. For each of the six dimensions of quality, the rubric identifies four levels of achievement (1, 2, 3, and 4) and for each level, provides a description of the typical features of work at this level. Because the teacher knows that the students have a copy of the full rubric, rather than detailing the features of the work, the teacher can provide feedback simply by giving a rating for each of the dimensions of quality, as shown in Figure 3.1. The students can then refer to the rubric to see what each of the ratings mean.

Figure 3.1: Use of a Rubric Summary to Provide Rapid Feedback

Focus	1	2	3	(4)
Organization	1	2	3	(4)
Grammar	1	2	(3)	4
Effectiveness	1	2	3	(4)
Length	1	2	(3)	4
Completeness	1	(2)	3	4

However, where the goal is to help students understand the learning intentions and success criteria, a more powerful activity is to get the students to do a self-assessment for each of the dimensions specified in the rubric and then for the teacher to look at the students' self-assessment and report back to the student, "I would have given you a higher rating in two of the categories and a lower rating in one of the categories. See if you can figure out which categories these are, and why." This is an example of making feedback into detective work, discussed in further detail in the chapter on feedback.

Find Out What Your Students Think They Are Learning

No matter how much the teacher involves the students in the "co-creation" of the learning intentions and success criteria, and no matter how well those learning intentions and success criteria are designed, there is always the danger that students' understandings are different from what was intended. It is therefore useful periodically to ask students what they think they are learning.

Go to www.learningsciences.com/bookresources to download figures and tables.

When we taught middle and high school math, we would both get our students to undertake "mathematical investigations"—open-ended (and often open-begun!) tasks to get students to understand how mathematics generates knowledge (as opposed to what knowledge mathematics generates). In one such lesson, Dylan was getting a class to investigate the number of "polyominoes" that could be made from a given number of squares, given that each square had to join edge to edge and corner to corner with other squares. The class quickly established that there were only five distinct tetrominoes (i.e., five different ways of arranging four squares, not counting rotations and reflections as different). He then asked students to find out how many pentominoes there were. When he asked students why they thought they were doing this particular investigation, they replied that they thought what was important was finding out how many pentominoes there were. It turns out there are exactly twelve pentominoes, but there is nothing interesting or important about this fact. This particular task had been chosen to prove a challenging (and somewhat messy) context for students to practice working systematically and logically, but the students did not realize this.

One particularly powerful way to find out what your students think they are learning is to ask them to make up test items, with correct answers, about what they have been studying. You will often find out what you think they are learning is not the same as what they think they are learning, which is useful, but this particular task of generating items is beneficial to students in itself.

It has long been known that learners remember responses they generate themselves better than those responses that are given to them, and this is now often called the *generation effect* (Slamecka & Graf, 1978). In particular, one hour students spend writing test questions on what they have been studying results in more learning for them than one hour spent working with a study guide, answering practice tests, or leaving the students to their own devices (Foos, Mora, & Tkacz, 1994).

Big Ideas, Learning Progressions, and Staging Posts

So far in this chapter, we have treated learning intentions and success criteria for one lesson as relatively isolated from those for another lesson. The problem with such an approach is that each lesson or unit stands or falls on its own, few connections are made, and the student's experience is fragmented. In this final section, we lay out an approach that you can use to begin to look for the "big pictures" in your curriculum. The idea is that instead of dealing with pine needles and twigs, you identify the trunk of the tree and the main branches.

In terms of the logic of Ralph Tyler's approach to curriculum and instruction we presented at the beginning of this chapter, you might assume that we should have started the book with this idea, but in our experience, it can take many years of teaching to be clear about the big picture of what we are teaching. Moreover, the idea that all our teaching should be focused on big ideas is likely to be unrealistic. Our state and national standards simply aren't well-enough designed for this to be possible, at least in any reasonable period of time. Our recommendation is therefore that you should work both bottom-up and top-down. Begin by clarifying learning intentions and success criteria lesson by lesson and unit by unit, and share them with your students. Over time, however, we encourage you to give some attention to a top-down process of starting from the big ideas in what you are teaching, mapping out the routes your students are likely to take in developing their understanding of the big ideas and figuring out what the most important staging points are along the way. As well as making the curriculum simpler and more manageable for teachers, focusing on the big picture in this way helps students see how what they are learning builds on what they have done before, and how their current learning prepares them for what is to come. This idea of progression in learning is particularly important in helping students develop what Carol Dweck calls a *growth mindset*, which is explored in more detail in Chapter 5.

We can, of course, define a big idea in any way we please. To us, the most powerful way involves more than using a label. To be useful as a big idea, a concept should provide a way of making sense of a number of related phenomena in an effective and efficient way. Most importantly, a big idea is *generative* in the sense that you can apply it in areas that the student has not yet encountered. It does not just make sense of what the student already has experienced, but it also provides a way of making sense of what the student encounters in the future. For this reason, the best big ideas form part of student learning over many years and can even bridge from elementary to secondary school.

Just how big an idea needs to be to qualify as big is, of course, a question that does not have a simple answer. When there are relatively few big ideas, obviously you can explore each idea to some depth, but the risk is that the ideas become so vague as to be difficult to use. A relatively large number of big ideas allows for more comprehensive coverage, but the danger is then that the ideas become small atoms of content, and their relationship to the other content is lost. One group of researchers that looked at this recommends that for each school subject, the number of big ideas should be between five and ten (Popham, Keller, Moulding, Pellegrino, & Sandifer, 2005), but there could be many good reasons for more or fewer.

A group of science education researchers from around the world led by Wynne Harlen proposes a list of ten big ideas of science that could provide a focus for the learning of science from kindergarten to high school (Harlen, 2010, p. iv):

1. All material in the Universe is made of very small particles.
2. Objects can affect other objects at a distance.
3. Changing the movement of an object requires a net force acting on it.
4. The total amount of energy in the Universe is always the same but energy can be transformed when things change or are made to happen.

5. The composition of the Earth and its atmosphere and the processes occurring within them.

6. The solar system is a very small part of one of millions of galaxies in the Universe.

7. Organisms are organized on a cellular basis.

8. Organisms require a supply of energy and materials for which they are often dependent on or in competition with other organisms.

9. Genetic information is passed from one generation of organisms to another.

10. The diversity of organisms, living and extinct, is the result of evolution.

In addition, the group looks at how scientific knowledge is created and suggests four big ideas about science (Harlen, 2010, p. v):

1. Science assumes that for every effect there is one or more causes.

2. Scientific explanations, theories, and models are those that best fit the facts known at a particular time.

3. The knowledge produced by science is used in some technologies to create products to serve human ends.

4. Applications of science often have ethical, social, economic, and political implications.

Because big ideas are meant to have traction over a number of years, they aren't of much use as learning intentions, so it is generally helpful to break big ideas down into smaller elements. This may seem paradoxical. The whole purpose of a big idea is for it to be a single concept, and breaking it down into smaller concepts seems to undermine the entire purpose of having big ideas. However, students' understanding of big ideas is meant to develop over time, so there is nothing inherently contradictory in having a big idea that can be broken down into a number of developmental steps.

In recent years in the United States, these developmental sequences have been called *learning progressions*—indications of the stages through which students typically progress in reaching an understanding of a big idea. For example, learning progressions in science is defined as "empirically grounded and testable hypotheses about how students' understanding of, and ability to use, core scientific concepts, explanations, and related scientific practices grow and become more sophisticated over time, with appropriate instruction" (Corcoran, Mosher, & Rogat, 2009, p. 20).

Perhaps not surprisingly, most of the early work on developing learning progressions focuses on science and mathematics, because the developmental trajectories of learners in these subjects have been studied in some detail in recent years (see, for example, Corcoran et al., 2009; Daro, Mosher, & Corcoran, 2011).

However, as far as we are aware, the idea of learning progressions applies equally well in all school subjects. For example, the following is a learning progression proposed by a working group in England looking at students' developing conceptions of chronology and cause and effect in history (National Curriculum History Working Group, 1990, pp. 121–125):

- Recognize everyday time conventions.
- Place a few straightforward events in chronological sequence; demonstrate, by reference to the past, an awareness that actions have consequences.
- Demonstrate awareness of a variety of changes within a short time span; demonstrate an awareness of human motivation illustrated by reference to events of the past.
- Employ appropriate chronological conventions by using time lines or other diagrammatic representation of historical issues; understand that historical events usually have more than one cause or consequence.
- Demonstrate a clear understanding of change over varied time periods; understand that historical events have different types of causes and consequences.
- Recognize some of the complexities inherent in the idea of change, when explaining historical issues; when explaining historical issues, place some causes and consequences in a sensible order of importance.
- When explaining historical issues, show a detailed awareness of the idea of change; when examining historical issues, draw the distinction between causes, intentions, motives, and reasons.
- Apply extensive understanding of change to complex historical issues; produce a well-argued hierarchy of causes for complex, historical issues.
- Demonstrate an awareness of the problems inherent in the idea of change; demonstrate an awareness of the problems inherent in the idea of causation.
- Demonstrate a clear understanding of the complexities of the relationship between cause, consequence, and change.

Now, different social studies teachers might have other views about the appropriateness of this particular learning progression, but the important point is that this does attempt to lay out how the student improves when he gets better at history.

It might be assumed that, to save teachers all over the country from "reinventing the wheel," learning progressions could be developed at a national or at least state level. However, because the sequence in which topics are taught vary from state to state, district to district, and even building to building within the same district, progressions developed nationally or at state level are likely to need adaptation if they are to faithfully trace the learning journeys students take in any particular school. For some ideas about generating learning progressions that meet the needs of your students, see Leahy and Wiliam (2011).

After learning progressions are developed, it is then possible to select particular points along the "learning journey" as learning intentions. Most often the learning intentions relate to what a teacher can cover in a particular instructional period, such as a lesson or unit of work, but it is also sometimes useful to define learning intentions as what David Perkins calls *troublesome knowledge* (Perkins, 1999), which is discussed in more detail in the next chapter. The important idea here is if we know there are particular things that are difficult for students, then we need to find out whether they understand them.

The goals of education in play, of course, strongly influence the nature of big ideas, and what might be a big idea for one person might be trivial or even irrelevant for another. Big ideas may not even be "true" in fields where knowledge is contested, but they always provide ways of making sense of experience.

Tips

Get the Grain Size of Big Ideas Right

When developing big ideas for their curriculum, it is difficult, but important, to get the *grain size* of big ideas right for the task at hand. When the grain size is too large then the idea tends to be so loosely framed that it is not helpful in guiding learning. For example, one group of teachers adopted the following list of big ideas for social studies: government and civics, cultures and societies, economics, geography, and historical perspective (NTI Social Studies, 2014). These are useful ways of dividing up the content matter, but they provide little guidance about what the students should be learning in this subject.

On the other hand, when the grain size is too small, the number of big ideas becomes large, and ultimately unmanageable. Think of this: in the context of teaching about the American Revolution, we could adopt as potential big ideas the nature of patriotism, whether the bravery of the founders was an admirable quality, or whether the British government was fair to the colonists (Propel, no date). The problem with this list is the grain size of these ideas is so fine that dozens, and even perhaps hundreds, would be needed to cover just one year's work in social studies.

Table 3.2 shows examples of suggestions for big ideas that seem to us to be sufficiently general to be powerful over a number of years of a child's development but also sufficiently precise for determining whether students are improving.

Table 3.2: Suggestions for Big Ideas

Subject	Big idea
English language arts	The "hero's journey" (Campbell, 1949/2004) as a structure for understanding myths and legends.
Social studies (geography)	Patterns of human development are influenced by, and in turn influence, physical features of the environment.
Social studies (history)	All historical sources are products of their time, but understanding the circumstances of their creation helps us resolve conflicts of evidence.
Mathematics	Fractions, decimals, percentages, and ratios are all ways of expressing numbers, and every real number can be represented as a point on a number line.
Science	All matter is made of very small particles.

Cautions

Not All Useful Learning Intentions Will Be Big Ideas

Even with a clear focus on big ideas, there is always a need for some "mopping up" of individual pieces of content that don't fit neatly anywhere else. For example, it is useful for students to know how to read Roman numerals, but understanding Roman numerals is not a big idea in the sense we have described it here. Moreover, the Roman numeral system is highly idiosyncratic, using bases of both 5 and 10, so learning about the Roman numeral system doesn't help you do anything apart from using Roman numerals; the topic of Roman numerals is probably best treated as a "one-off."

In our view, it is generally possible, over a period of several years, to organize the curriculum so that at least half of the content is in the form of big ideas. This may seem modest, but the clarity brought to the curriculum, for both the teachers and students, is a huge advantage. If you can get two-thirds, you're doing well, not least because state standards were never designed to be coherent, so imposing some order on them is challenging.

Learning Progressions Need Both an Empirical and a Theoretical Basis

The fact that students happen to learn something in a particular sequence does not mean that the sequence is an appropriate learning progression. After all, the particular learning sequence might just be an accident of the particular way that students had been taught. To be useful as a learning progression, there has to be some underlying rationale that students are likely to follow in using this particular sequence in advancing their work. However, as every teacher knows, by itself, a compelling logical rationale that students should learn something in a particular sequence does not mean that they will do so.

We have all taught students who, for whatever reason, seem to find easy things difficult and difficult things easy. That is why Denvir and Brown (1986) suggest there should be both a logical and an empirical basis for the learning progression: there should be clear reasons why the elements of the progression are arranged in a particular sequence, and it should be rare (if not impossible) for students to reach the later parts of the progression without going through the earlier parts.

Enhancements

Involve Students in Clarifying the Big Ideas

As students get more involved in their own learning, they become clearer about their own learning, and over time, develop views about what the subjects they are studying are really all about. In the same way that we recommended that students are involved in the co-construction of the learning intentions and success criteria, it can be useful to ask them for their views about what the big ideas are of the subjects they are studying. This helps students develop a more strategic view of the subject and also provides useful information for you about the students' experiences. For example, if your students tell you that mathematics is all about getting the correct answer quickly, or English language arts is all about reading and writing, that is a cue for you to change what you are doing. Perhaps most importantly, our students can sometimes help us think about the subjects that we teach in a way that had not occurred to us and help us move our own thinking forward as well.

Case Studies

In this section, we present two case studies of teachers sharing learning intentions and success criteria with students. The extracts are transcripts of videos taken from Wiliam and Leahy (2014). We encourage you to read the transcripts, and then think about what you have read by responding to the reflection questions at the end of the transcript before moving on. The two case studies in this chapter, and the two in the chapter on "activating students as owners of their own learning," are both taken from secondary schools. You may be surprised by the extent to which the conversations between teachers and students, and among the students, are dominated by what they need to do to get a good grade on an examination. Of course doing well on tests or examinations is not the only—or even the most important—reason to educate young people, but they are, in many schools and districts, a feature of classroom life. We have included these examples to show that using formative assessment to improve the quality of instruction is entirely compatible with success on tests and examinations. Indeed, we know of nothing else that you can do to have a bigger impact on your students' test and examination performance. The point is that if high-stakes tests and examinations are a part of the system in which you work, then formative assessment can be used both to deepen student learning and increase test scores at the same time. You don't have to choose between teaching well and increasing test scores. You can do both.

English

A group of tenth-grade students is preparing for a formal written examination that will assess their understanding of English literature. The examination consists of two examination papers, each seventy-five to ninety minutes long, during each of which the students will attempt two or three questions, so they will have thirty to forty-five minutes for their response to each question.

Chris Flack, the teacher, shares with the students the following handout, which includes the four lists of success criteria associated with the four highest grades available—C, B, A, and A* (equivalent to an A+ grade)—in the examination they are about to take.

Handout

Match the four lists of criteria below to the correct grade. Which one is C, B, A, and A*?

- Shows originality of analysis and interpretation
- Sustained evidence of enthusiastic and personal response
- Shows concise textual analysis and understanding

- Demonstrates insight
- Explores connections between texts
- Explores how meaning is conveyed through language, structure, and form
- Explores connections between texts—refers to some detail

- Demonstrates analytic skill
- Shows independent understanding
- Shows layers of meaning—how meaning is conveyed through appropriate detail
- Shows relevant comparisons

- Demonstrates analytical and interpretive skill
- Explores alternative approaches and interpretations
- Considers and evaluates the way that meaning is conveyed through language, structure, and form

With a partner, the students discuss the key differences between each grade. Here is a transcript of the video:

Teacher:	Exams are creeping up on us now. We are going to try to work out how you are going to be assessed in this thing. You've got a sheet in front of you. It's got the GCSE criteria for C, B, A, and A*. Have a read, and try and work out which one is which first of all. So where's the B, which one is the A, which one's the dirty C? Obviously once you have done this, I want you to work out why, because anyone can write a grade next to a sentence. Try to work out why that grade is what you are thinking it is.

Two students working together, followed by a whole-class discussion:

Polly:	For a C you don't actually have to analyze anything.
Sofia:	You just have to show that you understand it.
Polly:	Yes, basically that you understand. And for B it's more.
Teacher:	Thirty seconds.
Ana:	And it says sustained evidence so it's not just like you . . .
Teacher:	Right, then. Which one is the A then? Steph.
Steph:	Demonstrate an analytical and interpretive skill. Explore alternative approaches and interpretations. Consider and evaluate the way meaning is conveyed through language, structure, and form.
Teacher:	Good. It is that one. How did you know that it was an A? Someone else that isn't Steph.
Briony:	Because for the A* it says "originality of analysis," and you have been telling us that we need an original idea to get an A*.
Teacher:	Excellent. Good. So the difference between an A and an A* is that for an A* you really have to try to pin down that originality of analysis. What other differences did you spot between an A and an A*?
Polly:	For an A* you really have to have an opinion on it and be enthusiastic about it.
Teacher:	Yes, you do. We have had this discussion before. Enthusiasm doesn't mean you have to jump up and down and pretend you love the poem. It means you have to have an enthusiastic response. Good, anything else that you spotted? Prin.
Prin:	It uses words like *sustain* and *concise*.
Teacher:	Absolutely, you've got to get straight to the point for an A*. You've got to know what you are saying and get there as accurately as you can. Good, hopefully by the end of the lesson you will be another step nearer that A*.

The video ends with a student and the teacher reflecting on the process after the lesson:

Anika:	If they give a list of, like, A*, what you need to do for an A* and what you need to do for a C, you'll make sure you do more A* work than a C, because you know what you are doing. But if you don't have that success criteria you don't know what you are doing, what you need to do to get that grade.

Teacher:	It is slightly disingenuous because some of them aren't an A yet. They are not a miracle class. But by talking only about A and A*, the Cs and the Bs, you'll find they reach further toward an A. So if I keep talking about an A*, even those that aren't an A will still make progress.

Reflection

Before reading further, take a few moments to reflect on this transcript, and think about what how effective this kind of activity was in helping the students be clear about what they had to do to get a good grade.

German

Ian Storey is teaching a group of eighth-grade students in an accelerated class. Shortly, these students will be taking an examination that most students take at the end of tenth grade. The examination includes three pieces of school-based assessment—extended pieces of writing that the students complete individually, under controlled conditions— and before they redraft a piece of writing they have just completed and been given feedback on, the teacher wants the students to have a good understanding of the criteria against which their work will be assessed.

Teacher:	Going from a C/B to an A/A* for our coursework is what we are all aiming for. So, I thought the best thing to do would be to moderate some coursework, not yours but other pieces of coursework that have already gone through the process of GCSE examination and they've been moderated by a team of teachers. So remember, give your examiner a break and not a breakdown (class joins in).
	Thank you. Okay. So,
	Ihr habt zehn minuten. Ihr must jetzt diese drei Kurzarbeit Blätter lesen und . . . wie gut oder schlecht es ist. You have ten minutes. You must now read these three sheets of coursework, and say how good or bad it is.
	So, in English, we have communication, range of language, and accuracy mark. You will need your coursework descriptor sheets that we used a few weeks ago. It's this sheet that you are going to talk about in eight minutes (there is a countdown timer on the whiteboard).

Students in pairs looking at work, followed by a whole-class discussion:

Liam:	He spelt [*sic*] "hotel" wrong.
Ben:	It's got a wide range of vocabulary.

Liam:	But not used correctly.
Ben:	Language range. He has tried to use big words and complicated.
Liam:	But he hasn't used them successfully, so about a three or a four I guess.
Ben:	I'd say a three because there is some variety.
Teacher:	Oscar (choosing a student from small name cards held in hand).
Oscar:	Communication. For marks, I gave him between a seven and eight because there was a lot of detail, and he did lots of descriptions. He gave a lot of opinion.
Aria:	I think it would be a seven, but it were [*sic*] really good but he could have included a bit more information.
Teacher:	Yes, it was lacking a bit of information, but it definitely was a seven, and you are absolutely spot-on with that. Oscar, what did you give it for range of language?
Oscar:	Five. He was quite strong in the past tense, but he could have used more complex sentences.
Teacher:	Interesting, and you gave it six for accuracy?
Oscar:	Yes, because there was [*sic*] only a few minor mistakes.
Teacher:	Yes, right, okay. Rosie, tell me why you disagreed with Oscar and said that it should have a six rather than a five for range.
Rosie:	Because he used a large variety of sentence types and vocabulary. He expanded all the sentences a lot more.
Teacher:	Interesting. Christian, talk to me a bit about the work you and Rhiannah did.
Christian:	We gave it, for communication, a four because it had quite a fair bit of useful information but not enough to give it a five. Language range, a four, because again it used a lot but just not enough. And for language accuracy we gave it a four, as well, because although he used quite a lot of different words not all of them were spelt right or used in the right context.
Teacher:	Who agrees that this coursework is not worthy of a C?
Krishna:	All the stuff was not explained in detail.
Teacher:	Detail. That's the key word, isn't it?—Detail. If there is no detail you can't get anything above a C. Now we need to consider any feedback that we could give this student. What feedback could we give this student? David, tell me please.

David:	Widen his range of sentences a bit more.
Teacher:	Well, you are really on the right lines there. Well done. Zoe.
Zoe:	Use more opinions and a wider range of opinions, because he uses the same ones.
Teacher:	Good. Really important what Zoe was saying. Just bouncing off Zoe there. What she was saying about opinions. Opinions are really, really important.

After lesson ends:

Teacher:	From the lesson they have a clear understanding of what it is the exam board is looking for. They now know the marking criteria. They were given student-friendly assessment criteria grids as well. I did change it slightly because sometimes the exam board language isn't that student-friendly. So from that point of view they now know what to expect in a piece of coursework. They also had a chance to talk to their peers, they got ideas, they exchanged ideas about what they could include in their coursework drafts, and, all in all, they demonstrated to me that they can develop their coursework and take it forward so that they can gain not just C and D grades but looking at As and A*s.

Reflection

As with the previous case study, take a few moments to reflect on this transcript, and think about how effective this activity was in helping the students understand the criteria against which their work would be judged. In particular, note any similarities and differences between this example and the previous case study.

––––––––––––––

We end the chapter with a recap, followed by a reflection checklist you might find useful to complete, a planning sheet for using a technique with a class, and a peer observation sheet (so that you can ask a colleague to give you feedback).

Each of the sheets are at the back of this book for you to copy if needed, so feel free to write all over the following sheets!

RECAP

The aim of any learning intention or success criterion is not to help the students complete the activity—it is to help them learn.

- Sometimes you should not set a learning intention at the start of the lesson.
  - You may not know exactly where the lesson is going—it is the experience rather than the outcome.
  - It may spoil the journey.
  - It may not inspire students.
- Keep the context of learning out of the learning intention.
  - Get students to apply in other contexts what they have learned.
  - Mix it up.
  - Differentiate success criteria, not learning intentions.
  - Make learning intentions and success criteria generic.
  - Be aware of the strengths and weaknesses of analytic and holistic learning intentions and success criteria.
- Start with samples of work rather than rubrics, to communicate quality.
  - Use anonymous work.
  - Compare two or more pieces of work.
  - Use a document camera.
  - Use examples where deep features are not aligned with surface features.
  - Use rubrics as the starting point for a dialogue between you and your students.
  - Recognize that sometimes, quality cannot be put into words.
  - Help students develop a nose for quality.
  - Don't abdicate responsibility for quality.
  - Find out what your students think they are learning.
- Use big ideas, learning progressions, and staging posts.
  - Over time move to a top-down process starting from the big ideas.
  - Develop learning progressions.
  - Get the grain size of big ideas right.
  - Understand that not all useful learning intentions will be big ideas.
  - Ensure that learning progressions have both an empirical and a theoretical basis.

REFLECTION CHECKLIST FOR STRATEGY 1:
Clarifying, Sharing, and Understanding Learning Intentions and Success Criteria

	I don't do this	I do this sometimes	This is embedded in my practice	I could support someone else
I know what the learning intention of the lesson is, although sometimes I do not tell the students at the start of the lesson.				
I keep the learning intention and success criteria for a lesson context free.				
I communicate quality by using at least two pieces of anonymous work.				
At the end of a lesson I sometimes ask my students what they have learned.				
I use rubrics to discuss quality with my students.				
Other techniques for this strategy that I use to improve student learning:				

LESSON PLANNING SHEET

The technique I am going to use:
Why I am planning to use it and the results I am hoping for:
Class and date:
Preparation for the lesson:
What I am going to do less of:
Reflecting on how the technique worked, including evidence to support my claims:
What I am going to do next:

PEER OBSERVATION SHEET

Class to be observed:
Peer's name:
Technique to be observed:
What I want my peer to comment on:
Peer's comments:
Reflections after reading peer's comments and/or talking through the observation:
What I will do next:

Chapter 4

STRATEGY 2: ENGINEERING EFFECTIVE DISCUSSION, TASKS, AND ACTIVITIES THAT ELICIT EVIDENCE OF LEARNING

OVERVIEW

Questioning, together with a range of related techniques for eliciting evidence about student achievement, is a staple in classrooms all over the world. But in most classrooms, the greater part of the "intellectual heavy lifting" is done by the teacher, with students delegated to a supporting role, or even, in many cases, "absent without leave." This chapter looks at ways that you can generate evidence about what your students can and cannot do and provides a range of classroom techniques to improve questioning, including how to create and capitalize upon more "teachable moments," and the defining characteristics of effective diagnostic questions. The chapter also explores ways of eliciting evidence that do not involve questions— for example, by making statements or engaging students in tasks that are likely to reveal important aspects of their developing capability.

WHY USE THIS STRATEGY

To teach well, we have to find out what students already know. But students do not always learn what we teach. That's why finding out what students *do* know is essential to good teaching.

GETTING TO UNDERSTAND THE STRATEGY

Finding out what learners know is difficult for two main reasons. First, in many subjects, the evidence has to be sought. We can't peer into a student's brain and see why he or she is having difficulties understanding texts, for example. We have to go looking for the information. Even in so-called practical subjects, working out what is going wrong requires expertise. If a right-handed child is throwing a baseball with her right foot two feet in front of her left foot, it might look ungainly, but unless you know that, for a right-hander, throwing a baseball is best done with the left foot in front of the right, you won't be able to help the child. Evidence about student learning doesn't just present itself to the teacher. It has to be sought, and teachers have to know what to look for.

Second, students are often reluctant to share their thinking—it is a source of some mystery to many teachers why students are so reluctant to allow teachers to see their scratch work. It may be tempting to view this as a problem for the student, but actually, it's more of a problem for the teacher. You can't do your job unless you find out what your students already know. If you create an environment in which students are reluctant to share their thinking with you, that's not the student's problem; it's yours.

At the outset, we should say that we believe that the best way to find out what students are thinking is by talking to them. When we engage students in dialogue, if they aren't clear what we are talking about, they can ask for clarification, and if they say things that aren't clear to us, we can ask them to expand on their answers. Even in small groups, relatively unstructured dialogue, guided by the teacher's expertise, is often the best way to find out what students are thinking. However, as the size of the group gets larger, it becomes increasingly difficult for teachers to ensure that they have high-quality evidence about what the students are thinking. Obviously, when you are trying to get some idea of the thinking taking place in thirty different minds at the same time, you are going to have to make compromises in terms of the quality of that information. In an ideal world, teachers would have time to work more intensively with smaller groups getting rich information about their students' capabilities and emerging ideas. However, most teachers don't have the luxury of being able to work exclusively with individuals or small groups of students, so a significant amount of time needs to be spent in teaching students in larger groups. In the rest of this chapter, we discuss a number of practical techniques that you can use to get better evidence about what your students are able to do, so you can decide what to do next, whether you are teaching individuals, small groups, or whole classes.

TECHNIQUES

No Hands Up, Except to Ask a Question

Walk into a classroom almost anywhere in the world and you will see the same script being played out. The teacher asks a question, and a number of students raise their hands to signal they wish to respond. If only a few students raise their hands, sometimes the teacher says something like, "I want to see more hands up" and waits a while until more students signal their willingness to participate. Then, the teacher almost always selects one of the students with her hand raised, and that student responds to the question. Sometimes the teacher picks on a student who has not raised his hand, but in most cases, this is because the student gave some indication that he is "off task," and the teacher selects him in order to make a point.

This script is so entrenched that calling on a student who has not raised a hand is seen as unfair by many students, unless he was misbehaving in some way. But if the aim of questioning is to help the teacher find out what the students know, it makes little sense to select a respondent from the volunteers, because generally, students raise their hands only when they are confident they have the correct answer, as the following responses from students who participated in *The Classroom Experiment* TV show illustrate:

Emily:	I try to put my hand up quite a lot because I feel I'm getting more involved in the lesson.
Chloe:	I think the smart people put their hands up when the teacher asks a question because most of the time they know what they are doing. The shy people tend to stay out of that.
Katie:	I put my hand up in class when I feel that I've got the right answer, but I don't do it as often as the other students, because there are only a few lessons that I think I'm quite good at.
Sid:	I put my hand up in class when I feel I'm one hundred percent confident that I've got the right answer, because if I'm not one hundred percent confident I feel like everyone would laugh if I got the wrong answer, even though that's not the case really. That's just what I feel.

This is why having students raise their hands to show that they have an answer is such an ineffective strategy, even though it is almost universal. Instead, if the teacher is asking the question, it should be the teacher who selects the student or students to respond, ideally, at random. It does make sense to encourage students to raise their hands if they want to *ask* a question, and this is why we call the basic technique "No hands up, except to *ask* a question."

Teachers think they can select students at random, but our evidence is that they cannot. Especially when time is tight, they are drawn to the "usual suspects"—the students whom they expect to give a good, strong response so that the teacher can wrap up the matter at hand and move on. Instead, teachers need to find a way to choose students at random. Interactive whiteboards generally have randomizers built into the software, and there are many online resources that teachers can use. They can even create a simple randomizer in PowerPoint by having each student's name on a slide and then setting the time interval between slides to zero seconds. When the slide show is set to automatic, pressing the *s* key starts the slide show, and doing so again stops it at a random slide. There are even apps for smartphones that teachers can use. Simplest of all is having each student's name on an ice-pop stick or, better, a tongue depressor (since there's more room for writing!) in a cup.

When you start selecting students at random, it is important to be aware that you are likely to encounter considerable resistance. Students who didn't raise their hands dislike it because they were used to a quiet life, and now they have to pay attention and be ready to answer:

Katie:	If I know the answer to a question I feel the need to put my hand up, but if I don't know it my name always seems to get picked out on questions that I don't know.

Students who do raise their hands regularly also dislike it because they can't show off they know the answer:

William:	Normally, I get frustrated if they don't pick me with my hand up, but this is more frustrating I think.

However, very quickly (typically within about two weeks) students accept it because they see the advantages:

Sid:	Before, what would happen is, you would get a group of about six people who would always be answering the questions, but now it's a lot more; everyone's in the same group, just a lot more people getting picked out, so everyone has to know the answer.
	Before, it used to be, for some people, it used to be a laid back sort of feel in some lessons, but now you've got to know the answer all the time because there's a chance you could get picked.

Even the higher-achieving students began to realize the benefits:

Chloe:	I thought you had to be right all of the time, otherwise you're stupid. But now I realize that making mistakes is learning.
Emily:	I want people, when they make mistakes, to realize that it doesn't matter. You are learning from it, so don't worry about what other people think, because they're obviously going to make mistakes too.
William:	Because it's fair, because everybody gets a go with sticks.

Teachers are often concerned that students will be somehow embarrassed or humiliated if they give incorrect answers to questions—and this can be an issue in some classrooms—but the most common result is that students become more supportive of each other.

Teacher:	I notice more confidence in what they are saying. Also, just the fact that they are willing to have a go.
William:	It feels like a happy environment for people to work in.
Chloe:	I've realized that everyone else learns more this way. Because they struggled learning the other way, it's better because everyone gets to learn more, not just the people that find it easier to remember things and get higher grades. Everyone learns more.
Teacher:	I feel like they are different students now. They are more actively engaged in classroom discussion, in work, in talking to their peers, and asking for help from the teacher, which most of them didn't do earlier.

One of the most interesting benefits is that students came to appreciate the contributions of their peers more. When students were able to raise their hands, the classroom discussion tended to be dominated by those who were quickest and not necessarily those with the most interesting or important things to say.

| Emily: | I listen to people more, because I've actually noticed that some people are a lot smarter than I used to think, because they have had their chance to share now. |
| William: | I never knew my classmates were so smart. |

Finally, it is worth noting that one of the main benefits of random questioning is that you get to hear responses from students who would never share them with you but are nevertheless insightful and illuminating:

| Teacher: | Sid, what do you think a domestic servant might be? |
| Sid: | I have no idea, but something tells me it's sort of undemocratic. |

Tips

Allow Volunteers *After* Random Selection

As noted earlier, higher-achieving students can feel left out when they are unable to show you they know the answers. One way to address this is to allow volunteers to contribute responses but only after at least two individuals selected at random respond. This retains the essentially random nature of the questioning, but still allows those who want to have their say to do so.

Using Numbers Rather Than Names on Ice-Pop Sticks

If you teach a large number of students every week, it can be tricky keeping track of sets of ice-pop sticks for each group. As an alternative, have a set of sticks numbered from one up to the size of the largest group you teach. You can then select students by their number on the class roster.

Don't Let "Don't Know" End the Conversation

When you pick students at random, the most common response, at least to begin with, is "Don't know." This may, of course, signal that the student really does not have an answer, but it is far more likely to be an indication that the student does not want to engage in the conversation. That is why you cannot let "Don't know" end the conversation; as Doug Lemov points out, there must be "no opt out" (Lemov, 2010). When there are many possible answers to a question (e.g., with higher-order questions), you might collect responses from other students before asking the original student to choose which of the responses is the best. When there is a single best answer, you can provide support for the student in a variety of ways. For example, if the question is in multiple-choice format, you can ask the student to identify any options that are definitely incorrect. If there aren't options to choose from, you can ask students if they need additional information, or invite students to "ask the audience" or "phone a friend." Initially, it probably doesn't matter if a peer tells the student the answer, and the student just repeats it to you. The important principle we establish is that if you ask a question, "Don't know" can never end the conversation.

Cautions

Allowing Students to Raise Their Hands Anyway

Some teachers accept that they should select students at random, regardless of whether they have raised their hands , but still think it is valuable to have students raise their hands if they know the answer—they say it's useful to know who knows the answer and who doesn't. But that's not what raised hands show. Raised hands show only which students think they know, and while knowing which students are confident may have some use (whether they are right or wrong!), it seems to us that any positive benefit is outweighed by the disadvantages. First, having a sea of hands actually makes it difficult to see who does not have their hands raised. Second, it encourages game playing on the part of students who may raise their hands even though they don't want to answer the question, because they think there may be less chance that the teacher selects them to respond if they have their hands up than if they have their hands down. We want students to be focusing on the learning at hand rather than playing a game of "guess what's in teacher's head."

Choosing the Student First, Then Asking the Question

Many teachers choose the student first and then decide on the exact question to ask. The problem, of course, is that as soon as students realize they have not been chosen, they can relax and no longer need to pay attention. Teachers often defend such practices by saying, "What's the point of asking a student a question you know he can't answer?" This is, of course, a fair point, but the best response is not dumbing down the questions you ask your students but rather reframing the questions in a way that all students in the class can actually engage with.

Not Replacing Sticks

In using ice-pop sticks, some teachers go through all the sticks to make sure that everyone has a turn to answer a question. This has the advantage of being fair, but the problem is that as soon as students answer a question, they know they are off the hook until every other student in the class answers a question. To avoid this, some teachers place a dividing screen inside the cup that holds the ice-pop sticks, so as sticks are selected, they are moved from one section to the other. As long as the students know that the teacher can, at any time, select a stick from the "used" section as well as the "unused" section, all students know that there is a chance they will be called on for a response. As a compromise, some teachers have little cards (e.g., 1" by 2") on which the students' names are printed. You can go through the cards systematically, but as soon as it looks like some students believe they are off the hook because they have just answered a question, you can ostentatiously shuffle the deck of cards, and there is nothing to stop you from occasionally dealing off the bottom of the deck.

Losing Sticks

A number of teachers find that unless they are very careful to guard the ice-pop sticks, sticks can disappear from the cup. When teachers are told that sticks are missing, they naturally assume that it is likely to be the lowest-achieving students who are secretly removing their sticks from the cup, in order not to have to answer questions in class. However, we find that it is the high-achieving students who are most likely to try to remove their sticks from the cups. Many of the students that teachers assume have their hands raised all the time are, in fact, raising their hands only when they are certain of being correct. For these students, their reputation as smart students is more important than anything else (see the discussion of mastery and performance goals in the next chapter). Although being completely excluded from classroom conversation is unattractive, it appears to be preferable to being asked a question that they cannot answer.

Enhancements

Having a Student Look After the Sticks

Using ice-pop sticks can pose problems for you if the students do not believe that the sticks really are being selected at random. This is why handing the cup of sticks over to a student can be very effective. For some reason, students often seem to believe that one of their peers is less likely to "fix" which stick gets picked than you are.

Hand Signals

While having students raise their hands to show they have an answer does not make much sense, it is useful to have students give other sorts of signals to provide you with information about the kinds of contributions they want to make to the discussion. For example, some schools train their students to use different hand signals in whole-class discussions to show that they want to build on something someone else has said, ask someone to explain something they have said, or put forward a different view from a previous speaker. When students use these kinds of signals, you can choose from those who are signaling, and those who are not, to create much more logically sequenced, organized, and effective classroom discussions.

Basketball

After you select a student to respond to a question, you could evaluate the response yourself, but as an alternative, it can be useful to ask another student (again chosen at random) to decide whether the response is correct. One teacher calls this "pose-pause-pounce-bounce": *pose* the question, *pause* for at least three seconds, *pounce* on one student, and then *bounce* that student's response to another student, who can then be asked for an evaluation of the first student's response (i.e., is it correct?). A third student can then be asked for an explanation of whether the response provided by the first student and the evaluation provided by the second are correct. In other words, rather than having all conversations directed through the teacher, pass questioning around the classroom like a basketball.

Hot-Seat Questioning

Choosing students at random does increase student engagement but can lead to a rather flat classroom dialogue. Going from one student to another makes it harder to build deep dialogue with students. For that reason, it is sometimes helpful to put a student in the hot seat. After a student responds to a question, you can follow up with a second, third, and fourth, or even fifth question to probe in depth the student's thinking about the matter at hand. The danger, of course, is that other students in the class may be off task, relieved that they are not in the hot seat. However, the students are likely to be listening carefully if they know that at the conclusion of the hot seat session, you will select another student at random, and ask her to summarize what the student in the hot seat said. It is not enough for other students to be quiet when a student is speaking. If we want to create a community of learners, we need to ensure that students are listening appreciatively when their peers are speaking.

Time for Thinking

When teachers begin using the technique of "no hands up, except to ask a question," they find that the students they select often don't have a response. The problem is that with the traditional approach of picking volunteers, as noted earlier, teachers get used to pacing their lessons on the basis of the students who are quickest in their thinking, not necessarily those who have the most interesting or important things to say.

Pace is valuable in teaching, but it is important to realize that pace is not the same as speed. Videos purporting to illustrate well-paced lessons often show teachers asking questions and students responding immediately with answers. The problem with such rapid-fire question-and-answer teaching is that there is relatively little thinking going on. As Daniel Willingham (2009) points out, "memory is the residue of thought" (p. 54; students remember what they have been thinking about), so giving students time to think—about the right things of course—is one of the most valuable things a teacher can do.

Unfortunately, a lot of research shows that teachers often don't give their students a lot of time to think. In the 1970s, Mary Budd Rowe showed that it was common for teachers to allow less than a second after the end of a question to allow students to begin their response (Rowe, 1974a, 1974b). What is as interesting is that teachers also left less than a second of gap between the end of a student's response and the teacher beginning to respond to what the student had said, and that often the length of this second sort of wait time was actually negative—the teacher began to evaluate the answer before the student had finished speaking!

In order to distinguish between these two types of wait time, Mary Budd Rowe calls them "wait time 1" and "wait time 2," but we find it more helpful to call them "thinking time" and "elaboration time," since these terms give some idea as to what is meant to be going on. Thinking time allows students time to think about what they want to say, and "elaboration time" allows students to extend and develop their answers. And when they're talking, they're thinking, and when they're thinking, they're learning.

Most teachers find increasing wait time difficult partly because changing any habituated practice is hard, but also because when the teacher is driving the lesson forward, it feels more purposeful. If the objective of teaching is to "cover the standards" or "deliver the material," then obviously leaving space for thinking seems like a waste of time. But if, on the other hand, the aim is to find out what students have been learning before plowing on, it is essential to give students time to think up their answers and elaborate them. When teachers allow students at least three seconds for thinking and elaboration, students provide more correct and complete responses to questions, their responses are more likely to exhibit higher-order thinking, they are less tentative in their responses, and they score higher on standardized achievement tests.

Tips

Plan the Question

Most teachers rarely plan the questions they are going to ask their students, so they end up making up the questions as they go along, adding phrases as they think of them to try to make the meaning of the question clear. As a result it is common to find teacher questions consisting of thirty, forty, or even fifty words, so the students may well have forgotten the first part of the question by the time the teacher finally asks them to respond. Thinking of at least a few of the questions when planning the lesson gives you time to refine the wording to make the question really clear and focused precisely on the key ideas. In other words, the teacher should make sure the question is worth asking and answering.

Increase Wait Time Slowly

Increasing wait time is difficult. This reflection from a teacher sums it up nicely: "Increasing waiting time after asking questions proved difficult to start with—due to my habitual desire to 'add' something almost immediately after asking the original question. The pause after asking the question was sometimes 'painful.' It felt unnatural to have such a seemingly 'dead' period, but I persevered. Given more thinking time students seemed to realize that a more thoughtful answer was required. Now, after many months of changing my style of questioning I have noticed that most students will give an answer and an explanation (where necessary) without additional prompting" (P. Black, Harrison, Lee, Marshall, & Wiliam, 2004, pp. 11–12).

Explain Any Changes You Are Making in Classroom Routines to Students

A teacher decides to increase wait time but does not tell his students why he is doing this. At the end of the lesson, one student comes up to the teacher and says, "Sir? You were really slow today." If you are going to change the classroom rules, it's a good idea to tell the students what you are doing and why you are doing it. It is also a good idea to prepare students for their changed roles by giving them ideas of what they should do in the time you give them to think (see Walsh & Sattes, 2011, for examples).

Cautions

No Maximum Wait Time

While researchers seem to agree that wait times of less than three seconds are not helpful, other researchers claim that increasing wait time beyond about five seconds leads to a loss of pace in classrooms. It is obviously very convenient to have simple rules like "three to five seconds: good; everything else: bad," but the truth is in education, things are rarely, if ever, that simple. Five seconds may be enough for some questions, but for others longer periods may be appropriate. It is up to you to judge whether the students are engaged in productive activity.

This is starkly illustrated in an interview with an Illinois science teacher named Daniel Ferri on the NPR program *All Things Considered* (Ferri, 2005). A journalist was coming to interview four eighth-grade students (two boys and two girls) about a mini "science museum" they had constructed. Because the teacher was aware of the tendency of the boys to dominate discussions, he asked the journalist to ask the students from left to right and arranged for the two girls to be sitting on the left. At the first question, the two boys' hands shot up but the journalist, as requested, asked the girl seated on the extreme left to answer first. After a while (during which time the boys were, in Daniel Ferri's words, squirming in their seats), the first girl answered, and then the second girl gave a brief answer, and then the boys gave theirs. Afterward Daniel Ferri asked the girls if they had enjoyed their interview. One of the girls replied, "Yeah, it was fun, but . . ." "But what?" "Well, we didn't really get a chance to say what we wanted to say. We needed time to think. And the boys were all anxious to answer and everything, so we just said anything. And by the time the boys were done, we knew what we wanted to say, but by that time the reporter was asking us the next question, and we had to think about that."

Common Errors in Questioning

Over twenty years ago, George Brown and Ted Wragg drew up a list of "common errors in questioning" from their extensive research in classrooms (G. Brown & Wragg, 1993). We reproduce the list here (Table 4.1) because it seems as relevant now as it was then.

Table 4.1: Common Errors in Questioning (from G. Brown & Wragg, 1993)

Asking	Failing to
• too many questions at once	• correct wrong answers
• a question and answering it yourself	• indicate a change in the type of question
• questions only of the brightest or most likeable	• give students the time to think
• a difficult question too early	• pay attention to answers
• questions in a threatening way	• see the implications of answers
• irrelevant questions	• build on answers
• the same kind of questions all the time	

Enhancements

Think-Pair-Share

One technique that teachers find very useful for structuring wait time is "think-pair-share." The technique became popular in higher education in the 1980s, but, of course, the fundamental idea is much older than that; indeed, good teachers have probably always used such techniques to get students thinking and talking. The basic structure is that the teacher poses a question and then gives students some time to think about their response; depending on the kind of question and age of the students, this could be

Go to www.learningsciences.com/bookresources to download figures and tables.

anything from a few seconds to several minutes. The teacher asks students to share their responses with a peer, and then the teacher selects students to share their own or their peer's responses with the whole class.

Avoiding Questions Altogether

Many years ago, Hugh Mehan pointed out the conversations that take place in school classrooms are often very different in character from those that take place outside school classrooms. Here is a normal, out-of-classroom exchange:

Teacher: What time is it?

Student: Two-thirty.

Teacher: Thank you.

Here is an exchange that could occur only in a classroom:

Teacher: What time is it?

Student: Two-thirty.

Teacher: Well done.

(Mehan, 1979)

There are, of course, times when teachers need to check that students are secure in the knowledge they need in order to move on. But in general, question-and-answer sessions where the teacher just, in effect, inventories the knowledge the students hold in their heads with rapid-fire, short-answer questions (to which the teacher already knows the answer) represent wasted opportunities to explore students' thinking.

James Dillon points out that part of the problem is with the whole idea of asking questions in the first place (Dillon, 1988). Asking questions tends to close down discussion, because students usually just answer the question. More importantly, when you are asked a question, you can be wrong. You cannot be wrong responding to a statement. As noted earlier, you cannot do your job without finding out what students know, and anything that makes it more likely for students to volunteer what they know helps the teachers. Here are some alternatives to teacher questions, based on the work of James Dillon and others:

Declarative statement: In response to a student saying, "The Republican party believes in private health care," the teacher could say, "But the Democrats also believe in private health care."

Reflective restatement: In response to "The Republicans and Democrats believe in private health care," the teacher could say, "So you're saying that both major political parties believe in private health care."

Statement of mind: "The last two things you said seem contradictory. I don't see how you can believe in both."

Statement of interest: "I'm interested in hearing a little more about what you just said."

Student referral: "It seems to me that what you just said contradicts what we heard from David."

Teacher opinion: "That certainly hasn't been my experience."

Student question: "I wonder if you could express your confusion in the form of a question."

Class question: "If you had to ask one question now, what would it be?"

Phatics and fillers: One of the most powerful things a teacher can do to get a student to expand a response is use expressions that do not convey information but rather indicate the listener is interested in what the speaker is saying, such as "Uh-huh" or even "Hmmm." Such responses are a natural part of conversations outside classrooms—they are, if you like, the grease that lubricates normal human exchange, and signal to the student that you are interested in what he or she is saying, and they encourage the student to elaborate and extend his or her answer.

Pass: Once a class is used to the idea of individuals being drawn into the discussion at the direction of the teacher, you will find that a hand gesture, or even a glance, is enough to "pass" the conversation to another student. Such signals are common in graduate seminars, and there is no reason why the same should not apply in discussions with younger students.

Silences: As noted earlier, just not saying anything can be the most powerful response of all because it encourages the student to expand her answer. However, being silent is difficult because as teachers, we are so used to filling the space.

This list is not, of course, exhaustive, but it does highlight the fact that there are many ways of finding out where learners are in classroom discussions without asking questions.

You can also learn about students' thinking by encouraging them to complete "learning logs." These provide valuable insight for you about the students' learning and have the added benefit of prompting students to reflect on their learning. We provide a sample learning log sheet at the end of the chapter. One particular feature of this learning log sheet is that students are not asked questions but rather offered prompts for writing. While some teachers ask students to respond to all the prompts, in general such learning logs seem to be more effective when teachers ask students to choose no more than three prompts to which to respond. For other ideas about prompts for use as learning logs, see Keeley (2008, p. 191).

Tips

Interpretive Rather Than Evaluative Listening

In the second example from Mehan above (asking for the time) the teacher was listening *evaluatively*. In other words, the teacher was listening for the correct answer. This is particularly noticeable when a student gives an incorrect answer, because the teacher generally allows the student another opportunity to provide the correct answer so that the teacher can get on with the lesson. Some teachers also try to make the students feel okay about providing an incorrect response by saying things like, "That's a great wrong answer, and if you think that then I'm sure other members of the class think the same." The problem with such responses is that they are, in effect, attempts to make the students feel okay about not providing the correct answer.

In contrast, the best teachers listen *interpretively* (Davis, 1997). They are listening not for whether the student provides the answer the teacher is hoping for but rather what the teacher can learn from attending carefully to what the student actually says. Correct responses are not particularly interesting, because they just reveal that the student "got it." On the other hand, interpreted appropriately, incorrect answers reveal something about the student's thinking that you can use to improve instruction.

What is most interesting is that when teachers shift from listening evaluatively to interpretively, students notice. As one seventh grader says, when asked whether she has noticed any changes in her teacher's questioning style over the course of a year, "When Miss used to ask a question, she used to be interested in the right answer. Now she's interested in what we think" (Hodgen & Wiliam, 2006, p. 16).

Cautions

Overstructuring the Learning Environment

One of the things that students find both confusing and frustrating is that they seem to be able do things when the teacher is supporting them but not when the teacher goes away. This occurs, of course, because of the "scaffolding" that the teacher is providing. While such scaffolding is undoubtedly helpful when students are learning new concepts, ultimately because the goal is to make the student independent of the teacher, teachers need to be careful to reduce the amount of support they give. This way, students are able not just to execute particular steps but also decide for themselves which steps they need to take.

Enhancements

Minimal Encouragers

One of the criticisms that students make of novice teachers is that they give too much help. One student summed this up by saying, of a pre-service teacher on placement, "I asked a question and got a lecture." One particularly important technique that teachers can develop is the idea of giving what might be called *minimal encouragers*—responses to requests for help that are supportive, but, as far as possible, leave the learning with the learner. As Linda Allal points out, only learners can create learning (Herbst & Davies, 2014). When the teacher takes control of the learning process, the teacher takes the learning away from the learner. Sometimes a request for help is really just a statement of anxiety. Students look at a carefully structured task, which takes them through material step by step, and because they cannot immediately see how to complete the final step, they ask for help. In such situations, often, all that is needed is to say to the student something like, "Copy that grid, and I'll be back to help you fill it out."

Model-Revealing Activities

Once the focus is on eliciting evidence, rather than questioning, anything that can reveal how the student is thinking about something can provide useful information to a teacher. Instrumental music teachers often have particular pieces of music that reveal weaknesses in technique that may not be apparent in other pieces of music. Sports coaches have particular routines that they can use to reveal deficiencies of skill. In the same way, teachers of less practically oriented subjects can develop particular tasks or activities that they can use to reveal facets of students' thinking. One classic example is the "concept cartoon" that depicts students discussing how to preserve the snowman they have made from the increasing temperature (Naylor & Naylor, 2000). Student A suggests putting a coat on the snowman, while student B argues that doing this will warm up the snowman and make him melt. Student C points out that the sun is shining and the black coat will absorb more heat. When you ask students which of the three students are right and why, they quickly reveal their mental models of heat transfer. For younger students, it may be useful to start with simple cartoons with just two points of view, but for older students, it can be useful to build in four or more. It can also be useful to have points of view expressed in the cartoons that are correct but incomplete, to provide an element of differentiation and challenge. As another alternative, to avoid "catching students out," tell the students which of the individuals in the concept cartoon is right and ask them to say why that individual is correct, and the others are incorrect. All these activities are helpful in revealing the implicit models students are using, which provides you with insight about what to do next.

All-Student Response Systems

When you need to make a decision about whether sufficient time has been spent on a topic, so the class is ready to move on, or whether further reinforcement, repetition, development, or discussion is needed, obviously getting responses from students you select at random is likely to be far more useful to you than responses from confident volunteers. But the evidence available to you will still be a poor guide to the learning needs of the whole class. That is why we recommend that, at least every twenty minutes of group instruction, you use an all-student response system in which you get a response from every single student. Perhaps the simplest way to do this is via a class poll where every student gives a quick response to a question, such as, "Was George right to do what he did?" The problem is that even if you conduct the poll briskly, it is still going to take thirty seconds to get round the class, and you have to remember the responses each student gives if you want to draw on their responses in developing the instruction. Also, once students regarded by others as more likely to know the correct answer do respond, that is likely to influence the responses of the other students. This is why we believe that the best all-student response systems require students to respond simultaneously and allow you to collect the information in real time.

Many companies sell what are called *electronic voting systems* or, more commonly, *classroom clickers*. These seem to us to be very valuable in higher education, where teachers are working with groups of 200 or more, but the expense of such systems is unlikely to be cost-effective in K–12 education, where group sizes are much smaller, and the teacher can get a fairly good grasp of the understanding of a class with simpler and less expensive systems.

Vendors of electronic voting systems cite two particular virtues of such electronic voting systems. The first is that teachers can record every single response that students make. Actually, that does not sound like a good thing to us. The idea that every single incorrect response one has ever made in a classroom is recorded in a spreadsheet somewhere until the end of time sounds distinctly creepy to us—as if George Orwell's 1984 has finally arrived. If we are serious about creating classrooms where students are happy to share their ideas with us, even if they might be incorrect, the last thing we should do is record every single response.

The other virtue that vendors claim for such systems is that they are capable of collecting all students' responses anonymously. This is an important issue because if a teacher uses a physical rather than electronic student response system, students can see each other's responses.

For example, the simplest alternative to an electronic voting system is to give students cards bearing letters of the alphabet. These can be sourced commercially, but it is easy to make up sets in-house for less than $5 for a class set. A letter-size card (ideally made of 110 lb. card stock) cut into quarters, with letters in 300-point Helvetica, produces sets of cards that students can easily see in most classrooms. You can keep the cards in an envelope, on a stationery ring, or by using "treasury tags" (two plastic toggles connected with a short piece of string, available from Amazon.com). Most teachers find just four letters per set, A, B, C, and D, are enough, but there are occasions when it is useful to have a larger number of options for students to choose from (see the section "Hinge questions"). Some teachers find it useful to have up to eight options in their questions, so each student response set has nine cards: A, B, C, D, E, F, G, H, and T (for "true," since the set already includes the "F" for "false").

Because students can see the responses other students make, some teachers tell them to put their hands over their eyes while displaying their responses, and some teachers have even gone as far as asking the students to put their heads down on their desks while they show their answers. However, most teachers find that while initially there is a lot of looking around within the class, after about two weeks, students worry less about how others are voting and are more focused on their own learning.

As an alternative to using cards, you can use "finger voting" in which each student holds up one finger to indicate they think "A" is the correct response, two fingers for "B," and so on, and the student can hold up a clenched fist if she thinks none of the options are correct. Note this is most emphatically *not* the same as what some people call *from fist to five* voting. With the fist to five system, students are indicating their confidence in an answer they have given or that they understand a particular idea. Such responses are self-reports and have very little value as indicators of how well students understand something.

For younger children, ABCD cards and finger voting are likely to be too complicated, so we recommend using something much simpler, such as green and red cards or discs. For example, a teacher was working on phonemes with a kindergarten class, and she had told the class that the guard of a magic bridge would only allow people whose names began with a certain letter to cross. Once the "letter of the day" has been revealed to the class, the teacher reads out a list of names and students are asked to show, by holding up a green or red disc, whether someone with that name would be allowed to cross. Depending on the phonological awareness of the students it might be best to start with continuant consonants and vowels as the letter of the day before moving on to plosive consonants.

Below are a number of other ways of using red and green discs in elementary language arts instruction.

A teacher has been teaching a class about how to construct sentences, and she has been stressing three features: start with a capital letter, have finger-sized spaces between the words, and end with a "stop sign" (i.e., "." "?" or "!"). The teacher uses an interactive whiteboard to display sentences to the class that may, or may not, contain deliberate mistakes. The students have to vote whether the sentence is correct (green) or not (red). Students who vote red are asked what is wrong with the sentence, the change is made, and the class votes again. The process continues until all the students vote green (provided the sentence really is correct, of course).

Students are shown a picture and a number of sentences are read to the class. For each sentence, students have to vote (by showing red or green discs) whether the sentence correctly describes the picture.

Students are presented with two statements, and are asked to show a green disc if there is a cause-and-effect relationship between the two, and a red disc if not.

Students read a story, and the teacher then reads out a number of questions. For each question, students vote green if the question is about details in the story and red if not.

The main mistake that teachers make with ABCD cards or finger voting (or indeed any technique that needs students to select rather than construct an answer) is trying to make up a multiple-choice question on the fly. They realize that they need to check students' understanding before moving on, which, of course, is a good idea. But constructing good multiple-choice items requires a great deal of thought—our experience is that it typically takes sixty to ninety minutes for each item—so it is generally better to use questions where students construct their answers rather than select them, and to display them to the teacher using dry-erase boards.

The mini dry-erase board is, of course, little more than a modern reinvention of the slate. Students write their answers to a small number of questions (ideally only one or two) and display their responses to the teacher, and the teacher makes a decision about what to do next.

The benefits to the teacher of using all-student response systems are obvious. The teacher gets real-time information about what the class is learning. What is less obvious is that all-student response systems also benefit students directly, because of a strange feature of human learning known as the *hypercorrection effect.*

Most teachers tell their students that mistakes are okay—that one can learn from one's mistakes. What is not widely appreciated is that making mistakes is not just okay but also better than not making mistakes. When students make mistakes, especially if they are confident they are correct, and they receive corrective feedback, they are more likely to remember the correct answer (Butterfield & Metcalfe, 2001). Although this hypercorrection effect is not fully understood, it seems that answering questions puts the student in the position of having "skin in the game" so that they care about the answer when it is revealed, and remember it longer.

All-student response systems capitalize on this effect by routinely putting students in the position of committing to an answer and then later finding out whether they were right or wrong. These "uncertain rewards" have been shown to be an important factor in the attraction of computer games. When individuals make a commitment to a course of action, the level of dopamine in the brain increases (Howard-Jones, 2014, p. 33), and this seems to increase learning.

The problem is that students seem to mind being wrong much more in the classroom than they do when playing games (Clifford, 1988), and this is one of the fundamental challenges in teaching. Students learn best when they make mistakes, but students don't like being wrong, at least in classrooms. This is why the simple technologies just described are so powerful. Students can walk away from their mistakes. Once the response on a mini dry-erase board is erased or the letter cards are put away, there is no record of the mistakes the student made.

What all this means is teachers have to create a culture in their classrooms where students understand that being stuck and making mistakes are an inevitable consequence of intellectually demanding learning. Student athletes get this. They understand lifting weights that are not difficult for them to lift will not make them stronger. And in the same way, intellectual work that is not demanding does not make students smarter. That's why we tell students, "Mistakes are evidence that the work I gave you was tough enough to make you smarter."

Of course, this involves radical changes in what we think of as effective classrooms. People commonly assume that classrooms where students are answering teachers' questions quickly and correctly are good classrooms, and, of course, establishing what students know and determining future instructional steps are part of effective classroom formative assessment. But if the students are answering all the teacher's questions correctly, the teacher is probably wasting the students' time. One teacher in Scotland emphasizes this by displaying a poster in her classroom that just says, "Stuck? Good. It was worth coming in today." In an interesting example of the spread of ideas, the following poster was seen on a student notice board in the Darakshan Campus of the City School in Karachi, Pakistan.

Tips

Don't Get Students to Write Too Much on Mini Dry-Erase Boards

The mistake that many teachers make with mini dry-erase boards is getting the students to write too much. With thirty students in a class, if each student writes more than three words, you have over a hundred words to read while you scan the students' responses—a rather challenging data-processing task to achieve quickly. For longer responses, it is more appropriate to use three-by-five-inch index cards as exit tickets, described earlier. A few minutes before the end of the lesson, give students a question, and ask them to write their responses on the card. These can be anonymous or not (see "Cautions and Enhancements"). As they file out of the classroom at the end of the period, they hand in their exit tickets to you. At this stage, don't try to read the responses; simply check that each student made some attempt to complete the task properly. After the students leave, you can read through the exit slips, and decide how to begin the next lesson. If the whole class did well, you can move on to the next content. If all the students did badly, presumably you will review the content with the class. But if some students did well and others did badly, you can select (say) three exit tickets that best exemplify the different kinds of answers the members of the class made, and use these as a jumping off point for the next lesson. One especially effective way is to label the selected responses A, B, and C, for example, display them to the class on a document camera, and begin the next lesson by asking students to use finger voting to indicate which of the answers they believe is the best.

Cautions

Whatever Technique Is Used, Get All Students Responding at the Same Time

Some teachers appreciate the value of having each student respond, but they have them do so serially. In other words, they first ask students to raise their hands if they think A is the correct answer, and then they ask all those who think B is the correct answer, and so on. Some teachers claim to be able to remember which students voted for which answer (they can't!), but much more importantly, it is almost impossible to be sure that all students voted.

Don't Try to Remember All the Responses

When reviewing dry-erase boards, keep it simple. Focus on just two things: which aspects need to be reviewed with the whole class, and which students need individual attention. Sure, you are missing a great deal of evidence about what students can and cannot do, but just by collecting some of the evidence and using it, you are making your classroom much more responsive to your students' needs.

Choose the Method to Match the Question

One company produced a video for teachers showing a teacher using exit passes in his classroom where the question is in multiple-choice format. So each student just writes a single letter on a three-by-five-inch index card and hands it in as they leave the classroom. Since the response is a single letter, the teacher would have been better advised to get the students to respond with ABCD cards or finger voting, as described earlier. Similarly, some authors suggest using entrance tickets—like exit tickets but completed at the beginning of the lesson. This betrays a lack of understanding of the original rationale for exit tickets. Exit tickets are useful when the teacher needs time to review the students' responses, and can do so once the students leave. If students write extended responses at the beginning of the lesson, then the teacher is trying to read and make sense of twenty-five or thirty different student responses while the students are settling down at the beginning of the lesson, and then deciding what that means for the lesson. The whole point about the exit tickets technique is that it is designed for you to use in those situations where you need time to reflect on the significance of the students' responses and what that means for the next steps in instruction. At the beginning of the lesson, you would be far better off using a multiple-choice question, as discussed in the section on "Hinge Questions."

Decision-Driven Data Collection, Not Data-Driven Decision Making

In the description of exit tickets, we suggested that teachers should ask students to complete their exit tickets anonymously. Many teachers balk at this and feel that they need the students' names on the exit tickets so they can provide individual feedback. However, this misses the entire point of the technique. If students are going to write extended responses, and the teacher is going to grade and give feedback on their responses, the students may as well write their responses in their notebooks and turn them in for grading as they leave the classroom. The purpose of the exit tickets is to give the teacher a quick read of the whole class's understanding so that she can make decisions that apply to the whole class. The fundamental idea here is that teachers should not collect evidence of student achievement unless they know what they plan to do with it. Many people believe that teachers should engage in data-driven decision making, but when phrased this way, the focus always seems to be on the data, which is why teachers who espouse this approach collect all the data they can in the belief that it may be useful at some point. Indeed, it may not be going too far to term such people *data hoarders* (especially since they often keep their data in data warehouses). In contrast, those who believe in decision-driven data collection determine first what decisions need to be made and then figure out what kinds of evidence will help them make those decisions in a smarter way. As Howard Wainer points out, data becomes evidence only when it is interpreted with a particular purpose in mind (Wainer, 2011, p. 148).

Enhancements

Page Protectors

Dry-erase boards (or slates!) are very useful for getting a quick read of a class's achievement, but being blank, the uses are limited. In response, one commercial vendor of dry-erase boards produces them in twenty different formats (many of which are available in different sizes), including lined, graph paper, music staves, clocks, and a variety of maps. As an alternative, schools can use page protectors, and insert different sheets of paper for the specific lesson. One teacher was introducing a sixth-grade class to the French language, and after teaching the class the vocabulary for the parts of the body, she called out various parts of the body in French (e.g., "les oreilles"); each student had to draw an arrow to the corresponding part of the body of a picture of a cartoon character placed inside their page protector. Other ways of using page protectors include maps, for quick reviews of geographical knowledge, or graph paper so that students can produce graphs quickly, all to the same scale, which makes it easier for the teacher to review.

ABCD Corners

Where the use of ABCD cards reveals that most of the students understand the important point of the lesson, the course of action is relatively clear: move on, noting those students who appear to need individual help. If few students answer correctly, review the material with the whole class, perhaps drawing on those who answered correctly. However, when there is a range of responses, other options are possible. For example, some teachers go with just four options in the multiple-choice questions that they use with ABCD cards or finger voting, and if at least three students select each option, the teacher sends the students to the four corners of the classroom, which the teacher had labeled A, B, C, and D. The students who believe A is the best answer congregate in the A corner, the students who believe B is the best answer congregate in the B corner, and so on. The task for each group of students is then to determine how to persuade students in the other corners that their choice really is the best answer. Once each group has developed its argument and selected a spokesperson, the class debates the four responses.

Student Square Dance

A variation of ABCD corners for eliciting evidence from students is to present the students with a proposition of some kind, and ask them if they agree or disagree. Students who disagree are asked to stand in a line on one side of the room, and students who agree are asked to stand in a line on the other side of the room, while students who want to indicate that they need more information to be sure remain in the center of the room. Ask students in the center of the room what further information they need, which you then supply, and then they need to move to one side of the room or the other. The important point here is that students realize that "I need more information to be sure" does not allow them to avoid making a commitment. It just allows them to ask for more information before making a choice. This is, of course, just a special case of Doug Lemov's "No opt out" technique we discussed earlier.

Once the center of the room is clear, you can then quickly estimate the ratio of those agreeing with the proposition to those who disagree with the proposition. If, for example, a class of thirty breaks up into eighteen students who agree with the proposition and twelve who do not, suggest to the students that they form groups of five made up of three students who agree with the proposition and two who do not. Students can then engage in discussions and report back to the whole class about their discussions, and you can organize further votes, either by getting the students to move or by using the thumbs up/ thumbs down to signal agreement or disagreement with the proposition.

Exit-Ticket Placemats

As noted earlier, students' names do not need to be written on exit passes to make them a useful resource for the teacher. That said, if the students do write their names on the reverse side of the exit tickets, then, before the next lesson, you can lay out the exit tickets as "place settings" for the next lesson. You can group the students so that all the students experiencing difficulties with the material are in one group, in order to get support from you, while the others work on extension material. Alternatively, you could set up mixed-ability groups, ensuring that there are at least two students in each group with good answers (this last condition is important because if there is only one student in a group with a good answer, and that student happens to be absent the next day, there is no one able to steer the group in the right direction).

Placing Self-Adhesive Notes Along a Line

Having students place on a whiteboard self-adhesive notes on which their names are written can be a very useful technique for finding out about students' beliefs. For example, you might ask a class to think about whether climate change is natural or caused by human activity. You then draw a continuum line on a whiteboard and label one end "entirely natural" and the other "entirely anthropogenic." Students then place self-adhesive notes bearing their names somewhere along the line to indicate their beliefs about the causes of climate change (this technique is not too expensive, because the teacher can retain the self-adhesive notes for another occasion). Finally, lead a discussion with the class about the different views members of the class hold, and draw different students into the discussion at the appropriate time to express their opinions. You can also extend this technique: ask students to indicate, by how far to the left or right they placed their self-adhesive note, their beliefs about the causes of global warming, and by how far up or down they place their self-adhesive note, their beliefs about the seriousness of the issue or the degree of confidence they have in their response.

Student Scatterplot

As an alternative to placing self-adhesive notes along a line or in a two-dimensional space, you can use the classroom itself. For a one-dimensional issue such as the causes of climate change we mentioned in the previous paragraph, you can designate one side of the room as representing the view that climate change is entirely natural and the other side of the room as representing the view that climate change is entirely anthropogenic. Students can then come to the front of the classroom and move to the left or right, depending on their views about the causes of climate change. Ask various students to contribute to the discussion, knowing what views they expressed, and students can be encouraged to move to the left or right as their views about the causes of climate change develop.

If you have a relatively open space, you can develop this into a student scatterplot so that the distance left or right indicates their views of the causes of climate change, while their distance from the back of the classroom can be used to indicate, for example, their views about the seriousness of the problem. This will also help students' understanding of graphs (Swan, 1978), but it is important to note that, to begin with at least, students are likely to find this quite difficult.

Question Shells

In any classroom, the questions you ask affect the level of thinking. You can improve the questions you ask, and students can also be taught to ask questions. As noted in the previous chapter, there is a significant body of research that shows that one hour students spend devising questions about what they have been learning *with correct solutions* is more effective than one hour spent completing practice tests (see, for example, Foos et al., 1994).

For example, in the maze technique described by Guthrie, Seifert, Burnham, and Caplan (1974), one word in each sentence is selected as the focal word in the sentence, and a number of alternatives are presented. The alternatives can be stacked, as shown below:

$$Carla \left\{ \begin{array}{l} cried \\ ran \\ fell \end{array} \right\} into\ the\ house$$

or they can be presented linearly in a bracket: Carla [cried, ran, fell] into the house (this latter technique is harder for readers to read, but obviously is much easier to produce with a word processor). Students circle one of the three words to make the sentence correct.

Using this template, students can construct stories and then provide alternatives for one word in each sentence.

Other question formats that can be useful for getting students to generate questions include "three facts and a fib." After looking at a map, or reading a story, working in pairs or groups, students generate three true statements and one false statement about the map and the story. The teacher can then lead a whole-class session in which students not in the group are asked to vote (using green and red discs, for example) on the truth of each of the four statements.

Just as importantly, when students create questions about what they have been learning, they reveal what they think they have been learning. In the maze task above, the choices that students make in providing alternatives will give you an indication of their understanding of the reading process.

As another example, a teacher in a science class asks students to design an experiment to find out what kinds of conditions pill bugs (sometimes called sow bugs or woodlice) prefer: warm and dry, warm and moist, cold and dry, or cold and moist. The task is designed to help students understand the idea of a "fair test." However, when the teacher asks the students to make up some questions about what they have been learning, they focus on the kinds of conditions pill bugs prefer. They do not understand the purpose of the task, and this was made clear when they created questions. In other words, the questions that students generate are another way of eliciting evidence about their understanding.

Unfortunately, unless you give some guidance, when you ask students to generate questions on their own, they tend to pose factual questions. We can train students to ask better questions by providing them with a set of thought-provoking question "shells"—formats that illustrate different ways of asking questions—and suggest that students use these to compose their own questions. For example, you could give students the list of shells and then ask them to compose five good questions together with exemplary answers about the topic they have been studying.

Suggestions for How to Use Question Shells

- At the end of a lesson or period of work, ask the students to work independently using the question shells to generate two or three questions based on the material you covered. Then, either get the students to ask you the questions, or have them ask the class.

- At the end of a lesson or period of work, ask the students to work independently using the question shells to generate two or three questions based on the material covered. Next, in pairs or small groups, ask the students to engage in peer questioning, taking turns to pose the questions to their partner or group and answer each other's questions in a reciprocal manner.

- Get students to read a piece of relevant text. Then ask them to use the generic question shells to generate three or four thoughtful questions about the text.

- At the beginning of a topic, hand out the generic question shells, and ask the students to think of three or four thoughtful questions on this topic that they would like to know the answer to. Collect the questions, and make a poster of the best ten questions that you will attempt to answer during the course of the work.

Here are some possible ideas for question shells:

Question shell	Example
How are . . . and . . . different?	*How are the home lives of Juro and Camila different?*
What are the strengths and weaknesses of . . . ?	*What are the strengths and weaknesses of stone as a building material?*
What is the difference between . . . and . . . ?	*What is the difference between a fable and a parable?*
Explain why . . .	*Explain why you cannot have a probability greater than one.*
What would happen if . . . ?	*What would happen if there were no friction?*
Why is . . . an example of . . . ?	*Why is Romeo and Juliet a tragedy?*

(continued)

Question shell	Example
Compare . . . and . . . in terms of . . .	*Compare Malcolm X and Martin Luther King Jr. in terms of their views on integration.*
How are . . . and . . . similar?	*How are the governments of the United States and Canada similar?*
How would you explain . . . to a student in the . . . grade?	*How would you explain the idea of simile to a student in the third grade?*
What are the implications of . . . for . . . ?	*What are the implications of global warming for employment?*
How does . . . affect . . . ?	*How does temperature affect the rate of a chemical reaction?*
What is the strongest counterargument against . . . ?	*What is the strongest counterargument against democracy as a political system?*
Why is . . . happening?	*Why is the temperature of this boiling water not rising?*

Hinge Questions

You can use all-student response systems at any point in a lesson to check for understanding, and the most experienced teachers will have a huge library of such questions at their fingertips from which they can draw at any time in their teaching. However, for most teachers, it will be helpful to design such questions as part of their lesson planning. We call questions that are designed to be part of an instructional sequence *hinge questions* because the lessons hinge on this point. If the check for understanding shows that all students have understood the concept, you can move on. If it reveals little understanding, the teacher might review the concept with the whole class; if there are a variety of responses, you can use the diversity in the class to get students to compare their answers. The important point is that you do not know what to do until the evidence of the students' achievement is elicited and interpreted; in other words, the lesson hinges on this point.

Hinge questions can occur at any point in a lesson. When teaching an unfamiliar class, you might use a question to gauge the level of understanding that a class has of a topic. A teacher beginning a class on botany says that she likes to ask the students the following question:

> What proportion of the water taken in through the roots of a corn plant is lost through transpiration?
> A. 10%
> B. 30%
> C. 50%
> D. 70%
> E. 90%

She asks students to indicate their response by finger voting. What the teacher finds is that students with a poor understanding of how plants work tend to choose a small value because they know that plants die if they get too little water, and transpiration is therefore something that the plant needs to minimize. Students with a better understanding of botany choose options D or E because they know that transpiration is the process by which plants move water and nutrients from the roots to the shoots.

There are two important characteristics of a good hinge question. The first is that it is highly unlikely that a student will select the correct answer for the wrong reason. For example, if students have read a story about zebras, the two following questions are not equally useful:

1. Where did the zebras find food?
2. What color are zebras?

To answer the first question, the students have to have read the story, whereas many students will be able to answer the second from their general knowledge about zebras.

As another example, if students are asked to reduce the fraction $^{16}/_{64}$ to its simplest form, and students respond with $^{1}/_{4}$, it is tempting to conclude that they understand how to simplify fractions. However, the problem with this particular fraction is that, by a quirky coincidence, students can obtain the correct answer with the incorrect strategy of canceling the sixes: $^{16}/_{64}$. When a student can answer the question correctly with an incorrect strategy, the question is not much use as a check for understanding.

The second requirement of hinge questions is that they must be *diagnostic* questions, rather than *discussion* questions. Many of the questions that teachers ask really only work well when there is time to get the students to explain their answers. There is nothing wrong with such questions. Indeed, they are a potent source of high-quality classroom discussion, *if there is time for the discussion*. But if each student has to explain her or his answer for the teacher to find out whether the teaching has been successful, then the question is almost useless as a quick check for understanding.

During a lesson, it is particularly useful to focus hinge questions on what David Perkins (1999) calls *troublesome knowledge*—things that students are known to find difficult. Troublesome knowledge can be in the form of "threshold concepts," which are "a transformed way of understanding, or interpreting, or viewing something without which the learner cannot progress" (Meyer & Land, 2003, p. 1). In science, for example, it is generally more powerful to examine situations in terms of heat rather than cold. When it's a cold, windy day, we feel as if the cold is coming through our clothes, but if you ask a physicist what is happening, she will say that the wind is exacerbating the loss of heat from our bodies. This way of thinking is counterintuitive but powerful, and also necessary to progress in science. Knowledge can also be troublesome because of its alien character. In history, for example, it is very difficult to prevent students from applying current ways of thinking about the world to different epochs, perhaps best summarized by L. P. Hartley's quote: "The past is a different country: they do things differently there" (Hartley, 1953, p. 1). And knowledge can be troublesome just because it is burdensome. The formula for solving the quadratic equation is not simple: "negative b plus or minus the square root of b squared minus $4\ a\ c$, all over $2\ a$"; even if a student can derive this from first principles, it is useful to have it memorized, word for word.

When devising hinge questions that focus on troublesome knowledge, it is often useful to start from the mistaken, fragmented, or incomplete ideas that students are known to have. These are sometimes called *misconceptions* but some writers have argued that that this is a pejorative term, and prefer, instead, the idea of *pre-conceptions* (Novak, 1977), *alternative conceptions* (Driver & Easley, 1978), *children's science* (Gilbert, Osborne, & Fensham, 1982), or *facets of thinking* (Minstrell, 1992). That said, we find that students see the term *misconception* as quite useful. For example, students seem to find it easier to talk about having a misconception about a particular topic than to say that they couldn't do something or were incorrect in their ideas. In fact, one student thought it was a missed conception, which again made it seem less serious than a mistake. For this reason, we do not have any strong recommendations regarding terminology.

Some teachers find it particularly useful to engage students in an activity entitled "I used to think . . . but now I think" (Ritchhart & Perkins, 2008). Students are asked to reflect on their changing understanding of a topic by completing two sentences:

> I used to think . . .
>
> But now I think . . .

By stressing the idea that changing one's thinking is a normal and indeed expected part of learning, students can be encouraged to think of ability as malleable, an idea that is discussed in more detail in the next chapter.

Whatever we call students' developing, incomplete, or incorrect ideas, it is essential that we use them in devising effective questions. For example, in mathematics, if we want to check that students understand how to find the median of a set of numbers, we might start by looking at facets of thinking on this topic. We know that students confuse the median with the mean and the mode; we know that students sometimes think that the median is just the middle number (or the mean of the middle two numbers) regardless of whether the numbers have been ordered; and we know that students sometimes get confused when there are an even number of elements in the set, so there are two middle numbers rather than one. Finally some students think that the median is just the range of the numbers (i.e., the difference between the largest and smallest members of the set).

So, if we are going to ask a single question on this of a class, we need to have an even number of elements in the set, we need to ensure that the mean and mode of the elements are not the same as the median, that the average of the two middle numbers when they are not ordered is different again, as is the range (by now, you probably realize why it generally takes over an hour to make up a question).

Here is one possible hinge question on this topic:

What is the median for the following data set?

38   74   22   44   96   22   19   53

A. 22
B. 38 and 44
C. 41
D. 46
E. 58
F. 70
G. This data set has no median.

Options A, D, and E will be selected by students who confuse the median with, respectively, the mode, the mean, and the range. Option B will be selected by students who think that a set with an even number of data points has two medians (i.e., the middle two numbers when the elements of the set are arranged in order), while option G will be selected by those who think that such a set does not have a median. Option F is likely to be selected by students who find the middle number or numbers without first ordering them, while option C, of course, is the correct answer.

Tips

Use Multiple-Choice Formats for Hinge Questions

Let's face it: multiple-choice tests have a bad reputation. People say that they assess only students' abilities to spot or guess the correct response and that they cannot assess higher-order thinking. These are certainly properties of bad multiple-choice tests, but in fact, as the following example from Jonathan Osborne (2011) shows, carefully designed multiple-choice questions can assess higher-order thinking skills, such as observation and measurement.

Janet was asked to do an experiment to find how long it takes for some sugar to dissolve in water. How many repeated measurements would you advise Janet to take?

A. Two or three measurements are always enough.
B. She should take five measurements.
C. If she is accurate she only needs to measure once.
D. She should take measurements until she knows how much they vary.
E. She should take measurements until she gets two or more the same.

And multiple-choice questions have a particular advantage when used in classrooms. When students construct their own responses to a question and display them on dry-erase boards, that presents the teacher with a rather complex data-processing task: making sense of thirty possibly idiosyncratic responses in real time. Using multiple-choice questions makes the teacher's task easier because the students' responses are preprocessed into a small number of alternatives, and if the responses are designed to reflect facets of thinking, the meaning of students' responses is much clearer.

Use as Many Options in Multiple-Choice Questions as the Content Requires

The number of options that you should include in a multiple-choice question is the subject of much debate. Some people argue that four is the best number, while others are convinced that five are better than four. In fact, half a century ago, Amos Tversky (1964) showed that all other things being equal, three alternatives are enough. In other words, as long as there are at least three options in a multiple-choice question, the teacher should decide the number on the basis of what makes the most sense in terms of the topic of the question. For the foregoing question on the median, there were seven options, not because there is anything special about the number seven, but because, in terms of this particular aspect of mathematical knowledge, there are six well-known incomplete or incorrect facets of thinking, and the correct response.

Use Distractor-Driven Multiple-Choice Items

As noted earlier, the erroneous or incomplete ideas that students are likely to have should drive the number of options in a multiple-choice item. When generating questions, therefore, it can be useful to start with the "facets" of thinking, generate the multiple-choice options that students with those particular facets of thinking would choose, and then construct the question itself—what Sadler (1998) calls *distractor-driven* multiple-choice questions (*distractor* is just a technical term for one of the incorrect options in a multiple-choice question).

One such example that Sadler uses is:

The main reason it is hotter in summer than in winter is:

A. The earth's distance from the sun changes.
B. The sun is higher in the sky.
C. The distance between the northern hemisphere and the sun changes.
D. Ocean currents carry warm water north.
E. An increase occurs in greenhouse gases.

The correct answer (B) was chosen by only 12 percent of students in grades eight through twelve. More interestingly, the likelihood of choosing particular incorrect options changes with the ability of the student. Students of average science ability were most likely to choose option A, which was chosen by 45 percent of students overall, while students of above-average ability in science were most likely to choose option C (chosen by 36 percent of students overall). However, the very highest-achieving students (top 5 percent of achievement) chose the correct answer well over 50 percent of the time.

One noteworthy feature of this item is that the correct answer was chosen by fewer students (12 percent) than those who would have gotten the answer by chance (20 percent). This is an important property of well-designed multiple-choice questions. When questions are designed well, students who do not understand the content do worse than if they just respond randomly, because the incorrect options are so attractive. When the development of multiple-choice questions begins with incomplete or incorrect facets of thinking, single items can be rich sources of evidence about student understanding.

Cautions

Hinge Questions Are Always Works in Progress

Once you have a good hinge question—one that has worked well with different students for many years—it is tempting to regard the question as "as good as it can be." However, because we can never be sure that students are giving the right answer for the right reason, periodically it is useful to check—by asking students to explain their responses—that their choice of the correct response really does indicate that they understand the material you are teaching. For example, we might check on students' understanding of adverbs by asking them to use letter cards or dry-erase boards to identify the adverbs in the following sentence:

Jose ran the race well, but unsuccessfully

A   B   C   D   E

If a student indicates that he thinks "unsuccessfully" is an adverb but "well" is not, it would be tempting to conclude that the student believes all adverbs end in "-ly" (provided he realizes that such questions can have more than a single correct answer). Indeed, most of the time, this would probably be the correct interpretation. A teacher once used this question with a class, and one of the higher-achieving students gave such an answer. Because the teacher was fairly sure that the student did in fact know that not all adverbs end in "-ly," she asked him whether he thought "well" might also be an adverb. The student replied that it was not. After some discussion about whether "well" is an adverb, the student said, "Well, I kind of assumed that Fred was sick the day before." The student's interpretation of the sentence is entirely correct; when "well" is describing someone's health (a noun), it is an adjective. The important point here is that sometimes students get the correct answer for the wrong reason, but sometimes they get the wrong answer for the right reason. Good questions are never finalized. They are always works in progress, and periodically you will need to check that what you think your students' responses mean is correct.

Enhancements

Real-Time Tests

There is now a great deal of research evidence that shows regular and frequent testing increases learning (for a readable and up-to-date summary of the research, see P. C.

Brown et al., 2014). The important thing to note about this research, however, is that the benefits of testing come about because students are required to retrieve from their memories what they know. There is no further benefit when you record students' scores in a grade book. In other words, the important thing is that students are being required regularly to retrieve what they have learned. One way to do this is with "real-time tests," where teachers gauge what students have learned during the lesson, with enough time to address any issues before the end of the lesson.

For example, a teacher introduces a class to five different kinds of figurative language: alliteration, hyperbole, onomatopoeia, personification, and simile. To check the students' understanding of these terms, she reads out sentences and asks the students to use finger voting to show what kinds of figurative language they have heard: one finger for alliteration, two for hyperbole, three for onomatopoeia, four for personification, and five for simile. The teacher then reads out the following statements:

"He was like a bull in a china shop."

"This suitcase weighs a ton."

"The sweetly smiling sunshine . . ."

"The cat meowed menacingly at the mouse."

"He was as tall as a house."

From the students' votes, she can see that most of the class understands alliteration, hyperbole, onomatopoeia, and simile, but some students thought that the first statement was personification, while many did not realize that the *third statement* was an example of personification. By engaging the class in a discussion of this point, the teacher manages to clear up the confusion before the end of the lesson.

You can also use real-time tests to bridge from one lesson to the next. For example, a mathematics teacher coming to the end of a lesson on solving equations with a seventh-grade class decides to ask some questions that would both look back at the lesson that was just ending and look forward to the next lesson. The focus of the lesson has been on equations with an unknown on only one side of the equation, and she plans, in the next lesson, to move on to equations with unknowns on both sides of the equation. To check whether the students in the class have understood the content of the lesson, she posts six equations on the board, which the students are expected to solve and put their responses on a dry-erase board. The six equations are:

1. $3x + 3 = 12$
2. $5x - 1 = 19$
3. $12 - 2x = 2$
4. $4 = 10 - 2x$

5. $4x - 3 = 2x + 5$

6. $3 - 2x = 13 - 4x$

The teacher has designed the first four equations to test, in increasing order of difficulty, the materials she covered in that lesson, but the real-time test also includes two equations that test material she plans to teach in the next lesson. This may seem to contradict the advice we gave earlier about keeping student responses on white boards brief, but because there will only be six numbers on each board it is easy for the teacher to check the solutions. Moreover, the teacher has cleverly arranged for the solutions to the equations to form a pattern, so it is easy to check whether the displayed answers are correct. When the students display their responses, the teacher sees that most of the students have correctly solved the first four equations but that few solved the last two. This confirms that what she plans to do for the next lesson is appropriate.

As with the previous chapter, we end this chapter with a recap, followed by a reflection checklist you might find useful to complete, a planning sheet for using a technique with a class, and a peer observation sheet (so that you can ask a colleague to give you feedback).

Each of the sheets are at the back of this book for you to copy if needed, so feel free to write all over the following sheets!

RECAP

It is very important that you plan questions in advance.

- No hands up, except to ask a question
  - Choose students at random
    - Interactive whiteboard randomizer
    - PowerPoint
    - Smartphone
    - Ice-pop sticks
      - With names or numbers
      - With or without replacement
      - With one name on multiple sticks
      - With a student looking after the sticks
    - Small cards
    - Two random responses, then volunteers
  - No opt-out
    - Return to original student—which answer is the best?
    - Multiple choice—find incorrect items
    - "Do you need additional information?"
    - Ask the audience
    - Phone a friend

- Hand signals
- Basketball
- Hot-seat questioning
- Time for thinking
  - Increase wait time to enable thinking and elaboration time
  - Incorporate think-pair-share
- Avoiding questions altogether
  - Make statements
    - Declarative statement
    - Reflective statement
    - Statement of mind
    - Statement of interest
    - Student referral
    - Teacher opinion
    - Student question
    - Class question
    - Phatics and fillers
    - Pass
    - Silences
  - Learning logs
  - Interpretive rather than evaluative listening
  - Minimal encouragers
  - Model-revealing activities
    - Concept cartoon
- All-student response systems
  - Electronic voting systems
  - ABCD cards
  - Finger voting
  - Mini dry-erase boards
  - Page protectors
  - Exit tickets
    - Anonymous
    - With names for placemats
  - ABCD corners
  - Post-it notes along a line
- Question shells
- Hinge questions
  - Multiple choice
  - Real-time tests

REFLECTION CHECKLIST FOR STRATEGY 2:
Engineering Effective Discussion, Tasks, and Activities That Elicit Evidence of Learning

	I don't do this	I do this sometimes	This is embedded in my practice	I could support someone else
I find out what every student knows at least once a lesson, by using an all-student response system.				
I ensure that all students have time to think about an answer to a question I pose before I choose who answers.				
I give a student a way out if unable to answer my question, but then I come back to that student.				
I ask a hinge question during a lesson when I need to decide whether I could move on.				
Students pose their own questions, which other students answer.				
I make "no hands up" a standard classroom policy.				
I use statements rather than questions to encourage more thoughtful answers.				
I use learning logs, exit cards, or another way of collecting extended responses from students.				
I test students, look at their answers, and then teach the areas that students have problems with before I move on.				
Other techniques for this strategy that I use to improve student learning:				

LESSON PLANNING SHEET

Technique I am going to use:
Why I am planning to use it and the results I am hoping for:
Class and date:
Preparation for the lesson:
What I am going to do less of:
Reflecting on how the technique worked, including evidence to support my claims:
What I am going to do next:

PEER OBSERVATION SHEET

Class to be observed:
Peer's name:
Technique to be observed:
What I want my peer to comment on:
Peer's comments:
Reflections after reading peer's comments and/or talking through the observation:
What I will do next:

STUDENT SURVEY

Here is an example of a student survey—use it with or without the students' names. There is a sheet with three surveys for copying at the back of the book.

Name: **Date:**

Circle one number for each line to show me what you felt about this lesson:

The pace	Slow	1	2	3	4	5	Fast
The difficulty	Easy	1	2	3	4	5	Difficult
My interest	Low	1	2	3	4	5	High
My understanding	Low	1	2	3	4	5	High
My learning	Poor	1	2	3	4	5	Good

STUDENT FEEDBACK TO TEACHER (no name please—just check one box next to each statement)

	Never	Sometimes	Often
Does your teacher tell you what is expected before you start an assignment?			
Do you compare anonymous pieces of work to understand what makes a good assignment?			
Does your teacher ask what you have learned at the end of a lesson?			
Does your teacher choose students at random to answer questions?			
Does your teacher wait three seconds after asking a question to give everyone a chance to think?			
Does your teacher wait three seconds after a student answers a question to allow that student to give a fuller answer?			
Does your teacher ask all students to answer a question at the same time?			
When your teacher grades an assignment, do you get comments that help you improve?			
Do you give feedback to other students?			
Do you work with others in a group to try to help everyone improve?			

My Learning Log   **Name:**   **Date:**

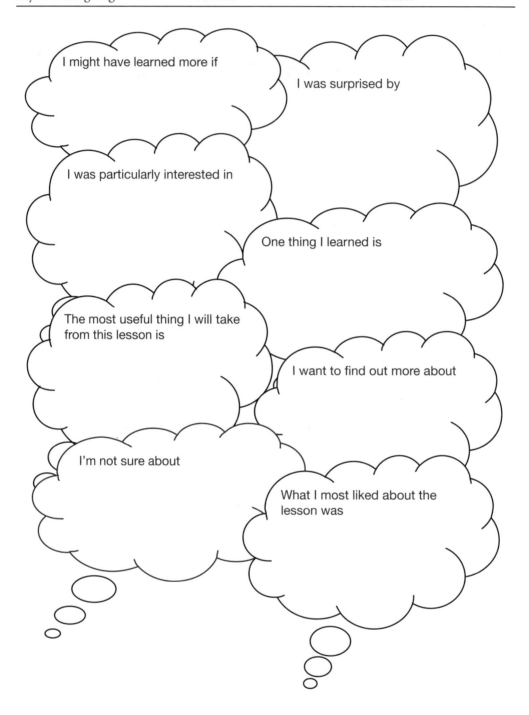

I might have learned more if

I was surprised by

I was particularly interested in

One thing I learned is

The most useful thing I will take from this lesson is

I want to find out more about

I'm not sure about

What I most liked about the lesson was

Chapter 5
STRATEGY 3: PROVIDING FEEDBACK THAT MOVES LEARNING FORWARD

OVERVIEW

In practically every educational institution in the world, teachers give students information on their progress while they are learning. Sometimes students are told how much progress they have made, sometimes they are told how much further progress is needed to reach some goal, and sometimes students are told how their performance compares with that of their peers. Even when it is not the teacher who does this, as soon as they receive the information on their performance, students often seek to compare their performance with their peers. This chapter looks at the research on the effects of different kinds of feedback on students' achievement, in both the short term and longer term, and suggests a number of techniques that teachers can use to harness the power of feedback to improve learning.

WHY USE THIS STRATEGY

When we elicit evidence about what our students have actually learned, we frequently find out it is not what we wanted them to learn; therefore, we need to provide feedback to get the learners back on track.

GETTING TO UNDERSTAND THE STRATEGY

At one level, feedback is a very simple idea. Take the room thermostat, for example. On the thermostat, we have a way of setting our desired temperature, and inside the thermostat there is a thermometer that measures the temperature of the air in the room. Inside the thermostat there is also a device that compares the actual temperature of the air with the desired temperature, and then there are wires that lead to a heating system, a cooling system, or both, depending on the design of the system. When the temperature in the room gets too low, the thermostat turns on the heating system, which then heats the room until it reaches the desired temperature. When the temperature in the room gets too high, the thermostat turns on the cooling system, which cools the room until, again, it reaches the desired temperature.

During the 1960s, in an attempt to make education more scientific, psychologists explored whether the use of feedback could improve learning. One major problem was deciding what kind of feedback would be the most effective.

Some psychologists—especially those who saw learning as a process that involves students actively constructing their own knowledge—argued that the most appropriate role for feedback was getting the learning back on track. They pointed out that (as we saw in the previous chapter) students often make sense of the world in ways that are different from what their teacher intended. If learners were making mistakes—for example, by consistently subtracting the smaller digit from the larger digit in multidigit subtraction—feedback that corrects the learner's inappropriate conceptions and strategies would be helpful.

Others, however—for example, those who believed that learning was mostly a matter of making associations between stimuli and responses—pointed out that repeatedly being told that one was doing things incorrectly could easily be demotivating. After criticism, learners would invest less effort, which would lead to more criticism, and so on in a vicious cycle leading the learner to give up entirely. They argued that feedback should instead act as reinforcement, telling the learner when she was on the right track, therefore prompting the learner to try harder, which would lead to more progress, which, in turn, would lead to more reinforcement in a virtuous cycle.

Intuitively, we can see that both kinds of feedback, corrective and reinforcing, can be helpful. If one is following a set of driving instructions, it is helpful to be told one is on the right track: "If you pass a RaceTrac gas station on your left, you know you're on the right road." But it is also helpful to be told when one has gone wrong: "If you pass under the interstate, you've gone too far."

One might assume that since we now have over 100 years of research on feedback we would have some clear answers to the question of what kinds of feedback work best. Unfortunately, this is far from the case. This is partly because it appears that different kinds of feedback are more effective for different kinds of learning, and we do not yet have a clear idea of which particular kinds of feedback are most effective for which particular kinds of learning. However, it is also clear that much of the research into the effects of feedback is of rather poor quality. Studies have been badly designed or poorly implemented, and researchers have too often ignored data that did not fit their theories.

Worse, those who have been involved in communicating research on feedback to teachers regularly substituted their own prejudices for rigorous evidence, with the result that much of what teachers are told about feedback is misleading, and often just wrong.

In this chapter, we look at why the research on feedback is so confusing and contradictory. We know that in the introduction to this book, we said that this is not a book about research, but, in the case of feedback, we think that understanding a little of the research is very helpful to giving good feedback. We also explore a number of practical techniques that you can use to improve your classroom practice, but we also see why with feedback, as with so much else in teaching, there aren't really any "hard and fast" rules.

TECHNIQUES

Focus on the Reaction of the Students, Not the Feedback

In 1996, two psychologists at Rutgers, the State University of New Jersey, published the results of a rather remarkable venture. They had tracked down a copy of every study they could find on the effects of feedback (Kluger & DeNisi, 1996). They defined feedback interventions as "actions taken by (an) external agent(s) to provide information regarding some aspect(s) of one's task performance" (p. 255). In other words, they included information that provided details of how well one was doing (e.g., "Your typing speed is 65 words per minute") as well as information that suggested ways in which performance could be improved (e.g., "Use your thumb only for hitting the space bar").

By going all the way back to 1905 (!) they identified 2,500 journal articles and 500 technical reports that were relevant. However, some of the studies were not well designed. For example, in some, the experimenters participated as subjects, while in others, they found that the reports of the experiments were not presented in sufficient detail to make an estimate of how much the feedback improved achievement. In some of the studies, feedback was combined with another intervention, such as target setting, so even where there was an impact on achievement, it was impossible to be sure whether it was the feedback or the target setting that was the cause of the improvement. Because errors of sampling are a significant problem with small data sets, they decided to exclude studies with fewer than ten participants (most statisticians would recommend a minimum of thirty). Finally, they also excluded studies that lacked a control group, since without a control group, it would be impossible to be sure whether any improvement was caused by the feedback, or would have happened anyway—for example, through maturation.

These criteria for exclusion seem sensible, and yet Kluger and DeNisi found that only 131 (i.e., fewer than 5 percent) of the original studies remained, which reported a total of 607 results about the impact of feedback on performance.

In order to compare the results of the different experiments, Kluger and DeNisi converted the result of each experiment into what is called a *standardized effect size*. You can find the details of how this is calculated in the appendix, but, to give some idea of what this means, an effect size of 1 would mean that giving someone feedback would take someone who was average just into the top one-sixth of the population, and an effect size of 2 would take an average person up into the top 2 percent of the population. Similarly, an effect size of −1 would take an average person down to the bottom sixth of the population, and an effect size of −2 would take an average person down to the bottom 2 percent. The effect sizes that Kluger and DeNisi found are shown in Figure 5.1.

Perhaps the most surprising thing about Figure 5.1 is that although there are some extreme values that can probably be discounted—it is hard to imagine what an effect size of 12 might mean, but it is almost certainly a spurious result—most of the values cluster quite closely around zero. The average effect size was 0.41, which equates to raising the performance of an average student up to the 66th percentile. Perhaps even more surprisingly, *38 percent of the effect sizes were negative.*

This is one of the most counterintuitive results in all of psychology. In each of the studies reviewed, feedback had been intended to improve performance, but in almost two out of every five experiments, feedback didn't just have no effect; it actually made things worse. The participants in the experiments would actually have done better if those providing the feedback had not given the feedback.

Figure 5.1: Bar Chart of Effect Sizes Found by Kluger and DeNisi (1996)

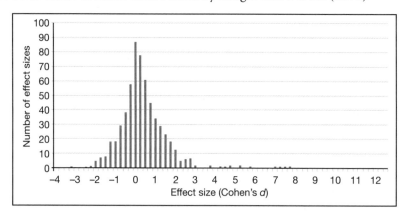

In a more recent study, focusing specifically on feedback in mathematics, science, and technology education, Ruiz-Primo and Li (2013) identify 9,000 potentially relevant studies, but after careful review, find that only 111 of the papers contain actual empirical evidence about the effects of feedback (with sixty, thirty-five, and sixteen focusing primarily on mathematics, science, and engineering/technology education, respectively). Like Kluger and DeNisi, Ruiz-Primo and Li find that feedback is generally effective, but the range is again wide. But more importantly, they conclude that hardly any of the studies they review are relevant to classroom practice. One "stunning" finding (their words, not ours) is that in over three-fourths of the studies, feedback is a single event, lasting minutes, with the whole experiment—teaching and testing the participants, giving feedback, testing the participants again—taking place in a single session of no more than three hours. There is not one single example of an experiment that looks at the effect of feedback on student achievement weeks, let alone months, later.

Go to www.learningsciences.com/bookresources to download figures and tables.

To understand why the effects they find in different studies are so variable, both Kluger and DeNisi and Ruiz-Primo and Li look for factors that make feedback more or less effective, and they find no simple answers. Kluger and DeNisi propose that the reason for this is that the only thing that really matters about feedback is the kind of reaction it triggers in the recipient, and hardly any of the studies they reviewed look at this.

Kluger and DeNisi suggest that when individuals are given feedback, they can do one of four things: change behavior, change the goal, abandon the goal, or reject the feedback. The problem is that—for some of these responses at least—whether the response is desirable depends on the context. For example, changing behavior is, presumably, desirable when the learner is falling short of the goal he or she has set. We want learners to increase effort in order to achieve the goal. But changing behavior is not desirable if the learner has already achieved the goal; we do not want learners to ease off and apply less effort because they are doing well. Instead, we want the learner to change the goal, by increasing aspiration and aiming for a higher goal. But changing the goal is undesirable if learners are falling short of the goal they already have; we do not want students saying, "I was aiming for an A, but I'll settle for a B." It is also, of course, undesirable if learners abandon the goal ("math is stupid") or reject the feedback ("my math teacher is stupid"). This is why feedback is so hard to get right. As shown in Table 5.1, when students are given feedback, eight things can happen, and six of them are bad (the two desirable responses are shown in bold).

Table 5.1: Reactions to Feedback, After Kluger and DeNisi (1996)

	Feedback indicates that performance	
	Falls short of goal	**Exceeds goal**
Change behavior	**Increase effort**	Reduce effort
Change goal	Reduce aspiration	**Increase aspiration**
Abandon goal	Decide goal is too easy	Decide goal is too hard
Reject feedback	Feedback is ignored	Feedback is ignored

The only thing that matters with feedback is the reaction of the recipient. That's it. Feedback—no matter how well designed—that the student does not act upon is a waste of time. This may seem obvious, but hundreds of researchers have ignored this basic truth, and tried instead to find out whether feedback should be immediate or delayed. Should it be specific or general? Should it be verbal or written? In the remainder of this chapter, we look at how to make feedback more effective, but ultimately, it comes down to the simple truth that the most effective feedback is just feedback that our students actually use in improving their own learning. We will explore ways in which you can increase the likelihood that your students use the feedback that you provide. While the quality of feedback does make a difference to how your students will respond, what is far more important is the continuing relationship you have with your students, and how they see themselves as learners.

Tips

Get to Know Your Students

Every teacher knows that the feedback he gives to one student may make that student try harder, but to another, similar student, that same feedback would make that other student give up. Only by getting to know your students will you be able to judge when to push and when to back off.

Build Trust With Your Students

As well as knowing their students, teachers need to build trust with them. If students do not believe that their teachers know what they are talking about and have the students' best interests at heart, they are unlikely to invest the effort needed to improve. In one study (Yeager et al., 2013), seventh-grade students were given critical feedback in a way that emphasized that the critical nature of the feedback was due to the teacher's high standards, combined with a belief that the student could meet the challenge (what the researchers called *wise feedback*). Students receiving wise feedback were more likely to submit a revision of an essay and more likely to improve the quality of the final drafts, than peers who were not getting wise feedback. Perhaps more importantly, the effects were more marked among African American students, and even stronger in those who were least trusting of school.

Cautions

Don't Believe Most of What Is Said About Feedback

In their review of feedback research, Kluger and DeNisi point out that many of the claims about what makes the most effective feedback ignore the available data. Sadly, the same problem is all too common today. Authors bombard teachers with advice that feedback should be verbal rather than written, immediate rather than delayed, and so on. This advice is certainly correct much of the time, and maybe even most of the time, but it is certainly not true *all* of the time. For example, a recent study finds that engineering undergraduates prefer feedback given immediately but actually learn more when feedback is delayed for a week (Mullet, Butler, Verdin, von Borries, & Marsh, 2014).

Perhaps the most common advice given to teachers about feedback is that it should be descriptive rather than evaluative. This is generally advisable, but there are also circumstances where it might be appropriate to give evaluative feedback. If the student can use evaluative feedback to improve or focus her learning, there seems to be little harm in doing so. For example, if a student is planning how to divide attention between different advanced placement courses, knowing that she is, at her current level of progress, likely to get a 5 in AP Calculus but only a 2 in AP English Language and Composition might help the student make a smarter decision about how to allocate her time. More importantly, the term *descriptive* doesn't really capture the most important feature of effective feedback, which is that it leads to useful action on the part of the student. The only good feedback is that which is *productive*.

Sometimes it might even be appropriate to refuse to give feedback. If a student turns in work that clearly indicates he didn't take the assignment seriously, the teacher could certainly give feedback about how the work could be improved. But it might be more appropriate to return the work to the student without any feedback, saying, "I'm not going to give you any feedback until you put more effort into producing a decent first draft."

Enhancements

Build Your Students' Capacity to Use Feedback

In their book *Thanks for the Feedback: The Science and Art of Receiving Feedback Well*, Stone and Heen (2014) point out that there are three "triggers" that can affect how recipients of feedback react to the feedback: *truth triggers*, *relationship triggers*, and *identity triggers*. Truth triggers are those related to the recipients' perception of the accuracy of the feedback. For example, if a teacher tells a student, "You didn't put enough effort into this assignment," the student is likely to reject the feedback if she thinks that she did, in fact, work hard on the assignment. For truth triggers the actual truth of the matter is irrelevant; it is the recipient's *perception* of the truth that matters. So if the student had actually been working on the assignment while watching a two-hour movie but the student's perception is that she spent two hours on the assignment, this will make it difficult for her to accept that she didn't put enough effort into the assignment.

Relationship triggers are cued not by what the feedback is saying but who is saying it. One category of relationship triggers includes feedback that the recipient regards as hypocritical. For example, if a teacher who is often not punctual criticizes a tardy student, the student may (justifiably!) reply or at least think, "Look who's talking." Relationship triggers also include feedback that the student rejects because the donor is regarded as overly critical—for example, when a student says, "No matter how hard I try, nothing's ever good enough for you." Particularly for high-achieving students— who are often used to getting a lot of approval and praise—critical feedback can sometimes be taken as signaling a change in the relationship. For example, a student might react to feedback that shows how a piece of work might be improved by saying, "But I thought you liked me." The actual content of the feedback is ignored because the recipient interprets the feedback as a statement about the relationship between the donor and recipient.

Identity triggers are reactions not to the truth of the feedback, nor to the person providing the feedback, but rather to the recipients' view of themselves. When feedback challenges a student's image of himself, the likelihood of one of the negative responses to feedback shown in Table 5.1 is increased. And it is important to remember that as humans, our brains' reactions to threats and unpleasantness are extremely rapid—typically these reactions occur about ten times faster than our responses to opportunities and pleasures (Haidt, 2005). Moreover, they are stronger and more difficult to inhibit.

While these triggered responses get in the way of responding appropriately to feedback, it is important to note that they are entirely reasonable. The problem is not that these are unreasonable responses to feedback but rather that they prevent our students from taking advantage of the available feedback to improve their capabilities. There is no simple formula for getting our students to like, value, or even accept our feedback—it can be an extremely painful process. But when teachers develop their relationships with their students—when students trust that teachers know what they are talking about and have the students' best interests at heart, and the students see feedback as a way of increasing their capabilities—it is more likely that feedback leads to productive action.

However, as noted earlier, it is also important to realize that individuals vary greatly in how they react to feedback (see next section on "mindset"). Some students are so focused on improvement that they don't need any sweet talk to soften the blow of what they need to do to improve—they just want to get on with getting better. Other students, however, may need a great deal of positive feedback before they can accept even the slightest criticism. There is no substitute for you knowing your students.

Model Responding to Feedback

One way to take the ego out of the students' responses to your feedback is to give them practice in responding to feedback in a less emotionally charged context, as was done in the second case study in the previous chapter. For example, you can write feedback on a piece of work by an anonymous student in another class, make one copy per group of students, and give each group a copy of the work, together with the success criteria for the original task. You can then ask each group of students to improve the work by following your feedback. Although students are not improving their own work, they will learn much from improving someone else's. Each group could then explain to the class the improvements they have made to the work, or they could display their improvements around the room for the class to view as they walk around.

You can vary this basic technique in a number of ways. Instead of using the same piece of work for each student group, you could differentiate the task by assigning different pieces of work, or even the same pieces of work but with different feedback, to different groups. By presenting the original work and feedback electronically (e.g., in Microsoft Word or Google Docs), it is easier for groups to redraft the work and for them to share their responses to the task with the rest of the class.

Develop a "Growth Mindset" in Your Students

One particularly important factor influencing how students react to feedback is the way that students make sense of successes and failures in school, which has been a major focus of a forty-year research program by Carol Dweck, now at Stanford University. When you ask students about the reasons for success or failure—for example, "When you get an A, why is that?" or "When you get an F, why is that?"—their answers differ in three important ways: *personalization*, *stability*, and *specificity*.

Personalization: Students attribute successes and failures to internal factors (how smart they are, how much effort they put in) or external factors that are outside their control (whether the teacher likes them, good or bad luck).

Stability: Students attribute successes and failures to relatively fixed factors, such as being smart, while others attribute successes and failures to transient factors, such as how much or how little effort they put into that particular task.

Specificity: Students differ in the way they generalize from particular examples of successes and failures to other areas of experience. Some students overgeneralize success or failure, so they take success or failure in one aspect of one's life as being indicative of the likely outcomes in completely unrelated areas. In contrast, others consciously limit the meaning of success to only the specific aspects of their experience in which they are successful.

Some samples of student attributions, showing how they differ in terms of personalization, stability, and specificity, are shown in Table 5.2.

Table 5.2: Personalization, Stability, and Specificity of Attributions of Success and Failure

Sample attribution	Personalization	Stability	Specificity
I got an A because I worked hard on this assignment.	Internal	Unstable	Specific
I got an F because my math teacher is a tough grader.	External	Stable	Specific
I got an A because I'm smart.	Internal	Stable	General
I got an F because I find it hard to concentrate at the moment.	Internal	Unstable	General
I got an F because I'm just not very good at taking tests.	Internal	Stable	General
I got an A because I'm good at math.	Internal	Stable	Specific

(continued)

Sample attribution	Personalization	Stability	Specificity
I got an F because the teachers I have this year are bad.	External	Unstable	General
I got an F because I'm not very good at math.	Internal	Stable	Specific

The way that individual students attribute their successes and failures in a particular situation obviously depends on a whole range of factors, including details of the current context, their previous experience of the teacher and the subject being taught, and so on. However, there is now a large body of evidence (see, for example, Dweck, 2000, for a summary) indicating that the most successful learners attribute both successes and failures to internal, unstable, specific factors: it's down to them (internal) and they can do something about it (unstable). Perhaps more simply, smart is not something you *are*; it's something you *get* (Howard, 1991).

One particular set of beliefs that strongly influences how students make sense of successes and failures in school, which in turn influences how they respond to feedback, relates to the students' view of the nature of intelligence—what Carol Dweck calls *mindset* (Dweck, 2006).

Some students have an "entity" view of intelligence. They believe that each person is endowed, either at conception, birth, or certainly very early in life, with a certain amount of intelligence that is pretty much fixed for the rest of one's life. As one student says, "There are smart people and not-so-smart people." Other students hold a more incremental view of intelligence. They believe that intelligence is inherently malleable and in particular that engaging in challenging work can increase it.

Students with different views of intelligence tend to pursue different goals in school. Compared with students with incremental views of ability, those with entity views are more likely to:

- Seek confirmation of their ability (Dweck & Leggett, 1988)
- Avoid situations where they might fail (Robins & Pals, 2002)
- Attribute failure to lack of ability (Hong, Chiu, Dweck, Lin, & Wan, 1999)
- Persist with clearly ineffective strategies (Robins & Pals, 2002)
- Give up when stuck (Robins & Pals, 2002)

What is rather striking is that very subtle differences in the way we praise children can have serious long-term effects. Very young children (one to three years old) whom their parents praise for their effort rather than achievement are likely to have an incremental view of intelligence five years later (Gunderson et al., 2013).

Go to www.learningsciences.com/bookresources to download figures and tables.

Fortunately, we now know that students' views of the nature of intelligence can be changed, and when students develop more incremental views of intelligence, they learn more (Aronson, Fried, & Good, 2002; Blackwell, Dweck, & Trzesniewski, 2007). Perhaps most surprisingly, even quite brief interventions can change students' views of intelligence. In the study by Blackwell et al. (2007) the only differences between the experimental group and the control group are four twenty-five-minute sessions. While the control group students are taught about short- and long-term memory and practice mnemonic strategies, the experimental group takes turns around the class to read an article that describes the changes in the brain that occurs during learning. Then they engage in discussions about the consequences for their own learning, centered around the key message "Everything is hard before it is easy."

Tips

Help Your Students See the Connection Between the Feedback and the Improvement

One of the ways to help students develop a growth mindset is to document and draw attention to the improvements that students make through effort, although this is much easier to do in some school subjects than others.

In practical school subjects it is very easy to help students see improvements in ability through responding to feedback. For example, a physical education teacher is introducing a class to putting the shot. He asks students to throw the shot three times with just one hand, using whatever approach feels most natural to them, and measures each student's attempts. The teacher then tells the students some of the key techniques of shot putting, such as holding the shot at the base of the fingers rather than in the palm, and raising the elbow of the throwing hand high. Over the course of a single lesson, the students see substantial improvements in their performance, often in excess of 50 percent. Because the improvement in performance is so clearly linked to the feedback, it is easy for the students to relate the two.

In academic subjects, it is much more difficult for students to see the link between the feedback and improvement, because the timescales tend to be longer, but it is still worth getting students to reflect on how they used the feedback to improve their work. Indeed, such reflection can also help the teacher ensure that the feedback is functioning correctly. After all, if your students can't tell you how they are using your feedback to improve their work, the feedback probably isn't having its intended effect.

Focus on Self-Efficacy, Not Self-Esteem

We all want our students to feel good about themselves—to feel that they are important and valued and have substantial contributions to make. However, the relationship between self-esteem and academic achievement is weak, with one review of research estimating that self-esteem accounts for less than 5 percent of the variation in academic achievement (Hansford & Hattie, 1982). Perhaps more importantly, self-esteem that is based on nothing but the approval of others is very shallow and brittle, and easily eroded. We actually don't want students feeling good about themselves because others tell them they are wonderful. We want students feeling good about themselves because of their confidence in their ability to reach their goals—what Albert Bandura calls *self-efficacy* (Bandura, 1977). The distinction is important because self-esteem actually discourages students from attempting challenging work, just in case they fail, whereas self-efficacy is all about engagement with challenge.

Help Students Develop Appropriate Learning Goals

Many psychologists classify the academic goals that students adopt in schools as either *performance goals* or *mastery goals*. Performance goals relate to how one is doing, and mastery goals relate to whether one is learning. These goals are then subdivided according to whether the student's main focus is on approaching the goal or avoiding it. For example, a student who wants an A has a performance-approach goal, while a student who wants to avoid getting an F has a performance-avoidance goal. In contrast, a student for whom understanding something is more important than the grade awarded has a mastery-approach goal, and it is widely assumed that mastery-avoidance goals are not relevant. After all, it is hard to imagine someone striving to get worse at something.

People often claim that mastery goals are superior to performance goals (see, for example, Rolland, 2012), which of course makes sense. Students who are focused on learning rather than getting good grades are less likely to cheat or take shortcuts in learning. It is also clear that the way that teachers provide feedback to their students can influence whether students adopt mastery or performance goals. For example, in a study of 1,571 students in eighty-four mathematics classrooms from fifth to twelfth grade, Deevers (2006) finds that although students' self-efficacy beliefs and motivation to learn declines steadily from fifth to twelfth grade, students provided with positive constructive feedback are more likely to display mastery orientation, even though teachers give less of this kind of feedback as students get older.

However, the experimental evidence just doesn't support any simple conclusions. For example, in a study of a five-week elementary school math unit, Linnenbrink (2005) finds that a combined approach, emphasizing mastery goals within small groups but emphasizing performance goals between groups, produces the highest achievement, provided the competition between groups is focused on relative improvement among the groups.

Performance-approach goals can, in fact, be effective in getting students to aim high (see, for example, Senko, Durik, Patel, Lovejoy, & Valentiner, 2013). Of course, when performance-approach goals get out of hand, students may well cheat to reach the goal, which is obviously not good; but getting students to aspire to a challenging goal is an important part of a teacher's repertoire. Researchers also tend to point out that performance-avoidance goals, such as not wanting to fail, can lead students to avoid challenge. However, in other cases, performance-avoidance goals can make students prepare diligently for tests, which tends to enhance learning. Finally, it is also worth noting that wanting to avoid getting worse at something, which some researchers confusingly term a mastery-avoidance goal, can lead to worse performance than the other three kinds of goals (see, for example, van Yperen, Elliot, & Anseel, 2009).

Cautions

Be Careful How You Praise

It has long been known that praise, in and of itself, has no simple relationship with student achievement. Indeed, a number of studies find that the most effective teachers praise less than others, but do so in a distinctive way; praise is specific to a task the student has recently completed, is seen as sincere and genuine by the student, and is related to something that is within the student's control (Brophy, 1981). However, most of the research into praise, like that into feedback, has not examined the relationship between the student and the teacher, so it is not particularly helpful.

As Carol Dweck points out, praising a student often sends an additional, negative message, as shown in Table 5.3 (Dweck, 2006).

Table 5.3: Praise Statements and Their Hidden Implications (after Dweck, 2006)

Praise statement	Hidden message
"You learned that so quickly! You're so smart!"	If I don't learn something quickly, I'm not smart.
"Look at that drawing. Martha, is he the next Picasso or what?"	I shouldn't try drawing anything hard or they'll see I'm no Picasso.
"You're so brilliant; you got an A without even studying!"	I'd better quit studying or they won't think I'm brilliant.

Over many studies with hundreds of children, Dweck and her colleagues find that praising children's intelligence harms both their motivation and their performance (Dweck, 2006). For example, four-year-olds given generic praise (e.g., "You are a good drawer") are more likely than those given specific praise (e.g., "You did a good job drawing") to abandon work with mistakes in it rather than attempt to fix the mistakes (Cimpian, Arce, Markman, & Dweck, 2007).

Give Task-Involving Rather Than Ego-Involving Feedback

As has been stressed several times already, there aren't any universal principles about what makes feedback effective, but the idea that feedback should focus on the task rather than the individual comes pretty close (Hattie & Timperley, 2007; Kluger & DeNisi, 1996). While some studies find that task-involving feedback improves achievement (see, for example, Butler, 1987), others find that task-involving feedback is often no better than no feedback at all but that ego-involving feedback is worse than either task-involving feedback or no feedback at all (Skipper & Douglas, 2012). It does, therefore, appear that the really important thing is to try, wherever possible, to avoid giving feedback that relates to the individual, and especially feedback that relates to an individual's value as a person.

Enhancements

Use Personal Bests, Not Ranks or Grades

Traditionally, in the United States, teachers include a range of factors other than achievement in awarding students grades. Elements that contribute to the final grade include contribution in class, tardiness, completion of homework, and so on. Some teachers routinely use grades as incentives for students to hand work in on time, or behave well— for example, during a visit to the library. It is therefore hardly surprising that Paul Dressel describes a *grade* as

> an inadequate report of an inaccurate judgment by a biased and variable judge of the extent to which a student has attained an undefined level of mastery of an unknown proportion of an indefinite material. (quoted in Chickering, 1983, p. 12)

In response to such practices, many schools adopt *standards-based grading*; although this term means different things to different people, the essence of the idea is that student assessment is based on the academic standards a student achieves. This seems to us eminently sensible, but it does bring in a number of problems. For example, with a "traditional" grading policy, students might lose points if they submit work late—a typical penalty might be 5 or 10 percent—but this would be inconsistent with a standards-based grading policy. If the student shows mastery of the required content, the logic of standards-based grading is that they get 100 percent even if the evidence arrives late. The problem then, of course, is that there is no incentive for the student to turn the work in on time. Similarly, if contributions in class are not graded, why should students contribute? If we do not grade effort, why should students make an effort?

As a result, many schools supplement standards-based achievement grades with effort grades. However, we think this brings in additional problems. Now, it should be clear from our discussion of the work of Carol Dweck and others earlier that we think effort is very important—we actually think it's the most important thing in school work. Our problem is with attempting to grade effort.

We think there are at least three problems with grading effort. The first is the asymmetry of the situation; the student knows how hard he tried and you don't. Students tell us routinely that they get angry when teachers say they haven't put much effort into a piece of work, when the students think they have. In the TV show *The Classroom Experiment*, the following exchange takes place between a student and teacher after the student sees that the teacher has commented in her notebook that she needs to make more effort.

Teacher:	"Have you got a question to ask me?"
Jessie:	"It says that I haven't got . . . that I have a lack of effort."
Teacher:	"Why do you think . . . what's a lack of effort . . . what activity was that for?"
Jessie:	"Well, nothing. I put loads of effort into this. Oh, I don't care."

Now, it may be that Jessie's idea of effort is very different from the teacher's. As suggested earlier, Jessie may think that she spent two hours on an assignment, when it was on her lap for two hours while she watched TV; but the thing is, Jessie now believes that the teacher has no idea what he is talking about. Conversely, when the teacher says, "Well done for putting so much effort into this," and the student knows that she hasn't put much effort in, again the impression is that the teacher doesn't know what he's talking about.

The second problem with effort grades is that they tend to be strongly correlated with achievement scores; it is not clear why, but whenever we have analyzed achievement grades and effort grades, we find a strong correlation—high-achieving students get high-effort grades and low-achieving students get low-effort grades. So the real message being sent is, "Not only are you no good at math, you're not even any good at trying."

The third problem with effort grades is that even if students are trying but not making any progress, it may be that they need to try something else. That is why we think there is great value in grading in terms of "academic personal bests."

The idea of a "personal best" is well established in sports, but in recent years, there has been a stream of research studies exploring the idea of a personal best in academic work (see, for example, Liem, Ginns, Martin, & Stone, 2012). The evidence so far is that focusing on personal bests in academic work can have just as much value as it does in sports. For example, many English language arts teachers have found it useful to give feedback to students in the form of comments, together with either a minus, an equals, or a plus, according to whether the work is not as good as, about the same as, or better than previous work done by the student in that genre. While students will, inevitably, compare scores, it is likely to be less harmful to their learning if they are comparing themselves in terms of progress, rather than achievement, not least because frequently it is the lowest achievers who make most progress.

Use Students' Reactions to Feedback as Clues to Their Mindsets

One long-standing debate in education is whether teachers should provide feedback in red or some other colored ink, or even in pencil. Some argue that because of the way modern societies use the color red (e.g., to signal "stop" in traffic lights), red is an inherently negative color (see Mehta & Zhu, 2009, for a brief summary of some of the research on this topic). Indeed, there are even some research studies that claim to show that grading in a more neutral color will increase student achievement (Dukes & Albanesi, 2013). Some teachers use green ink to signal things that are positive, and pink or purple to signal things that need attention (what they dub "the purple pen of progress").

However, even if students perceive grading in red as negative, and even if they would prefer another color, this doesn't mean it has to be this way. As noted earlier, educational research generally tells us what was, not what might be. Students with fixed mindsets may well regard feedback in red as strident and "spoiling their work," but the advantage of red is that it stands out. Students with growth mindsets may well prefer feedback in red, since it is easy for them to see what they need to do to improve. The important point here is that students' reactions to feedback can provide an indication of whether they have performance or mastery goals, which is strongly influenced by their mindset.

Be Aware of the Implicit Messages You Send

Imagine you are teaching an eighth-grade mathematics class and give the class a set of twenty equations to solve. The equations are reasonably challenging, so you expect the students to take around two minutes to solve each one, and the task should take around forty minutes. After about five minutes, one student brings his work to you, showing a correct solution to each of the twenty equations but with no details of how he derived the solutions. What would you say to the student?

When asked this question, most teachers say that they would ask the student to explain how he derived the solutions and show his scratch work. The second most common response is that teachers say that they would ask the student to check that his answers are correct. Other common responses include asking the student to make up some more equations of his own to solve or suggesting that the student provides support to other students who are finding the work more difficult.

We believe that a more appropriate response would be, "I apologize. I clearly underestimate your current capabilities, and I will try to do better in future." Every sports coach knows getting athletes to lift weights that are not heavy for them is unlikely to make them stronger. In the same way that weights are the resistance against which athletes develop their strength, challenging material provides the resistance against which students can develop their intellectual capacities.

Of course, as Carol Dweck's work on mindset that we discussed earlier shows, whether students believe this depends on their view of the nature of capability. If they think that capability is malleable, they welcome challenge because it is a chance to increase their capability. Athletes who are serious about their pursuits do not welcome easy workouts, because they know that such workouts will not develop their capabilities. Indeed, in his study of sporting excellence, David Hemery (winner of the gold medal for the 400-meter hurdles at the Olympic games in Mexico City in 1968) finds that a determination to push themselves when no one is pushing them distinguishes the very best athletes from others (Hemery, 1986).

Design Feedback as Part of a System

The defining idea of feedback is that, by eliciting evidence about what students can—or cannot—do, the teacher is able to give some guidance to the learner that is more effective than the guidance she would have been able to give without the evidence. Feedback in education is therefore, by definition, responsive. The problem is the nature of the response is often not clear.

When a thermostat determines that a room is too cold, there is only one response that the system can make—to turn on the heating system to warm up the room. The whole feedback loop is designed as a *system*. If a thermostat is connected only to a heating or cooling system, there is no point in having the thermostat measure humidity, because the system of which it is a part is not designed to affect the humidity.

In education, however, what the feedback should do is not obvious. In particular, as noted in the introduction to this chapter, it is not clear whether the feedback should focus on telling students what they are doing right (reinforcement) or what they are doing wrong (correction).

It therefore seems likely that, depending on the situation, both kinds of feedback—that which reinforces and that which corrects—may have a role to play. If students are on the right track, feedback that confirms this can be helpful. If students are not on the right track, however, feedback has to be concerned with getting the learners back on track. The important point is that both kinds of feedback—reinforcement and correction—require planning.

As noted in the previous chapter, even if feedback is intended merely to reinforce learning, it is necessary to collect the right evidence before we can be clear about whether the learning is proceeding as intended. When students give appropriate responses to tasks, questions, or in discussion, there is a temptation to conclude that the learning is, indeed, heading in the right direction. But of course, as the previous chapter showed, when questions and tasks are not well designed, correct and incorrect ways of thinking about the matter at hand can lead to a correct response. Asking the right questions in the first place is essential to all feedback. If you don't find out what's going wrong, you can't give effective feedback.

However, when feedback needs to get students back on the right track, things get much more complicated because there are infinitely many responses the teacher can make. What is most challenging, of course, is the teacher has to use the same task for both reinforcement and correction because we don't know, ahead of time, whether the students are going to respond correctly.

Many teachers find that while grading student work, they realize the work needs improvement but are not sure what kind of feedback would be most effective. This is most often because the teacher didn't design the task with feedback in mind.

For example, you are grading work on subtraction with decomposition from a group of eight-year-olds. Obviously if all of a student's responses are correct, it is appropriate to show this by placing a check next to each subtraction solution, although we would be tempted to try to "stretch" the student by asking her to make up three further examples of their own— one easier, one at about the same level, and one more difficult than those she has already answered. However, when students answer incorrectly, what to do is less obvious. Often, all we learn by looking at students' responses is that they haven't gotten it yet, so we must teach it again, but somehow better this time. This is an important illustration showing that if the teacher hasn't designed the task specifically to support feedback, it is unlikely to do so.

As an example, consider the following question from *Embedded Formative Assessment*:

Which of the following is the correct translation for "I give the book to him"?

A. Yo lo doy el libro.
B. Yo doy le el libro.
C. Yo le doy el libro.
D. Yo doy lo el libro.
E. Yo doy el libro le.
F. Yo doy el libro lo.

The teachers who designed this question know that their students often have difficulties with pronoun selection, pronoun placement, or both. Because of the design of the question, if students answer correctly, it is likely that they understand which pronoun should be used and where it should be placed—it is unlikely that they choose the correct answer by chance. More importantly, if students answer incorrectly, the teacher knows what the students are having difficulty with. In other words, while the teacher doesn't know how the students will respond, the teacher has a plan of action about what she will do when she gets the responses. For each of the possible outcomes, the teacher knows what feedback she will provide. The feedback is part of a system.

Tips

Don't Give Feedback on Everything Students Do

Our work with teachers in the United States and elsewhere suggests that it is common for teachers to spend about twice as much time grading books as they do planning instruction. In our view, it would be better for these proportions to be reversed. In other words, we think it is preferable for teachers to spend twice as much time planning instruction as grading. Moreover, giving feedback in the form of comments rather than scores or grades takes about twice as long. So our advice is that teachers should plan on giving detailed feedback on about one-fourth of the work their students do and quickly look over another one-fourth of their students' work. Peer assessment can provide feedback on another one-fourth, and self-assessment activities can provide the final one-fourth. This "four-quarters" approach to feedback will, of course, be very unfamiliar to parents, so it will be important for schools to communicate to parents why things are changing and what kinds of differences parents can expect to see in their children's notebooks. However, it is our experience that when parents understand the reasons for the changes in the kinds of feedback the teacher is providing, most (although not all!) parents are positive about the changes. A sample letter to parents that teachers can adapt for their use is at the back of the book.

Cautions

Feedback Should Focus on What's Next, Not What's Past

When *Inside the Black Box* (P. J. Black & Wiliam, 1998b) was published, one of the recommendations that garnered particular attention was that feedback is generally more useful in the form of comments rather than grades (see next section). To their credit, many teachers started giving feedback in the form of comments rather than grades. However, many of the comments were not that helpful. Often, the comments they gave to students were, in effect, saying something like, "This would have been a better piece of work had you done the following things, but you didn't, so it isn't."

When people see that the second half of the word "feedback" is "back," there is a temptation to think that feedback should be backward-looking—that it's what we see in the rearview mirror rather than through the windshield. Or, as Douglas Reeves points out, it's like the difference between having a physical and a postmortem. But in the same way that a room thermostat attempts to use information about the temperature of the room *in the past* to regulate the temperature of the room *in the future*, feedback has to use what we know about our students' capabilities from their past work to improve their learning in the future.

Don't Give Feedback Unless You Allocate Class Time for Students to Respond

In many, perhaps most, classrooms in the United States, teachers spend hours crafting feedback for their students but much less time ensuring that the students use the feedback appropriately. This seems to us a wasted opportunity. Providing feedback is, after all, one-to-one tuition (we don't know of a single teacher who can grade two books simultaneously), and one-to-one tuition is the most expensive form of education it is possible to imagine—what Benjamin Bloom calls "the gold standard" in education (Bloom, 1984). Providing the most expensive kind of education to students and then not ensuring that students are responding appropriately therefore seems perverse. That is why, as a general rule, we recommend that you should not give feedback to your students unless you build in time on the next occasion they are with you for the students to respond to the feedback. Put simply, if it's worth your spending time generating the feedback, it's worth taking instructional time to ensure students respond.

Of course, ensuring that students respond to the feedback also takes time, so it is useful to put in place systems that help teachers monitor this. Some teachers use feedback sheets where the upper portion of the page is for the teacher's feedback and the lower portion of the page is for the students' responses, while other teachers ask students to maintain a "feedback log"—a separate notebook where the teacher enters the feedback, then students enter a response. If there is no response to the feedback, the teacher doesn't provide any more feedback until there is.

One particularly useful way of tracking the responses of students to feedback is to ask the students to respond to the feedback on strips of paper that they then staple over the work that needs improvement. Provided the work is stapled only on one edge, it is easy for the teacher to see the original work, the comments they provided, and the response of the student. Ultimately, the systems themselves are less important than the fact that the teacher has a way of checking that the students are doing something with the feedback.

Feedback Should Be More Work for the Recipient Than the Donor

Robyn Renee Jackson suggests that one of the most important principles for teachers is "Never work harder than your students" (Jackson, 2009). We regularly ask teachers whether they believe their students spend as long taking onboard the feedback they are given as it takes the teacher to provide it. Hardly any teachers believe this. We spend far too much time giving feedback that the students either completely ignore or give scant attention to. One corollary of Jackson's principle is therefore that feedback should be more work for the recipient than the donor.

Focus More on the Longer Term

Those who teach young people how to play musical instruments are all too aware of short-term improvements in performance that can lead to a longer-term worsening of performance by building in bad habits that are difficult to correct later on. In the same way, it can be difficult to get young children to hold a pen or pencil in an appropriate way. Young children may prefer a way of holding the pen that works reasonably well for them when they are learning to write, but may fundamentally limit how quickly or clearly a student can write when older. In their review of the research on feedback,

Kluger and DeNisi find a number of studies where the feedback intervention produces improvements in performance in the short term but leads to lower long-term performance. An extreme example of this is giving students feedback that helps them pass a test but leaves them less prepared for the next phases of learning. Sometimes, such a trade-off will be justified, but the teacher needs to make a careful appraisal of the trade-offs between costs and benefits.

Beware of the Halo Effect Around Feedback

Even where feedback improves performance in a sustainable way, it still may not be a good idea. For example, if the feedback improves the performance by increasing students' motivation for a task but the teacher has to continuously provide the intervention to maintain the improvement, it may not be a good idea. There must be an "exit strategy" from the feedback.

Don't Make the Feedback Too Specific

If the feedback relates only to the particular task at hand, it will improve the student's ability to do that task, but not others, which is not particularly helpful, since the student is unlikely ever to do that task again. In giving feedback, we need to be clear about the goal of the feedback. Is it to improve this particular piece of work, or is it to improve the student's capabilities more generally in some area? If the goal is to improve that particular piece of work, specific feedback may be entirely appropriate. However, in general, the goal of feedback is to improve the student's general capabilities, and the particular task is just an index of that general capability. Telling students how to improve a particular piece of work may just be the equivalent of placing ice cubes in the mouth of a patient with a fever. When you measure the patient's temperature with a thermometer under the tongue, the measured temperature may be lower, but this doesn't mean the patient is better.

Provide an Appropriate Balance of Critical and Supportive Feedback

One of the most common pieces of advice about feedback given to teachers is that feedback should not be critical. Of course, when feedback is too critical, it is less likely that students will act on the feedback, but the problem is often that feedback *needs* to be critical to improve performance. For example, as mentioned earlier, when young children are learning to throw a baseball, some right-handed children choose to throw the ball with the right foot in front of the left (i.e., off the "wrong foot"). I have yet to see a baseball coach react to this by saying, "You've clearly developed your own personal style for throwing a baseball; now let's see if we can work with that." Invariably the coach says that the child is doing it incorrectly, and that having the left foot in front of the right will give the child greater velocity on the throw (although perhaps less accuracy—right-handed darts players tend to have the right foot in front of the left).

Be Careful With the Bad-News Sandwich

A particular technique some teachers use to balance critical and supportive feedback is what we sometimes call "the bad-news sandwich." The idea is that the feedback to the student begins with a positive or supportive comment, followed by a more critical remark about how she could improve the work, but then, presumably to make the student feel better about the negative comment, the feedback ends with a positive comment.

Many students do seem to prefer their feedback to be "sugar-coated" in this way, and accentuating the positive can be as helpful to students as pointing out what needs work, because they may well not be aware that some parts of the work are better than others. The danger, of course, is that when teachers praise certain features, students tend to overuse those features in subsequent work.

The bad-news sandwich has other potential drawbacks. By having twice as much positive as negative, it may send the message that the work is acceptable and any further improvement is therefore optional. Also, older students may regard such feedback as manipulative. Indeed, as discussed earlier, for students with a growth mindset, positive feedback to soften the blow may well be completely unnecessary. Students who are focused on improvement just want to be told what they need to do to get better.

Make Feedback Into Detective Work

As we have stressed several times already, the most important thing about feedback is what it does to the recipient. With students who are hungry for feedback, it might be appropriate to leave it to the student to decide how to use the feedback. However, for most students, it makes more sense for the teacher to specify the process by which they will use the feedback to improve their work.

For example, Chapter 5 of *Embedded Formative Assessment* (Wiliam, 2011a, p. 130) describes how an English language arts teacher named Charlotte Kerrigan increases the attention that her students give to her feedback by changing the way she provides comments to her students. Aware of the potential harmful effects of scores and grades on learning, she has for many years given her students feedback in the form of comments, but she is dissatisfied with how much attention her students have given to the comments. To get the students to read the comments more carefully, she changes the way she provides feedback: A class of students has written essays on a Shakespeare play, and rather than writing her comments on the students' essays, she wrote them on strips of paper. She returns the four essays and the four associated strips of paper to the students, who are in groups of four. Each group's task is then to match the comments to the essays.

This way of giving feedback is smart because it keeps the ego out of the learning situation. When a student picks up one of the comments, he has no idea whose comment it is, so he is more likely to look for the meaning of the comment rather than its personal significance; in other words, the students read the comment for what it says, rather than what it says about them. This is because this way of giving feedback gives the student a concrete, well-defined task to undertake. The task is concrete because the students have to match each comment to a single essay, and it is well defined because the students should be able to decide for themselves whether they have successfully completed the task. If any group manages to match three of the comments to three of the essays, but the remaining comment does not match the remaining essay, that group should quickly realize that their matching is not correct.

Tips

Link the Feedback to the Learning Intentions and Success Criteria

One common problem with the way teachers give feedback is that it is not related to the learning intentions or success criteria for the activity. Teachers develop rubrics for tasks, either on their own or in collaboration with other teachers, and share them with students or even co-construct the rubrics in collaboration with their students as discussed earlier, but then fail to refer to the rubrics in the feedback. If you do give students criteria for success, whether in the form of rubrics or some other way, make sure you close the loop by linking the feedback to the success criteria.

Cautions

Steering a Fine Line Between Prescription and Vagueness

Feedback has to steer a fine line between prescription and vagueness. If the feedback is too tightly specified, all the student has to do is follow the steps indicated. In other words, the student is just following the teacher's instructions for improving the work. On the other hand, if the feedback is too vague, students don't know what to do with it. As a general rule, feedback should always give students something that they can take from the current task into their future learning.

Enhancements

Categorizing Strengths and Weaknesses

Described in *Embedded Formative Assessment*, one way of giving students feedback is "Find it and fix it." For example, if a student has done twenty subtraction calculations, five of which are incorrect, then simply tell the student, "Five of these are wrong; find them and fix them." In English language arts, on a final draft of a piece of writing, you can place a dot in the margin in each line where there is something that needs attention, and, for students who need more support, you can write a "p" for a punctuation error, "g" for a grammar error, and an "s" for a spelling error. As an alternative, you can use pink and green highlighters to annotate the student's work, with green to highlight positive features and pink to highlight weaknesses. The student's task is then to decide what is positive about the features highlighted in green and what is weak about the features highlighted in pink, and annotate the piece of work accordingly.

This basic idea has been extended by a Spanish teacher who was feeding back to her class on a piece of writing her students had just completed. On each student's work, she used a colored pen simply to indicate the location of errors in the text. She returned the work to the students, who had to identify the kinds of errors they made (e.g., tense, adjective-noun agreement, subject-verb agreement, and so on) and draw a bar chart that shows the errors they made most often. The teacher then encouraged the students to find someone with complementary strengths and weaknesses to theirs so they could "buddy up" and provide mutual support.

Comment-Only Grading

In an experiment conducted in the 1980s (Butler, 1988), teachers give eleven- and twelve-year-old students two divergent thinking tasks and then feedback on how well they have done. In four classes, the teachers give a comment to the students about how they can improve their work, such as, "You thought of quite a few correct words; maybe it is possible to think of more short words/more long words/even more words." In four other classes, the teachers give the students grades, produced by scoring the students' work on a curve (so that the students' scores range from 40 to 99 with a mean of 70). And in another group of four classrooms, teachers give the students both a grade and a comment, side by side, in their notebooks.

A couple of days later, the teachers give students a second pair of divergent thinking tasks; later the same day, they give more feedback of the same kind as the students received after the first session. The teachers then ask the students to work on the same tasks that they undertook in the first session.

The students who are given comments produce much better work in the final session— between a half and one whole standard deviation higher than their first attempts. The students given grades actually perform worse in the third session than they did on the same tasks in the first session. Perhaps even more surprisingly, the students given both grades and comments did even worse in the third session than those given just grades (although the difference is small).

Now, of course, this is just a single study, and it would be unwise to place much emphasis on a single study, but the fact is that many subsequent studies find the same thing. Providing grades with comments seems to make it much harder for students to learn from the comments. As Sid, one of the students in *The Classroom Experiment*, says,

> What you get normally is that all the people who have seen their grade and got a 6 [a high score] or something, they are always looking around and asking other people, "What grade did you get?" and I think it's partly because they want to raise their own self-confidence to think, "Oh, yeah, I got better than everyone else."

The response of a fifteen-year-old student named Åsa, in the Swedish town of Borås, neatly illustrates this. The same teacher instructs Åsa in Swedish and philosophy, and after hearing about the work of Butler and Dweck, she decides to give comments, but not grades, when marking philosophy homework; because of the importance of the grades for Swedish for entry to higher education, the teacher continues to give grades for Swedish homework. Åsa, reflecting on her experiences of getting just comments in philosophy and comments and grades in Swedish, writes the following:

> I have gone through the comments, but when there is a grade given, you become a little blinded by it and focus too much on it. So personally (even though I quite possibly would complain if I did not get the grade) I would prefer you not to do it, because I have noticed that I pay more attention to the comment and learn more when the grade is not written on the paper.

This doesn't mean that we shouldn't give grades to students. In high school, grades have an important role to play in indicating to higher education institutions the quality of work students do in high school. Indeed, high school grade-point average is a better predictor of college freshman grades than SAT scores (Kobrin, Camara, & Milewski, 2002), which is pretty extraordinary when you consider that it is often difficult to get teachers in the same high school English language arts department to agree on their grading criteria. Rather, what we need to do is reduce the frequency of grades, and, as far as possible, give grades only at the end of sequences of learning; in Alfie Kohn's words, "Never grade students while they are still learning" (Kohn, 1994, p. 41).

Tips

Don't Mix Up the Different Functions of Feedback

Some teachers, when they hear about the effects of giving grades and comments together, ask whether the problem can be solved by giving the comments to students one day and the grades the next day. This will certainly get the students to read the comments, because for twenty-four hours, that's all they have to go on, and they may be reading the comments only to try to figure out what the grade is going to be; but at least they're reading the comments. However, if the purpose of the comment is to help students improve their work, then giving them a grade the following day that merely evaluates the quality of the unimproved work seems a little odd. If they have taken the comments to heart, their work would now be better, so the grade is beyond its "sell-by" date. We believe a more appropriate response would be to give comments on the work, allow the students a period of time to improve the work, and then assign a grade for the final revised piece of work. When Anna Shepard, the history teacher of the class featured in *The Classroom Experiment*, tries this, she is genuinely surprised at the seriousness with which the students study the comments: "I think that is the most I have seen any students read comments—like, ever."

In other words, use feedback *either* to tell the students how to improve the work *or* to tell them how good it is, but don't try to do both at the same time. Earlier, we mentioned Alfie Kohn's advice: "Never grade students while they are still learning something." He goes on to say, "And, even more important, do not reward them for their performance at that point" (Kohn, 1994, p. 41), because, as Condry and Chambers (1978) show, rewards are most destructive when skills are being developed.

Focused Feedback

Many schools have a grading policy that requires that all teachers must correct work before returning it to students. The rationale behind such a policy is entirely under-standable based on the associationist views of learning described in the introduction to this chapter. If we return incorrect work to students without some indication that it is in fact incorrect, the concern is that students may believe the work is correct, and we will have reinforced inappropriate beliefs.

However, even though the idea of correcting everything that needs attention might be well intentioned, the result is too often, especially for weaker students, work that is returned completely covered with teachers' comments. The reaction of this middle school student is typical: "When you get a lot of feedback, it means your work wasn't very good." When asked why she believes this, the girl says, "When you do really good work, you just get an 'A.' But when your work isn't as good, there are lots of comments all over your work." For this student, the more feedback you get, the worse your work must be.

The research from feedback in sports confirms the basic intuition here: too much feedback can be destructive. In particular there is a great deal of research into what is sometimes called *bandwidth feedback*. The idea of bandwidth feedback is that provided the performance is within some acceptable range (i.e., within the acceptable bandwidth), you should not provide correction. Provide feedback only when performance strays out-side some acceptable bounds. Studies in many sports show that bandwidth feedback is more effective in improving performance than feedback that corrects everything (see, for example, P. J. K. Smith, Taylor, & Withers, 1997), and other studies show that this is not simply because you give less correction with bandwidth feedback (Lee & Carnahan, 1990). Of course, this does not tell us how wide the bandwidth for feedback should be to be most effective—as with all other aspects of feedback, it probably depends on the relationship between you and your students—but it should help you feel okay about not correcting everything that is wrong with your students' work.

Focus on the Feedback Itself, Not Proving That You Have Given It

One issue that often arises when we discuss feedback with teachers is the issue of whether teachers should give feedback orally or in writing. For students who have difficulty reading, the answer is obvious, but teachers worry about how to prove that they give feedback to students if there is no written record. We suggest that if you give students oral feedback, make some record of the feedback event. We came across one school that has a "video pod" in a corner of a kindergarten classroom; when students receive oral feedback from the teacher, they go to the video pod and record a summary of what the teacher said to them and what they are going to do about it. This video recording can later be reviewed by the student and in fact can also be viewed by the student's parents or guardians if they have access to the Internet. When you give older students oral feedback, ask them to return to their seat and make a note of the feedback interaction. This has three benefits: it develops literacy skills, provides a reminder for the student of the conversation that took place, and proves that you are doing your job and giving your students regular feedback.

Blur the Boundary Between Feedback and Teaching

Feedback that involves giving students a grade or score or even using a rubric always has something of the air of a formal event, divorced from teaching. If, instead, we think of the role of feedback as "keeping learning on track" (Wiliam, 2007b) then our whole perspective changes. There are times when we collect students' notebooks and provide formal feedback, but there are also times when we just notice that something needs attention on a student's work. By thinking about this as a continuum, we can get ideas about how the techniques we use one way we also might use another way. For example, in the next chapter we discuss the technique of "two stars and a wish," in which students give feedback to each other on self-adhesive notes, but you can also use such a technique yourself. So, for example, if you notice that there is something that needs attention in a student's work, but right now the student is engaged in another activity, you could make a note, either physically or electronically, and give it to the student when he completes the activity. Ultimately, when feedback is truly integrated with instruction, it will be impossible to tell where one ends and the other begins (Wiliam & Thompson, 2008).

Cautions

Don't Expect the Students to Like Comment-Only Feedback

We know of many schools where teachers have radically reduced—and in some cases, completely discontinued—the use of scores and grades, but we don't know of a single one where the majority of students like this. When students are used to receiving grades, they react negatively to the absence of the grades. Here are some of the reactions from the students in the *Classroom Experiment* documentary:

Jessie:	It's the only reason I done it.
Chloe:	Well, I don't get it unless I get my grade.
Emily:	I would be happier knowing what grade I got. I want to know what I got out of the work I've put in.

However, another student, Sidney, notes,

> Everyone was kind of annoyed, but I noticed that it seemed to be the people who seemed to be getting the good grades mostly who seemed to be the most annoyed, which I think that's probably because of . . . they just wanted to know whether they'd done as good as they normally do or not.

The longer that students are used to receiving grades, the more difficult doing without grades will be.

Even if you stop giving grades, your students may still find a way to compete. In the documentary program *The Classroom Experiment*, a social studies teacher tries giving students feedback in the form of comments rather than grades. When students receive their work with comments from the teacher, the following exchange takes place between Chloe and Emily, the two highest-achieving students in the class:

Chloe:	Emily? Where did you get the all *excellent*s and everything? Oh, I got one *excellent* and all the rest *good*.
Emily:	Oh, I got all *excellent* but then two *good*s.

Even when given no grades Emily and Chloe still find a way to compare their performances.

Feedback May Not Mean the Same to the Recipient as the Donor

As noted in Chapter 3 on learning intentions, those who give feedback often forget that the words they use may not mean the same to the recipient of the feedback as they do to the donor. For example, softball and baseball coaches often tell young players to "keep your eye on the ball." In fact, this is impossible. The human eye cannot physically track a baseball or softball over the final part of its journey to the plate (Epstein, 2013). More importantly, even if the human eye were capable of doing this, "keeping your eye on the ball" is actually a complex undertaking because the action of swinging the bat requires the batter to rotate the torso in a counterclockwise direction (for a right-handed batter), while keeping your eye on the ball requires rotating the head in the opposite direction. Unless the player realizes that he needs to rotate his head further in order to counteract the rotation of the torso, the advice is not helpful (Roberts & Green, 2014).

A similar issue arose in an eighth-grade science class where a teacher writes in a student's laboratory notebook, "You need to be more systematic in planning your scientific investigations." When asked what this meant, the student replies, "I have no idea. If I knew how to be more systematic, I would have been more systematic the first time round," which, when you think about it, is a reasonable response.

Enhancements

Make It Clear What the Student Is Meant to Do With the Comment

Even when you give comments, what, exactly, the student is meant to do with the comment is sometimes not clear. Comments are likely to be more effective if it is clear what the student should do and how she should do it. It is especially helpful if you give the feedback in such a way that students can determine for themselves whether they have responded appropriately. Some examples of how you might refine and improve comments are shown in Table 5.4.

Table 5.4: Examples of Comments in Science Requiring Definite Responses From Students

Vague	Better	Better still
Add some notes on seed dispersal.	Can you suggest how the plant might disperse its seeds?	Give one advantage and one disadvantage of seed dispersal.
Work on your graphing skills.	Think about the accuracy and neatness of your graphs.	One of the axes of your graph is much better than the other. Which one is it, and why is it better?
You need to be clear about the difference between power, energy, and force.	Check your glossary for the meaning of power, energy, and force, and then redraft this sentence correctly.	In two seconds, a machine lifts six meters from the ground a mass weighing ten kilograms. Describe what is happening using the words energy, force, and power.

Practice Giving Comment-Only Feedback

In their book *Practice Perfect*, Lemov, Woolway, and Yezzi (2012) point out that because classrooms are such busy places, changing what one does in the classroom is hard because there is rarely enough time to think decisions through carefully and therefore we react out of habit. One way to provide time to become more reflective about the kind of feedback given to students is for two teachers to arrange to meet for an hour or so and each to bring with them half-a-dozen student notebooks. The teachers spend about five minutes on each student notebook, thinking through, in conversation, what the most helpful thing would be to say to that student right now. Most teachers find that by practicing in relative tranquility the things you will say, they are able to improve the quality of the comments they give. If you are the only person in your school interested in improving the quality of comments, you could begin by looking through the following list of comments. For each of the comments, decide whether it is a comment that you feel would be appropriate for your students or not. Either way, see if you can put into words why you feel the way you do about the comment.

- "Hoshi, the start you have made is very pleasing, and the detail in your answers is improving. Read your responses again, and see if you think they are complete—is all of the relevant information there?"
- "Levi, although you've used a green traffic light on everything—and I don't doubt your confidence with it—you need to include more scientific words and phrases in your answers."
- "Look back at the way we worked out the scale for graph axes, and pinpoint the mistake you are making. Either have another go or come and see me for help."
- "Ling, generally your answers show a good understanding of the topic of plant reproduction. Start to add a few more of your own thoughts and ideas if you can."
- "This is generally fine, but you are mixing up the terms particle, element, and compound. Look at the glossary we made, and use it to check through this piece again."
- "Darius, you seem to know what 'self-pollination' is, and you can distinguish between this and 'cross-pollination.' Can you suggest why a plant would 'self-pollinate'? Could this be an advantage?"
- "Carlos, a disappointing attempt. You have already shown me that you can do these calculations. Please go through and complete your corrections by next week. Can I be of any help?"
- "Sunita, you have completed a lot of work, and it is very neatly done. However, your answers could be more sensitive."
- "There are two key aspects that you need to work on. You must show all your working out so that we both know you understand all the stages to get the answers. Also, you must keep up with the work in class even if you have to finish at home."
- "Excellent review of your test, Gabriela, and it got you a good result. But you are making mistakes with multiplying parentheses. Going forward, try to explore and correct multiplying out parentheses."

Respect the Student's Work

In a short story entitled "The Grammar School Master," Graham Wilson (1999) describes one English language arts teacher's approach to feedback:

His subject was English and through this he could influence minds not already blunted by the cudgel of the Mortgage Repayment. His message centered around the significance of the individuality of the task. He would stand before his class, a new exercise book [note book] held aloft. "This," he explained, "is not what it appears. It is not the commonplace staple of paper covered in red cardboard that you have received before. In this book I will find you, because only you will write in this book, and you will write what you think, what you believe, what you know. It will be a privilege for me to be allowed to enter your book. As a visitor I will consider and respect your point of view and your opinions. If I offer mine, it is with respect and in the way of help, as a guest might suggest a way to unblock a sink or rid the garden of a pest that is attacking the roses. This school exercise book is unique as it does not set out to produce a content that is marked right with a tick or wrong with a bad-tempered cross. There is no 'right' answer, no QED. Here is an empty space that demands no preconditions, waiting for you." (pp. 91–92)

Such an approach to feedback may be rather idealistic, but the respect the teacher shows for his students' work seems to us to be a model to which every teacher should aspire.

As with the previous chapters, we end the chapter with a recap, followed by a reflection checklist you might find useful to complete, then a planning sheet for using a technique with a class, and a peer observation sheet (so that you can ask a colleague to give you feedback).

There is a copy of the each of the sheets at the back of the handbook for you to copy if needed, so feel free to write all over the following sheets!

RECAP

Feedback should be more work for the recipient than the donor.

- Focus on the reaction of the students, not the feedback.
  - Model responding to feedback.
- Develop a growth mindset in your students.
  - Focus on self-efficacy, not self-esteem.
  - Be careful how you praise.
  - Give task-involving rather than ego-involving feedback.
- Design feedback as part of a system.
  - Don't give feedback on everything students do.
  - Don't give feedback unless you allocate class time for students to respond.
  - Don't give feedback that is more work for the donor than the recipient.
- Focus more on longer time for feedback.
  - Beware of the halo effect around feedback.
  - Don't make the feedback too specific.

- Provide an appropriate balance of critical and supportive feedback.
- Be careful with the "bad-news sandwich."
- Concentrate on personal bests, not effort or ranks.
- Make feedback into detective work.
  - Have students match the comments to the essays.
  - Link the feedback to the learning intentions and success criteria.
  - Steer a fine line between prescription and vagueness.
  - Categorize strengths and weaknesses.
    - "Find it and fix it"
    - Margin marks
    - Pink and green highlighters
    - Colored pen, students define type of error, draw bar chart, and "buddy up"
- Provide comment-only grading
  - Don't mix up the different functions of feedback.
  - Don't expect students to like comment-only feedback.
  - Be cognizant that feedback may not mean the same to the recipient as the donor.
  - Make it clear what the student is meant to do with the comment.
  - Practice giving comment-only feedback.
  - Respect the student's work.
- Use focused feedback

REFLECTION CHECKLIST FOR STRATEGY 3:
Providing Feedback That Moves Learning Forward

	I don't do this	I do this sometimes	This is embedded in my practice	I could support someone else
I focus on student response to my feedback rather than the feedback itself.				
I praise students for effort rather than ability.				
I give students task-involving feedback rather than ego-involving feedback.				
I limit the written feedback I give to students, and give class time for students to respond.				
I give "balanced" written feedback.				
I make feedback into detective work for my students.				
I use comment-only grading.				
Other techniques for this strategy that I use to improve student learning:				

LESSON PLANNING SHEET

The technique I am going to use:
Why I am planning to use it and the results I am hoping for:
Class and date:
Preparation for the lesson:
What I am going to do less of:
Reflecting on how the technique worked, including evidence to support my claims:
What I am going to do next:

PEER OBSERVATION SHEET

Class to be observed:
Peer's name:
Technique to be observed:
What I want my peer to comment on:
Peer's comments:
Reflections after reading peer's comments and/or talking through the observation:
What I will do next:

Chapter 6
STRATEGY 4: ACTIVATING STUDENTS AS LEARNING RESOURCES FOR ONE ANOTHER

OVERVIEW

The idea that students can learn from each other has been with us for hundreds, possibly thousands, of years. And particularly in higher education, there is a great deal of research into whether students can accurately evaluate each other's academic achievement. However, in recent years, there has been increasing interest in the idea that students might be able to assess each other formatively—that is, assessing each other's work not to judge it but to improve it. In this chapter we explore how what we know about collaborative and cooperative learning can be combined with principles of effective formative assessment to help students act as learning resources for one another.

WHY USE THIS STRATEGY

Engaging students in assessing the work of their peers is not just a labor-saving device for teachers. Implemented properly, it can substantially increase student achievement, both for those who get help from their peers, and peers who provide the help.

GETTING TO UNDERSTAND THE STRATEGY

Children have probably been learning from other children, especially older siblings, since humans first started using language (and maybe earlier!), and learning from older peers has been an important feature of educational settings for at least 300 years (Wagner, 1990). While the idea has intuitive appeal, evidence about the impact of collaborative or cooperative learning on academic achievement is mixed. Like so much else in education, "what works" is the wrong question because everything works somewhere and nothing works everywhere. The interesting and important question is "under what circumstances does this work?"

Before examining this issue in more detail, it is worth noting that there are two rather distinct purposes that people express for cooperative and collaborative learning. The first is that because adults are required to work together in their jobs and communities, schools should prepare young people to work in this way. The second is that having students work together can produce greater learning of subject matter than would be possible by having students work individually or in competition with their peers. The first of these is outside the scope of this book because it deals with what students should be learning, and the stance we are adopting here is that classroom formative assessment is independent of any choice about what students should learn. The second, however, is directly relevant because once you decide what it is you want your students to learn, formative assessment can help you increase the likelihood that your students do, in fact, learn what you want them to learn.

Some authors regard the terms collaborative learning and cooperative learning as interchangeable, while others draw a clear distinction between the two. Unfortunately, the way they make this distinction is not consistent. In higher education, a number of authors suggest that the key distinction between collaborative and cooperative learning is that the former takes place when students work together in unstructured groups and create their own "natural" learning situation, while the latter occurs in highly structured learning situations created by, for example, a teacher (D. W. Johnson, Johnson, & Smith, 1998; Matthews, Cooper, Davidson, & Hawkes, 1995). Others stress that collaborative learning is more a personal philosophy, while cooperative learning constitutes a set of structures that help groups achieve a specific goal (Panitz, 1999).

In looking at research on collaborative and cooperative learning, therefore, we need to be very careful to understand what, exactly, is being researched. The fact that two research studies both claim to be addressing cooperative learning does not mean they are researching the same thing, and the fact that one study looks at collaborative learning and another at cooperative learning does not mean they are looking at different things. To understand what is going on, we need to look behind the labels, and see who decides on the goals (and whether the goals have to be the same for all members of the group), who decides how the learning is organized, who decides on the roles that different members of the group play, and what will count as a successful outcome for the group.

David and Roger Johnson—two of the leading researchers in the field—define cooperative learning as taking place when students work "*cooperatively* to accomplish shared learning goals" (D. W. Johnson et al., 1998, p. 28, emphasis in original). This is in contrast to individualistic learning, where students work on their own to learn something, and competitive learning, where students strive to be better than others.

The Johnson brothers point out that there is now very strong evidence that cooperative learning can increase achievement but of course does not always do so. They found that students learning cooperatively scored 0.66 standard deviations higher than those learning competitively (128 studies) and 0.63 standard deviations higher than those learning individualistically (182 studies). However, reminiscent of the findings of Kluger and

DeNisi discussed in Chapter 5, over one-fifth of these studies yield a negative result—that is, cooperative learning results in *less* learning than competitive or individualistic approaches in 24 percent and 21 percent of studies, respectively (R. T. Johnson & Johnson, 1994).

According to the Johnson brothers, five conditions appear to be particularly important in maximizing the likelihood that cooperative learning increases student achievement (Johnson & Johnson, 1994):

Clearly perceived positive interdependence: Perhaps the most important requirement for effective cooperative learning is that students believe that they are "all in the same boat" so that the success or failure for each individual cannot be separated from those of others in the group. Students are therefore responsible for: (a) making sure that they learn the assigned material, and (b) that the other members of the group also learn the material (what psychologists call "positive interdependence"). This means that there can be no "free riders."

This can be achieved by linking the goals for the group members (positive *goal* interdependence), providing additional rewards for the extent to which the group works effectively together (positive *reward* interdependence), arranging for each member of the group to have unique resources necessary for the group to succeed (positive *resource* interdependence), or assigning unique roles to members of the group (positive *role* interdependence).

Considerable promotive (face-to-face) interaction: Although positive interdependence can work to increase student motivation on its own, its effects are considerably amplified when students have the opportunity to interact face-to-face. Students can help each other, exchange resources, provide each other with feedback, challenge each other's thinking and generally support the group's work.

Clearly perceived individual accountability: Ensuring that students believe they are individually accountable to the group for the quality of their contributions is, perhaps, the most difficult of the five conditions to implement consistently. There is obviously no single best way to do this, but as a starting point, it is certainly worth considering arranging for the performance of individual students to be assessed, and for the results of the assessment to be available to everyone in the group, so that the individual can be held responsible by the other members of the group for his or her contributions.

Frequent use of the relevant interpersonal and small-group skills: One of the most important findings from research on group work is that very few students acquire the skills necessary for small group work without some formal training and modeling of how to work effectively with others. Also, students have to be motivated to use such skills. Specifically, students need to develop mutual trust, communicate effectively, accept and support all members of the group, and resolve any conflicts that arise in a respectful and constructive fashion.

Frequent and regular group processing of current functioning: As well as possessing the skills needed for small group work, to be most effective, students must choose to use them while working cooperatively, and this is best achieved by regularly allocating time for reflection on the cooperative learning process so that

    a. groups can work on maintaining good working relationships between members;

    b. members can learn cooperative skills from each other;

    c. members can get feedback on their contributions from other members;

    d. members think at the metacognitive level (see next strategy); and

    e. there is a formal opportunity to celebrate successes.

This process is usually more effective if a member of the group has been given a specific role as a peer-observer (although it can sometimes be helpful if the peer observer does not lead the review activity).

While much, if not most, of the reflection time should be spent in small groups, there is also value in periodically having the teacher lead a whole class review of the work of the groups, contributing her or his own views, and drawing on the views of students, based on what the teacher has observed while the students were working in groups.

Of course, the focus of this chapter is not on cooperative learning in general but cooperative learning as a specific aspect of formative assessment, and in particular, the role that peers have in identifying specific issues in students' learning and providing appropriate feedback to help students move forward. The problem, however, is that much of the research in this area, particularly in higher education, focuses on the question of whether students are able to grade each other's work accurately. This research is often described as being on "peer assessment," which is, of course, a perfectly reasonable description provided it is understood that this is primarily about *summative assessment* rather than formative assessment. In other words, the research questions most of the studies in this tradition address are in terms of the extent to which the scores or grades that students award each other agree with the scores or grades that their teachers would award.

This kind of research seems to us to be of dubious value for a couple of reasons:

First, the question of whether students can grade each other's work as well as a teacher can is of no interest except as an academic exercise, unless the teacher proposes to use peer assessments in forming a judgment about the quality of a student's work. And if the teacher does plan to use grades or scores peers award as part of a formal assessment, this seems to us difficult to justify, not least because of the potential for a range of irrelevant factors to influence grades.

Second, even if it is shown that students can accurately assign grades to their peers' work, there is no reason to assume that such a relationship would continue to hold if the results of such assessments become highly consequential for students. That is why for us, the only reason for having students assess each other's work is to advance their own learning and that of their peers. In other words, returning to the definition of formative assessment in the introduction to this book, peer assessment functions formatively in a classroom to the extent that evidence of student achievement is elicited, interpreted, and used by students and their peers to make decisions about the next steps in instruction that are better, or better founded, than the decisions that would have been taken in the absence of that evidence.

Three of the five principles of effective cooperative learning the Johnson brothers identify are related to the *process* of cooperative learning— face-to-face interaction, development of interpersonal skills, and reflection—and can readily be incorporated into group work. The other two—positive interdependence and individual accountability—are features of how the cooperative learning situation is structured, and present particular problems for teachers, not least because they cut across norms and expectations about how classrooms should operate.

In the remainder of this chapter, we explore how what is known about cooperative learning and collaborative learning in general can be applied to formative assessment, focusing specifically on techniques that incorporate the two structural components of effective cooperative learning identified earlier: group goals and individual accountability. Almost all of the techniques can be used with students working in pairs, or in larger groups, but, as is explained below, it may be preferable to start with pairs.

Peer Feedback

As noted earlier, much of the research on peers helping each other involves settings in which students are learning cooperatively in groups. However, when students are involved in giving each other feedback, there are at least two reasons why having students work in pairs, at least to begin with, may be preferable:

First, in most classrooms, setting up a short session of pair work usually takes less time than getting students into groups. Most of the research on cooperative learning looks at extended learning activities lasting the whole lesson or even extending across multiple lessons. For feedback, however, sessions of five to ten minutes may be all that is needed. The time you take to get students into groups may not be worthwhile for such a brief episode.

Second, when students work in pairs, roles are clearer, with one student directly addressing the other. Because all the students either are speaking to or being spoken directly to, the level of engagement is generally higher.

As a simple example, a teacher has made up sets of 100 small cards on which are printed the 100 most common words in the English language (sometimes called "Fry words," after Edward Fry, 1980). Pairs of students are given three circular IKEA floor rugs (around two feet in diameter) in red, yellow, and green and students take turns in testing each other on the words. One student selects a card and shows it to the other, who has to read the word aloud. If the student reads the word correctly on the first attempt, the card is placed on the green rug. If he or she does so on the second attempt, the card is placed on the yellow rug, and if the student is unsuccessful, the card is placed on the red rug. The student doing the reading can then use the cards on the red rug as a review list, by taking a photo. The students then swap roles.

Even if students are to work in pairs, it is often helpful to begin any peer-feedback activity with a whole-class session. As noted in the case study of coursework moderation in the German lesson in the chapter on sharing learning intentions, one particularly effective way of getting students started with giving feedback to peers is to ask them to provide feedback on the work of an anonymous student, so there is little or no emotional engagement, and the students can therefore focus on giving the most appropriate feedback. Once students are used to giving feedback on the work of anonymous students, you can begin to use actual samples from the class. For example, after a class completes a task, you might select two or three pieces of work and place them on the document camera for students to critique. As students become more comfortable with the process, they are happy for the work to be identified as theirs. Indeed, many teachers find that students often request that their work is one of those the teacher chooses for discussion, because they want the feedback. Such a request marks an important point in the student's development. Students who see feedback as providing an opportunity for them to improve their work, rather than as a verdict on their last work, are clearly operating with a growth mindset, as discussed in the previous chapter.

One general and widely applicable technique for getting students started with peer assessment and feedback is "Two stars and a wish." The idea is that when students are giving feedback to each other, they identify two features of the work that are positive (the "stars") and one suggestion for how they can improve the work (the "wish"). For example, a student can read a short passage to a partner (or a group) and the other student(s) respond by saying two aspects of the reading that were good, and one that requires work.

While this might seem like a version of the bad-news sandwich discussed in Chapter 5, it is important to recognize that students, at least to begin with, are not skilled at giving feedback. The two stars and a wish technique provides a structure that helps build students' ability to give sensitive and constructive feedback to their peers.

What teachers typically find is that students are able to be much tougher on each other than the teacher would feel able to be, because the power relationships are different. This is an important observation since it suggests that, done appropriately, peer feedback may be more effective than teacher feedback because students are more likely to act on feedback from their peers than they would on feedback from a teacher.

Tips

Start by Agreeing on Ground Rules for Peer Feedback

When you begin work on peer feedback with a whole-class session as recommended earlier, it can be useful to summarize the discussion in the form of "ground rules" for peer feedback, much in the way that success criteria can be co-constructed with students as discussed in Chapter 3. You can then post the ground rules in the classroom, or display them when students are giving their peers feedback. Inevitably, the suggestions will, at least initially, be rather bland and vague, such as, "Make sure comments are helpful." However, if the ground rules are treated as dynamic summaries of the class's understanding of how to feed back to peers and are continuously updated as the students become more adept at this, then the ground rules will become more sophisticated and more useful. You are also likely to find that the advice of your students will help you give better feedback to your students. After all, few teachers ever get any training in how to give feedback; what better way to learn about effective feedback than from the client? Bearing in mind the limitations of rubrics discussed in Chapter 3, the ground rules will never capture all the nuances of how to give effective feedback; but they will provide a useful focus for students to reflect on how to improve the feedback they give their peers and help you give feedback that your students find more useful.

Get Students to Write Their Comments on Self-Adhesive Notes

From the previous chapter, it is clear that many students will regard any annotations placed on their work, whether by a teacher or a peer, as spoiling their work or as indications that the work is not good enough. For this reason, we suggest that students write their peer feedback on self-adhesive notes. That way, if the recipient does not find the feedback helpful, she can peel off the notes and discard them.

Model and Discuss Effective and Ineffective Feedback

When students begin giving peer feedback, you may need to give them some guidance about what sort of comments to write. Before engaging in a peer-feedback activity, therefore, it is often helpful to give students some examples of different kinds of feedback comments and ask the students to think about whether these would be helpful comments to be given on one's work. Students can then reflect on these comments on their own, in pairs, groups, or as part of a whole-class discussion, or, even better, do all four of these in sequence. Some teachers build this into the way they use two stars and a wish. First, they ask students to use different colored self-adhesive notes for the "stars" and the "wishes" (e.g., green for the stars and pink for the wishes). When students have had a chance to read and respond to the comments, the teacher collects the pink self-adhesive notes and places them on a document camera. The teacher can then lead a whole-class discussion about the relative merits of the various comments. This technique has two particular benefits. First, it improves the comments that students are able to give their peers, by getting students to be more reflective about the comments they give, and helps them understand the characteristics of effective feedback. Second, it introduces a measure of accountability into the activity. Even though the comments are displayed anonymously on the document camera, students say that they nevertheless feel the need to make their comments as good as they can be. As one student says, "Even if no one knows that it's your comment being discussed, you still feel bad if people say it's not a helpful comment."

Provide Sentence Starters for Peer Feedback

When students are just beginning with peer feedback, it can be helpful to provide them with "sentence starters" to prompt them:

"I like the way you . . ."

"You did an excellent job of . . ."

"I thought it was very effective when you . . ."

"My favorite part was . . ."

"I was surprised that . . ."

"I didn't understand . . ."

"I was puzzled that . . ."

"I think it would be clearer if . . ."

For younger children, it is perfectly acceptable if students begin with a personal reaction to the work. Ultimately, however, as students get better at giving feedback, it is important that their comments relate to the learning intentions and success criteria for the task at hand. One particularly powerful "anchor" for feedback is to ask students, when they are feeding back on a piece of work, whether the work is complete enough to provide a useful basis for review for an upcoming test. This will help students focus on what is missing as well as what is present in the work.

ABC Feedback

A variation of the sentence starters for peer feedback described earlier is to follow a specific protocol for the prompts. One example of this is the "ABC feedback technique," where students respond to a peer's work under three headings:

A   Agree with: highlighting areas of agreement

B   Build on: suggestions for how arguments could be strengthened

C   Challenge: suggestions for additions or more substantial developments

Cautions

Start With Peer Assessment of Anonymous Work

As mentioned in the previous chapter, giving and receiving feedback are emotionally charged processes, and the emotions involved frequently detract attention from the more important issues about the quality of the work. That is why we suggest that before students assess work done by their peers in the class, they gain some expertise in giving feedback by practicing on the work of anonymous students. They will then be in a position to engage in assessment of the work of peers in the classroom, which, in turn, will help them undertake self-assessment more effectively. Without substantial preparation, few students are able to undertake self-assessment appropriately, because it is emotionally charged and also inherently difficult. That is why we recommend that although effective self-assessment should be the goal, the stepping stones to get there are first, assessing the work of unknown peers; second, assessing the work of known peers; and third, assessing one's own work.

Enhancements

Use Structured Protocols for Peer-Assessment Activities

Depending on how much experience your students have in working with peers, it may be helpful to provide students with tightly timed protocols for peer-assessment activities. Obviously the format of the protocol will depend on the nature of the task; a suitable protocol for responding to a piece of persuasive writing is likely to be very different from a protocol for providing feedback on a laboratory report in science. One possible protocol for a twenty-minute peer-feedback session for students working in pairs is:

1. Three minutes for students to read their peer's work
2. One minute for them to think up questions of clarification they might have
3. Two minutes for each student to ask questions of their peer, and get any needed clarification (×2)
4. Two minutes for each student to generate appropriate feedback
5. One minute for students to read the feedback, and decide on any questions they want to ask about it
6. One minute for each student to ask their questions about the feedback (×2)
7. Five minutes for students to incorporate the feedback into their work

Astute readers will note that the timings in the foregoing protocol add up to eighteen rather than twenty minutes, but since almost everything that teachers do with students takes longer than intended, we think it is prudent to build in a 10 percent margin.

As students become more used to the protocol, the need to time different phases of the activity to the nearest minute diminish, and the protocol can become more of a "checklist" to guide the students through the activity. However, the checklist is likely to remain useful because it highlights the need (a) for the students to seek clarification from each other about what is meant in the original work and (b) for students to get clarification from each other about the meaning of any feedback given. You can find many other examples of structured protocols in the work of Spencer Kagan and his colleagues. Although most of the techniques focus on cooperative learning in the broadest sense, you can easily adapt several of them to place a greater emphasis on formative assessment. For further details, see Kagan and Kagan (2009).

Getting Peers to Mediate Teacher Feedback

Peers also have a role in helping students take onboard feedback from the teacher. As has been stressed several times already, students are likely to see feedback as emotionally charged, particularly if they have a "fixed" rather than "growth" mindset. One way for you to provide feedback that makes it easy for the student to act on it is for you to give the feedback in writing to the student's peer, who looks at the original work and feedback, and then relays to the student what the feedback suggests for improvement. Inevitably, this is somewhat of a balancing act. Some students may prefer to receive feedback in private rather than having their peers see criticisms of their work, although this problem is largely alleviated if the focus of the feedback is on how the work might be improved rather than how good it is. Alternatively, even if you give the feedback to the student directly, building in time for peers to help make sense of the feedback—if that is something the student requests—can be useful.

Similarly, you can ask students to comment on the responses a student makes to teacher or peer feedback. Again, while this may require sensitivity on the part of the student, anything that depersonalizes the feedback as a criticism of the individual student and instead focuses on what the student should do with the feedback, is likely to be helpful.

Emphasizing Group Goals in Classroom Work

Cultures differ in the relative importance that they attach to individuals and groups. In the United States, many believe that "the squeaky wheel gets the grease." On the other hand, an old Japanese proverb holds that "the stake that sticks up gets hammered down" (出る杭は打たれる or "Deru kui wa utareru"). Obviously both sayings embody a great deal of truth, but as the research of Robert Slavin and the Johnson brothers cited earlier shows, even if our primary concern is with how much individuals learn, the best way to ensure that individuals do learn is often to use the power of groups. In other words, there is often much less tension between individual goals and group goals than many people believe. People often say to us, "I would love to do more group work, but I have to stretch my most able students, and I have to ensure I am meeting the needs of those with special needs." The assumption underlying such a reaction is that the only way to meet individual needs is individually. Indeed, teachers tell us that when they use group-based approaches in their teaching, parents of gifted children sometimes complain because they think their child is being held back when made to explain something to the other children.

However, as Slavin, Hurley, and Chamberlain (2003) point out, there are at least four mechanisms by which group-based activities could increase learning, all but one of which benefit high achievers. First, when the work is structured to provide positive interdependence, it is in each individual's interest to work hard—indeed, the individual cannot be successful without the group being successful. Second, in well-structured group work, students often come to care about the group and therefore try harder. Third, in small groups, students can get help from peers as well as the teacher, so they have more opportunities to get personalized help, and as a result are more likely to have individual needs met. Fourth, those who give help in groups are forced to think their ideas through more clearly, and this *cognitive elaboration* deepens learning and makes it more permanent. This is why studies of cooperative learning often find it is the highest achievers who benefit most.

There are many ways in which teachers can harness the power of formative assessment in cooperative learning settings, but the starting point for all of these is to emphasize to students that everyone is responsible for everyone else's learning. For example, in the chapter on eliciting evidence, we noted the very strong evidence about the importance of regular testing for helping students' longer-term learning, but we also noted that there is, as far as we know, no additional benefit to students when scores get recorded in grade books. As a result, some teachers do not return to students their individual scores but simply display to the class the distribution of the scores all the class members gain as a stem-and-leaf chart. Here is the chart one teacher posts:

9	127
8	1112445789
7	124556799
6	09
5	489

The teacher returns the individual answer sheets to the students, who then, in groups of four, have to construct the best composite answer sheet they can, and the teacher displays the new distribution of scores. Frequently, it is the case that the scores of each of the composite responses the groups produce are higher than the highest scoring individual in the first round, which gives the teacher a chance to emphasize the idea that "none of us is as smart as all of us."

Tips

Start With Pairs, Before Going on to Groups

Where students are not used to working in groups, as noted earlier, it is often more productive to begin peer assessment work in pairs. One particularly powerful, and general, technique is "choose-swap-choose," which works well wherever three conditions are met:

1. Students make multiple attempts at exactly the same task.
2. There is some relatively permanent record of the attempt at the task.
3. There is some degree of subjectivity in the assessment of the outcome.

Some examples of such situations are:

- Students in kindergarten learning to write a particular letter of the alphabet
- Students in a shop class practicing making electric arc welds
- Student gymnasts performing vaults that are recorded using portable video cameras
- Student musicians practicing musical passages that are recorded on digital recorders
- Students in a calligraphy class practicing a particular character

The idea is that the students undertake the task a number of times, review their attempts, and select one of their attempts they believe is the best. They then exchange their work with their partner, who selects which one of their partner's work samples they believe is the best. When this is done, they compare choices and discuss any areas of disagreement.

Cautions

If There Is No Individual Accountability, Monitor Carefully

The example of "best composite answer" described earlier does create a group goal—all students are working toward a single group response—but it does not create individual accountability. Some students may "free ride" and contribute little to the attempts of the group to produce the best group response. The teacher could increase the individual accountability by requiring all students to take the test again individually, after they produce the best composite response, but this might not be a particularly worthwhile activity. While individual accountability does improve the likelihood of the group working effectively, it can sometimes be difficult to ensure, and the cost of doing so may be disproportionate to the benefits. For that reason, you may decide to dispense with the requirement for individual accountability and just focus on ensuring that there are group goals. This is fine, provided you realize that without individual accountability, there is no built-in incentive for students to maximize their contributions to the group. They may choose to do so because the work is interesting, or the setting motivates them, but there is nothing in the task structure to create the incentives. In such situations, therefore, it is important that you, as the teacher, monitor the quality of the discussions in the groups, and if necessary, intervene to support the students' learning.

Enhancements

Joint Evaluation of Multiple Attempts at Tasks

The "choose-swap-choose" protocol described earlier involves students independently arriving at judgments of the quality of their own and their peers' work and then comparing them. As an alternative, students can jointly evaluate the relative merits of multiple attempts at a task. For example, some kindergarten teachers prepare a daily sign-in sheet—a large sheet of butcher's paper with the five days of the week as columns and the students' names down the side. Every day, each student writes his first name in the appropriate cell. Obviously, being kindergarten, some students are writing their names legibly and clearly, while other attempts are closer to "pretend writing." However, the differences in quality between students is irrelevant in this task; what matters is the differences in quality in the five sign-ins each student completes. On Friday, each student chooses a partner, and with the partner the student reviews their five sign-ins for the week; the student has to agree with the partner on which of the five versions is the best and place a gold star in that cell. Some teachers extend this by inviting parents or guardians to come to the classroom at the end of the day on Friday to join in the lesson, and give them a different colored star to place against the sign-in they think is the best. If they disagree with the selection the student and his partner make, they can talk about why.

You can use this technique wherever multiple attempts at the same task can be reviewed simultaneously. For example, if a student is constructing a wooden picture frame, the student could discuss with a partner which one of the four miter joints is the neatest. Students learning calligraphy could decide together which one of eight attempts at the same character is the best, and students reviewing a writing portfolio could decide which one of four pieces of persuasive writing is the most effective.

Prioritizing Individual Accountability in Peer Assessment

Two elementary school teachers, Kelly Exley and Kaydene Linton, explore the use of cooperative learning in their teaching of spelling—something that is generally regarded as a highly individual learning task. Both teachers are aware of the benefits of frequent testing, which we discussed in Chapter 4, so they institute a regular spelling test where they give students ten words at the beginning of the week and test them on the ten words on Friday. They encourage the students to keep "spelling learning journals" in which the teachers ask students to look at the ten words for that week, decide how difficult the test would be for them, and then, in turn, decide how much time and effort would be needed to ensure success on the test. One visual analogy the teachers use with the students is the idea of a "spelling cake," which is displayed on the wall. A big cake (i.e., a relatively difficult list) would require more of the key ingredients of time and effort than a small cake. Crucially, the teachers also allow for individual differences in their approach by stressing that a list might be harder for one student than another, but that is no reason for students to do less well; it just means that—building on the work of Carol Dweck on mindset discussed in the previous chapter—some students would need to work harder than others. As one student says, "Someone else might find this week's list easier than me—because I am not as good at spellings as he is *yet*—but that is not an excuse for me to get a lower score than him. I can do as well as him, if I put in enough effort" (Exley & Linton, 2014, p. 2).

By stressing the role of effort in creating ability, Exley and Linton find that when the students study for the test, previously low-scoring students perform better than their peers, and, in one of the teachers' words, "This began to mess with their own notions of their respective places in the classroom in terms of ability" (p. 3).

The two teachers then introduce group goals to the class. While students continue to receive individual scores each week, the teachers also report the proportion of students who score 10/10. As you might expect, the idea of a contribution to a group effort does not motivate all students. In such cases, a teacher or an aide intervenes directly with the student, saying things like, "We want to encourage you to improve your score this week, Sezer, and feel proud of yourself. We will feel proud of you too." They encourage other members of the class to help— for example, by asking Sezer spelling questions during recess. The following week, Sezer goes from 0/10 to 10/10. This obviously pleases Sezer, but, equally important, his peers are as delighted as he is.

Here is a typical entry from a student's spelling learning journal:

Upon receiving the list of 10 words

This week's spelling cake is big for me, so I know I will have to put lots of effort in to be successful. I think the words . . . are the hardest so I will have to spend the most time learning those. I am going to play Sadiyya's game [a game invented by a student in the class to assist in learning] with my mom and I am going to do look/cover/write/check. My prediction is that I will get 9/10 or 10/10.

After the test

I got 10/10 and I am very proud of myself. This is my 3rd 10/10 in a row and my 6th altogether. I am improving by adding another 10/10 to my pile of 10/10s.

This week 17 out of 29 people got 10/10. Although this is the same number as last week, it is a better score because last week it was 17 out of 30 people. 8 people just got one spelling wrong and no one got less than 6/10. We think that is successful.

I feel a bit frustrated though because I hoped we would beat our record of 22 people. We will have to try harder next week.

We are proud of Sezer because he got another good score of 8/10. We helped him learn his spellings so we think we have been good study buddies.

Now some teachers might object to the use of scores in such a context, but, in view of the very clear research on the benefits of frequent testing discussed in the chapter on eliciting evidence, we think that the above account represents an interesting approach that is worthy of consideration. One noteworthy feature of this account is the evolution of the teachers' practice, from an activity that students undertake individually to the introduction of group goals and then the addition of individual accountability to the group. At first, students keep their own journal accounts of their progress with spelling, so there is no positive interdependence (although there might be some negative interdependence if students feel the need to compete against each other). Then the teachers introduce a group goal, specifically the idea of a "personal best" for the class in terms of the proportion of the class scoring 10/10. This is in itself an interesting decision because there are many different choices the teachers could make. For example, they could choose the proportion of students getting a higher score than previously, or the average score of the class. The particular advantage of choosing the proportion of students getting 10/10 is that it focuses on excellence for each individual student and sends the message that the teachers believe all students can achieve this. Finally, the teachers introduce a measure of individual accountability through the way they communicate their own expectations for the class, and also encourage the students to bring peer pressure as well.

Tips

As noted in the previous paragraph, there are many ways that you can structure the goal of the cooperative task to encourage group goals and individual accountability. All of them have advantages and disadvantages, which means that you will need to think carefully about what kinds of goal and reward structures are likely to be most effective for your students.

In the introduction to this chapter, we discussed how researchers distinguish between interdependence in terms of goals and rewards. For example, a teacher tells a group of students that they have to work together to learn something, but at the conclusion of the learning, she will test them individually and award each student in the group the mean score for the members of the group. This is an example of positive goal interdependence because anything one student does to increase the achievement of another member of the group increases the score awarded. You could raise the stakes further by awarding each member of the group the score that the *lowest* scoring member of the group achieves. We want to stress that neither of these ways of assessing achievement are particularly valid for the individuals concerned, which would be a problem if the results were to be used summatively, but they do create incentives for students to take responsibility for the learning of others in the group.

Cautions

Be Careful When Using Subjective Criteria for Self-Evaluation

Some teachers introduce incentives for students to contribute to the work of the group by asking students, at the end of the period of cooperative work, to assess the relative contributions different members of the group have made. While knowing that one's contributions to the group effort may be evaluated can increase participation, it also introduces a degree of competition into the work of the group because reducing the evaluations others receive can increase one person's relative contribution. More importantly, it is very difficult for anyone, let alone the participants, to accurately evaluate contributions different members of the group have made. Some students seem to be active members of the group, but in fact end up holding the group back, while others say very little, but what they do say is crucial in moving the work of the group forward. In the end, the only way to be sure about the effectiveness of the group work is for you to be constantly monitoring the work of your students. Sometimes you will need to intervene to redirect a group back onto the right track. And sometimes, the smartest thing you can do is sit on your hands.

Start With Simple and Straightforward Tasks

One obvious precondition for students to be able to comment appropriately on others' work is that all students understand the learning intentions and success criteria. That is why it is often appropriate to start with very straightforward techniques, such as the "preflight checklist."

This technique is most suitable for tasks with a number of requirements that are relatively straightforward to verify, but which, for some reason, students find difficult to incorporate. For example, science teachers often have quite detailed requirements for reports on practical work that students undertake in the science laboratory, including a specific format for the presentation of the report (statement of problem, hypothesis, materials, procedures, results, conclusion); text in the form of grammatically correct sentences; diagrams drawn and labeled in pencil; student's name and ID number clearly given on the front page; all charts cited in the text are included (and all included charts cited in the text!), and so on. Before a student can submit a report, the student's lab partner has to check that all the required elements are indeed present and appropriate. The partner then signs the checklist, and the student can submit the work. Individual accountability is secured by the fact that if there is any element that is not adequate, the student's partner is regarded as being at fault.

Enhancements

Assign Specific Roles to Students

A teacher uses a variation of the preflight checklist while working on suspense stories with a group of fifth graders. The teacher begins the work the previous day by getting students to discuss the key elements of a suspense story, and, through discussion, the class agrees that a good suspense story needs at least four elements:

1. An expository section in which key individuals are introduced
2. A period of rising tension or build-up

3. A climax of some kind

4. A period of falling tension or resolution

In addition, the class agrees that the suspense stories would be enhanced by ensuring that each suspense story incorporates at least two pieces of figurative language.

The students write their suspense stories, working on their own. When they complete their stories, they partner up with another student and switch roles from being authors to editors. The partners exchange their stories, and then they use colored pencils to mark up their partners' suspense story, indicating the onset of each element with a different color and using a fifth color to underline the two pieces of figurative language. When the editor is satisfied that the suspense story contains the necessary elements, he returns the work to the author, who is allowed to submit the suspense story to the chief editor (i.e., the teacher). The important feature of this arrangement is that if the author submits work that does not conform to the agreed structure, it is the editor, not the author, who is regarded as being at fault because the editor has failed to provide the required support to the author. In other words, students are held accountable for the quality of support they give their partners.

In many of the Kagan structures mentioned earlier, the teacher assigns specific roles in a group, but one particularly effective way of improving the quality of conversations in group work is to appoint one student to the role of "challenger." The idea is that when students are working in a group, one student asks peers for further details whenever a member of the group makes a contribution that is not supported by evidence or needs more detail. It is based on the work of Neil Mercer and his colleagues, who find that encouraging middle-school students to challenge the contributions of others in science lessons if they fail to back up their contributions with reasons have a significant impact on the quality of talk in groups and on achievement. Students make longer contributions, use words like "because" three times as often, score about 0.3 standard deviations higher on standardized science tasks, and even attain higher scores on IQ tests (Mercer, Dawes, Wegerif, & Sams, 2004).

Another way to assign roles is to use a cube or a spinner. For example, in an elementary language arts lesson, students read a story, and then each group of students is given a cube with the words "who," "where," "when," "why," "what," and "how" written on the six faces of the cube. Students take turns rolling the cube, and must ask someone in the group (who can be chosen randomly, using ice-pop sticks or a spinner) a question beginning with the word that is facing upward.

Putting the Elements Together

Inevitably, because of the structure we have adopted for this book, we discuss each strategy separately. This, of course, allows us to focus in detail on the important aspects of each strategy, but this structure does not make clear the fact that we regard all five strategies as intimately interconnected, and, indeed, that some of the most interesting and creative teaching takes place at the boundaries between the strategies. The interconnections between the strategies are neatly illustrated in this example of formative assessment practice from Tommy Lucassi, a science teacher in Stockholm, Sweden.

In 2011, a new assessment system was introduced to Swedish high schools, in which teachers grade student work from A to E, with standards specified for grades A, C, and E, and the other two grades being interpolated. Lucassi names the process he came up with for communicating the learning intentions and success criteria to the students the "wall matrix," and it consists of eight steps.

1. Students answer a question individually and write down reasons for their response. This could be a diagnostic question or a discussion question, depending on the context.

2. The teacher shows students three attempts at a similar question: one that would be awarded an E, one that would be awarded a C, and one that would be awarded an A (e.g., in science the differences between the answers might be in terms of the frequency and accuracy of scientific words and concepts, the cohesiveness of the arguments, etc.).

3. The teacher asks students (at random of course!) which one of the answers corresponds to the A and why, and he records the reasons on the board.

4. The teacher asks students, who are in groups of three to four, to create three possible solutions to the first question together, at different levels of quality. All members of the group have to reach consensus on each of the three solutions.

5. Each group posts its three solutions on the wall matrix, making sure that each solution is shown against the correct grade. When all groups have displayed their work, the wall matrix contains many examples of different ways of answering the original question.

6. Each student returns to the original solution completed in step 1 and assesses it, either by themselves or in collaboration with peers, and writes down suggestions on how the work could be improved.

7. Students plan individually what they will do over the next few lessons, according to their needs.

8. At the end of the process, students respond to a similar question to the one answered in step 1, and the teacher evaluates this.

Three outcomes of this process are particularly noteworthy. First, over time, the teacher notices that the wall matrix becomes a reference point for discussions in subsequent lessons. Second, students sometimes notice differences in the standards different groups applied, saying things like, "We gave that answer a C, but the other group gave it an A.

Who is correct?" We are sure you can probably guess the teacher's reply: "Discuss it with the other group; I'll be back in five minutes." Third, sometimes the students dispute the teacher's grading: "Your suggestion for an A isn't good enough. We don't think that it is worth more than a C, because . . ." In such cases, the teacher generally takes the matter to his colleagues for a second opinion.

Case Studies

In this section, we present two case studies of students acting as learning resources for one another. The extracts are transcripts of videos taken from Alderson (2007) and Wiliam and Leahy (2014). We encourage you to read the transcripts and then think about what you have read by responding to the reflection questions at the end of the transcript before moving on.

Science

In a tenth-grade classroom, the teacher sets up a database in Excel that details all the standards the students are expected to master during the year. Periodically, the teacher organizes review activities in which students complete a self-assessment of the standards they have mastered and which they feel they have yet to master. When they identify gaps in their learning, they can either find resources to help them understand or find out which students in the class have indicated they already understand the topic, so they can ask them for help.

Rebecca:	This is my self-assessment. This is for module 2 of physics, and it lists all the topics in module 2. So you've got all the topics down the left hand side here (points to screen), and then here is how I feel about these topics (points to traffic light colors under "my current level"), and I can change it every time I go onto it. So I can update it when I have got better at something, or if I don't understand something. I select my level, either "I can do it" [green], "I can't do it" [red], or "I think I can do it" [yellow], if I'm not sure. Once I have updated my progress it goes on to the system, and then if I'm a red and I don't understand it I can check by pressing CHECK and it will show me who in the class does understand it, so that I can ask them if I get stuck. They can show me how to do it because they have already got it on green. If I can't speak to a classmate I can click on a topic and it will take me to a hyperlink to go onto a website or an activity, which will show me how to do it—teach me the work I didn't understand.
	My good friend Sarah should be able to explain it to me. I'll go and find her.

Sarah arrives and sits with Rebecca.

Rebecca:	How do scientists detect comets using their "red shift" or something like that? I don't really understand it. Could you help me please?
Sarah:	They use satellites and stuff. When a planet is further away from earth it goes into the red shift, and that's when it starts into the . . .
Rebecca:	So is the red shift the infrared beams?
Sarah:	Yes.
Rebecca:	So they produce electromagnetic beams?
Sarah:	Yes.
Rebecca:	So, is that why it is called red shift, because it is infrared beams?
Sarah:	Yes, and you can see that they have moved further away from the big bang.
Rebecca:	So, the universe is still expanding now.
Sarah	Yes.
Rebecca	Okay. I understand.

Reflection

Before reading further, take a few moments to reflect on this transcript, and think about how effective this kind of activity is in moving Rebecca's learning forward. In particular, how effective is Sarah in acting as a learning resource for Rebecca? A commentary on this case study appears after the second case study.

English

A group of tenth-grade students is preparing for a formal written examination that will assess their understanding of English literature. The examination consists of two examination papers, each of seventy-five to ninety minutes' duration, during each of which the students will attempt two or three questions, so students will have thirty to forty-five minutes for their response to each question.

The teacher arranges for students to work in twos and threes to prepare a review topic for the class. He assigns two boys, Samson and Zaeem, to prepare a "mini-lesson" for the class on how they might respond to questions on a poem entitled "Stealing" by Carol Ann Duffy (1987):

> *The most unusual thing I ever stole? A snowman.*
> *Midnight. He looked magnificent; a tall, white mute*
> *beneath the winter moon. I wanted him, a mate*
> *with a mind as cold as the slice of ice*

within my own brain. I started with the head.
Better off dead than giving in, not taking
what you want. He weighed a ton; his torso,
frozen stiff, hugged to my chest, a fierce chill
piercing my gut. Part of the thrill was knowing
that children would cry in the morning. Life's tough.
Sometimes I steal things I don't need. I joy-ride cars
to nowhere, break into houses just to have a look.
I'm a mucky ghost, leave a mess, maybe pinch a camera.
I watch my gloved hand twisting the doorknob.
A stranger's bedroom. Mirrors. I sigh like this— Aah.
It took some time. Reassembled in the yard,
he didn't look the same. I took a run
and booted him. Again. Again. My breath ripped out
in rags. It seems daft now. Then I was standing
alone among lumps of snow, sick of the world.
Boredom. Mostly I'm so bored I could eat myself.
One time, I stole a guitar and thought I might
learn to play. I nicked a bust of Shakespeare once,
flogged it, but the snowman was the strangest.
You don't understand a word I'm saying, do you?

Two further pieces of information may be useful in understanding the transcript. First, the teacher reports the examination outcomes on a scale where the highest four grades possible are, in increasing merit, C, B, A, and A*, and tells Samson and Zaeem to prepare their review mini-lesson with the intention of helping the students in the class reach the highest possible grade, A*.

Second, at one point, Samson uses the term "PQA." This is an abbreviation for "point, quote, analysis," which is a technique the teacher uses with the class for structuring their English literature essays. The idea is that the students make a point, support it with a relevant quotation from the text, and then provide an analysis that shows how the quote reinforces or illuminates the point. This is substantially the same as (but less rude than!) P-E-E or "point-evidence-explanation," an acronym used by many English language arts and social studies teachers in the United States.

Teacher:	We're going to do one more poem today. We're going to have a look at "Stealing." Two boys are going to come up, Samson and Zaeem, and hopefully they're going to do the same thing and show you how to really nail down an A* on this.
Samson:	Right, we know from when we looked at it before what "Stealing" is roughly about, but we want to look deeper into it so we can get higher grades with it.

Zaeem: Are there any points to link a family life to the character?

Samson: So at any point in the poem can you see a quote which you could analyze where you will be able to say, "This could link back to him having a problem or something different about his family life from any other person"?

Elijah: Maybe you could show that he had a troubled childhood, because you know normally children build snowmen when it snows just for fun and he stole it just to make them feel bad. Maybe he's trying to make them feel how he felt when he was a child.

Samson: Because obviously this thing about the snowman is symbolic. It's not for the snowman; it's for what it represents, and it could be representative of a childhood or something like that and a problem in childhood. Polly?

Polly: The fact that he pinched a camera shows he doesn't have any, like . . . he's pinching someone's memories and pictures that they have which could show he doesn't have any memories of his own, he doesn't have happy memories like family life.

Zaeem: Yes. It shows that he has taken memories of other people, but it could also mean that he's sort of annoyed at the people that are creating all these memories, which shows, again, he may have had a troubled past.

Samson: Yes, and by giving a double meaning it moves up your grades showing you can see layers, and you can that see it could mean more than one thing when you look at it. How would you say that the way that the speech has been written within the poem is used to affect the reader, because it has been written in a particular style, which is meant to be the style of the person? So what is it about the style that gives you an insight into the character? Polly?

Polly: I think it's like stereotypes about male and female. Like the way "he" is speaking is matter of fact and rough, and he says things as it is, like you expect a woman to be more flowery and elaborate more, kind of. It's like stereotype, kind of.

Samson: Yes; the way the person speaks makes you think that they're a male, which is a technique that's used by the writer that you could pick up and use in a PQA which shows you're looking into it, but the fact that it never says "he" anywhere within it means that it's all just done by the style of the writing and not by anything else.

Teacher: We'd like you to do a PQA and you're going to write the PQA and we're going to give you the question, and you're going to write through it, and we'll come round and help you with it. "What is significant about the things that are stolen in 'Stealing'?" That will be your question.

Students work in pairs, and Samson and Zaeem circulate around the class.

Sanjay:	He knows he doesn't need it. He's just taking it just for the fun. Maybe it's like a pastime. Who knows? It could be like, a hobby.
Prisha:	We're talking about how he stole the bust of Shakespeare. We're saying how Shakespeare's language is misunderstood a lot because of the context that it was in then and how it's perceived now.
Jayla:	It's like, casual. Okay, maybe I'll do this, maybe I'll do that.
Zaeem:	He's leaving his trace everywhere trying to build upon many relationships with other people, so it's almost as though he's searching for his own memories and even . . .
Jayla:	Identity.
Zaeem:	Yes, he's searching for his identity there.

Samson and Zaeem reconvene the class.

Samson:	Are we ready for feedback to go through it? We're going to try to grade some of your paragraphs and see where we are with stuff and see if we can improve them.
Polly:	The making of the snowman is like Rousseau's theory about how man is born free and everywhere he is in chains. You do it as a young child, so you're quite carefree and not aware of the chains, but as the snowman melts your childhood melts away.
Zaeem:	So you're going to boost your grade up. You're mentioning historical context.
Samson:	Yes, just show your knowledge. If you have the knowledge you need to show it.
Teacher:	Can I have a go? Samson said it there, but it's worth repeating that as soon as you start saying "this word could mean this" or "Duffy may have meant the word to have meant this," then you're getting toward the A there because it's alternative meanings. Just by showing you that you're aware of other meanings gets you access to the A and the A*.
Prisha:	The last line, "You don't understand a word I'm saying, do you?" The quote also shows how content he is with this fact that he's misunderstood, and he's almost arrogant, because he might see himself as misunderstood because he's above everybody else. He's kind of too high above for anybody else to be understood, and Shakespeare, he was considered a high part of society now because he has a massive influence on today.

Samson: When you brought in that second quote which we said about, it makes it a very, very, very strong paragraph because you've got the original idea and then you've brought in the layers, and a deep understanding of the poem is what gets you an A*. Anybody got any other ideas from their paragraphs that they'd like to say?

Reflection

As with the previous case study, take a few moments to reflect on this transcript, and think about what how effective this kind of activity is in moving the class's learning forward. In particular, what kinds of preparation would students need in order to play this kind of role in the learning of their peers?

Commentary

In the science lesson, the student is clearly very confident in using the system to manage her own review of what she understands and doesn't understand. She is aware that she doesn't understand one of the standards the teacher identifies for the year—the idea of "red shift"—and she is able to find out which of her classmates has indicated that they do understand the concept, and asks one of them for help. However—and this is a big problem—the advice Sarah gives to Rebecca is incomplete and at least partially misleading. The term *red shift* describes the phenomenon that the light spectrum of objects that are receding is shifted toward the red end of the electromagnetic spectrum, much as the pitch of a siren of a police car drops as the vehicle moves away. It may be that Sarah understands this—she certainly seems to understand two key pieces of evidence in favor of the big bang theory of the origin of the universe: the fact that almost all objects in the observable universe do, in fact, exhibit red shift and that more distant objects show greater red shift and are, therefore, presumably receding more quickly (a phenomenon known as Hubble's Law). However, she does phrase this in an odd way, which seems to undermine her own understanding. For a start, she talks about red shift as applying to planets, which are not receding from the earth (because they are orbiting the sun), and she says that planets "go into" the red shift, which suggests she does not understand that red shift is what happens to the light from distant objects rather than something that happens to the objects themselves.

This illustrates a fundamentally important principle in the use of students as learning resources for one another: *if the teacher chooses to allow students to assist each other, the teacher is still responsible for the quality of learning that occurs.* Many teachers, on hearing about the benefits of students leading the lesson, use the technique without appreciating the extraordinary amount of work that needs to take place to share students for this role. The result is usually a disaster. The high level of maturity that Samson and Zaeem show in leading their peers in a discussion of how to do high-quality work in analyzing a poem, like much expert performance, belies the amount of careful preparation that has been done in advance, over many years. Indeed, we do not think it is a coincidence that in the English language arts transcript earlier, the students have had the same teacher for several years. Here is the advice of the English language arts teacher, Chris Flack, for other teachers interested in having students teaching their peers.

> Keep it quite manageable at first. You don't want students trying to teach the whole syllabus—they can't do it. Give them something really short and manageable and bite-sized to teach the class. Something the students are already an expert in to start off with because then the confidence will come.
>
> Make sure the students know what a good lesson should look like because if they're going to come up the front and waste twenty minutes just talking to the class there's no point, so spend a lot of time with your students. Make sure they know what assessment for learning is. Make sure they know the different strategies, and "Trust your students" is the bottom line.

Chris Flack's comments on why we should do this are also worth listening to:

> We have to find a way of injecting some originality. They've all got good ideas individually, so we just needed a means of them sharing those ideas. If all the teachers up and down the country are saying the same thing, it's very hard for students to be original. They've got the best ideas; they'll listen to each other much more than they'll listen to the teacher, that's for sure. They respect each other more than they respect us.

_____

As with the previous chapters, we end the chapter with a recap, followed by a reflection checklist you might find useful to complete, a planning sheet for using a technique with a class, and a peer observation sheet (so that you can ask a colleague to give you feedback).

There is a copy of the each of the sheets at the back of the handbook for you to copy if needed, so feel free to write all over the following sheets!

RECAP

When students support each other, both those who receive and those who give help benefit, resulting in higher achievement for all.

- Cooperative learning—five important conditions
  - Positive interdependence
  - Face-to-face interaction
  - Individual accountability (difficult to ensure)
  - Interpersonal and small-group skills used
  - Reflection time on learning
- Peer feedback
  - Start with pairs and an anonymous student

- Employ "Two stars and a wish"
- Use self-adhesive notes
- Model and discuss effective and ineffective feedback
- Provide sentence starters
- Use structured protocols
- Get peers to mediate teacher feedback

- Group goals
  - Move from pairs to groups
  - Use choose-swap-choose
  - Monitor carefully if there is no individual accountability
  - Jointly evaluate multiple attempts at tasks

- Individual accountability
  - Encourage students to support each other to get the "best" class score
  - Emphasize that effort increases ability
  - Consider incentives for students to take responsibility for the learning of others in the group
  - Be careful about students self-reporting group contributions
  - Incorporate the preflight checklist
  - Assign specific roles to students

- Case studies
  - Science
  - English

REFLECTION CHECKLIST FOR STRATEGY 4:
Activating Students as Learning Resources for One Another

	I don't do this	I do this sometimes	This is embedded in my practice	I could support someone else
I have groups of students working cooperatively at times.				
Pairs of students look at anonymous work to comment on.				
My students use "two stars and a wish," or another technique, to give feedback to each other.				
I support some students with sentence starters.				
I discuss ground rules of peer feedback with students.				
I use a structured protocol to ensure well-paced feedback and response between pairs of students.				
I get peers to mediate my feedback to students.				
I use group goals.				
I prioritize individual accountability in peer and group work.				
Other techniques for this strategy that I use to improve student learning:				

LESSON PLANNING SHEET

The technique I am going to use:
Why I am planning to use it and the results I am hoping for:
Class and date:
Preparation for the lesson:
What I am going to do less of:
Reflecting on how the technique worked, including evidence to support my claims:
What I am going to do next:

PEER OBSERVATION SHEET

Class to be observed:
Peer's name:
Technique to be observed:
What I want my peer to comment on:
Peer's comments:
Reflections after reading peer's comments and/or talking through the observation:
What I will do next:

Embedding Formative Assessment © 2015 Learning Sciences International

Chapter 7

STRATEGY 5: ACTIVATING STUDENTS AS OWNERS OF THEIR OWN LEARNING

OVERVIEW

The curious task of teachers is to work toward their own redundancy. Not literally, of course, because there will always be new students, but for each of our students, we should be working toward a situation where our students need us less and less. This is always important, but in recent years, as automation and offshoring change the world of work and as society becomes more complex, what students learn at school will never be enough. No matter how much our students learn in our classrooms, if they leave school with the passion for knowledge extinguished, we will have failed them. That is why the fifth and final strategy is in many ways the most important—the one that the other four strategies have been leading up to. When students are owners of their own learning, all the other strategies fall into place. Students play a part in deciding what they will learn, and they understand that to help them, teachers need to find out where they are in their learning, so classroom questions, discussions, and activities are designed not to "catch students out" but diagnose and support what needs to happen next. Similarly, when students own their own learning, feedback is a support and not an indictment. And, of course, peers are helpful guides, rather than judges, on the journey.

WHY USE THIS STRATEGY

Most of what our students need to know hasn't been discovered or invented yet. "Learning how to learn" used to be an optional extra in education; today, it's a survival skill.

GETTING TO UNDERSTAND THE STRATEGY

Writing almost three-quarters of a century ago, Sir Richard Livingstone, president of Corpus Christi College at the University of Oxford, writes the following:

> The test of a successful education is not the amount of knowledge that a pupil takes away from school, but his appetite to know and his capacity to learn. If the school

sends out children with a desire for knowledge and some idea of how to acquire and use it, it will have done its work. Too many leave school with the appetite killed and the mind loaded with undigested lumps of information. The good schoolmaster is known by the number of valuable subjects that he declines to teach. (Livingstone, 1941, p. 28)

It seems to us that there are two particularly powerful messages in the quotation. The first is that the work of the school is to produce students "with a desire for knowledge, and some idea how to acquire and use it"—a rather prescient comment for 1941. The second important message is that this takes time, and this time cannot be created by jettisoning unimportant content from the curriculum, for the simple reason that in most school curricula, there is no unimportant content. The only way we can create time for developing students' ownership of their learning is to decline to teach valuable content in order to make time to properly cover the even more valuable content.

The idea of increasing students' ownership of their own learning is the specific focus of a study by Barkat (2014). Working with high-school teachers across a range of subjects (English language arts, food technology, geography, history, mathematics, physics) she identifies a number of factors that seem to be particularly important in helping students take greater ownership of their own work, which in turn increases their achievement.

The key factors are:

Setting learning activities in the context of personal goals—for example, by connecting school learning to career aspirations

Connecting effort investment to success, through ensuring realistic understanding of success criteria, recognizing things done well, encouraging proactive help-seeking, and ensuring students understand actions for improvement identified in feedback

Engaging students in the planning of the work, by providing opportunities for organizing tasks with the teacher, and providing a choice of tasks and structures such as templates and checklists for keeping track of the work

The first of these relates closely to the discussion of learning intentions and success criteria in Chapter 3, while the second relates to the discussion of feedback (Chapter 5). The third factor involves helping students think about their thinking—what psychologists sometimes call *metacognition.*

The term *metacognition* is usually attributed to John Flavell, who defines it as:

one's knowledge concerning one's own cognitive processes and products or anything related to them, e.g., the learning-relevant properties of information and data. For example I am engaging in metacognition (metamemory, metalearning, metaattention, metalanguage, or whatever) if I notice that I am having more trouble learning A than B; if it strikes me that I should double-check C before accepting it as a fact; if it occurs to me that I had better scrutinise each and every alternative in any multiple-choice type task situation before deciding which is the best one; if I sense that I had better make a note of D because I may forget it; if I think to ask someone about E to see if I have it right. (Flavell, 1976, p. 232)

This is obviously an extremely broad definition—even Flavell himself describes the definition as a "fuzzy concept" (Flavell, 1981, p. 37)—and could include just about any activity that involves any observation about, or reflection on, one's thinking. It is hardly surprising, therefore, that different researchers focus on different aspects of these processes. Some researchers focus on the strategies that students use to keep their learning moving forward in a productive direction, including planning, managing attention, monitoring progress, and taking action to redirect learning when it is not proceeding as intended. Other researchers focus on what motivates students, such as how interesting they find the work, whether they see value in pursuing it, the way they make sense of their successes and failures, and the social cost of failure (and sometimes success!), while others focus on the emotional side of learning and how to manage that best.

What most researchers seem to agree on, however, is that these aspects of learning all fall under the broad banner of "self-regulated learning." Boekaerts, Maes, and Karoly (2005) define self-regulation as "a multi-component, multi-level, iterative, self-steering process that targets one's own cognitions, affects [i.e., emotions], and actions, as well as features of the environment for modulation in the service of one's goals" (p. 150). Most importantly, self-regulated learning involves both metacognition *and* emotions (Boekaerts, 2006, p. 348).

Boekaerts (2006) suggests that when teachers give students a task, the students immediately engage in an appraisal of the task and its context and take into account a number of sources of information, including their current perceptions of the task, what they believe they know about the subject of the task, what they believe about their specific abilities and the role of effort in this subject, how interested they are in the subject, and their previous experiences of such tasks. They then decide either to focus their energies *either* on protecting their sense of well-being *or* they invest effort in order to increase their capabilities. This "dual-pathway" theory is deceptively simple but in fact is an extremely powerful way of integrating the various perspectives that different researchers bring to bear on the issue of self-regulated learning.

If students are inherently interested in the task, they are likely to "go for growth," and they may also do so if the teacher presents the task to them in a way that triggers their curiosity. If the students are not interested in the task, they may compare the value of completing the task versus the cost. If the task relates to personally important goals, or the student can see the relevance of the task, the student is more likely to engage in the task in order to increase competence. If there is a danger of failing the task, for example, the student's mindset will be important. To a person with a fixed mindset, failure means that you are not a smart person, which increases the likelihood that the student disengages from the task (on the grounds that it's better to be thought lazy than stupid). To a person with a growth mindset, the possibility of failure is not a problem—indeed, it is an indication that the task is challenging enough to increase one's ability. Sometimes, paying some attention to the well-being pathway can help students direct attention toward growth. For example, if the teacher makes it clear to the students that a number of resources are available to the students that can help if needed, then failure becomes less likely. Alternatively, the teacher may "lower the stakes" for failure by making it clear that the task is intended to be challenging, so unsuccessful first attempts are to be expected—and are in fact normal. This is a particular feature of English language arts instruction, where teachers stress the normality of drafting and redrafting work several times.

In the remainder of this chapter, we explore a number of ideas and techniques that you can use to help your students take greater control over their own learning. Some of them you can apply immediately, while others will take longer. Indeed, sometimes it may seem as if you are making little progress. However, if you really embrace the idea that, as teachers, we are preparing our students for a world that no one can possibly imagine, then everything falls into place. The future will belong to those who continue to learn.

TECHNIQUES

Use Self-Reports, but Don't Rely on Them

Perhaps the most depressing aspect of the implementation of formative assessment over the past twenty years is the way that it has become associated with a number of simple techniques, such as "traffic lights" for self-assessment. Of course, there is nothing wrong in engaging students in reflecting on the work they have done, relating it to the learning intentions and the success criteria, and evaluating whether adequate progress has been made. For example, one teacher mounted by her classroom door three ledger-sized (i.e., 11" by 17") sheets of paper—one in red, one in yellow, and one in green—onto each of which she placed thirty hook-and-loop circles approximately 1" in diameter. Each student had a name card with a hook and loop pad on the reverse. Two or three times a week, the teacher would ask the students a self-assessment question as they went out to recess, and they placed their name tag on whichever colored sheet matched their confidence in their understanding. This is, of course, a self-report, and we now have many years of research on self-reports that shows they cannot be trusted—for example, according to Svenson (1981), 93 percent of American car drivers believe they are better than average! The teacher is well aware that she cannot rely too much on the students' self-reports, but she can use the students' self-ratings to make adjustments to the instruction or how the students are grouped, by the time they return from recess.

However, too often, the self-assessment session is a tokenistic "add-on" to the end of the lesson, where teachers ask students to choose a color to indicate their understanding of the lesson goals, using green, yellow, and red to signify respectively good, partial, or no understanding of the content of the lesson, and nothing happens as a result.

There are several problems with such self-reports when used in K–12 classrooms. First, often students do not know what they do not know. It is hardly surprising that students with a better knowledge of the subject produce more accurate self-assessments than those with a weak understanding (see, for example, Longhurst & Norton, 1997).

Second, social pressures may influence students in their self-assessments. Students may inflate their estimates if they believe they are in competition with other students or that the teacher will think less of them if they report a low level of understanding. Students are also likely to increase their scores if they know that their score will contribute to a formal grade. On the other hand, students may underestimate their achievement if they are worried about appearing too arrogant or do not want to appear to be too successful. These effects may, of course, cancel out, but there is no reason to expect that they will do so. For example, when teachers use traffic lights to get students to self-assess, it is common to find male students giving themselves a green and a female student with a similar level of understanding giving herself a yellow. This could, of course, be diffidence on the part of female students, but in our experience, it is more likely to be overconfidence on the part of the male students.

Ross (1998) reviews eleven studies that compare second-language learners' self-assessments with those of their teachers. In all, the eleven studies produce sixty correlations, and the values of the sixty correlations are shown in Figure 7.1. Only ten of the sixty correlations are greater than 0.70, which means that in the other cases, the self-assessment accounts for less than half the variation in the scores the teacher determines (the proportion of variation accounted is the square of the correlation coefficient). We do not know whether these rather inaccurate self-assessments are the result of students not knowing how well they have done or whether social pressures influence students in their self-assessments, but there is no doubt that asking students to self-assess in terms of scores or grades makes it more likely that irrelevant factors influence the students' assessments.

Figure 7.1: Correlation of Self-Assessment With Teacher Assessment in Sixty Studies of Second Language Learners (Ross, 1998)

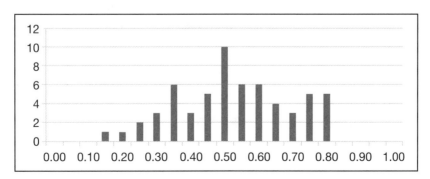

Focus Self-Assessment on Improvement, Not on Standards

For this reason, as with peer assessment, we think that you should not routinely ask students to evaluate their own work in terms of a score on a rubric or a grade. Of course, if students are using rubrics, then inevitably the way that the rubric is laid out will focus some attention on how good the work is. However, rather than focusing on whether, in terms of organization, a particular piece of persuasive writing is a "2" or a "3," we think that it makes far more sense for the student to focus on what one can learn from the rubric to improve the work. Alfie Kohn's dictum, "Never grade students while they are still learning," applies just as much to self-assessment as it does to peer assessment and assessment by teachers. More importantly, there is not much point knowing how good your work is if you do not know how to improve it.

Tips

Anchor Self-Reports to a Clear Standard

In some ways, it is hardly surprising that students' self-assessments are difficult to interpret because in many cases, students are not clear about the criteria they should use in deciding whether to signal red, yellow, or green. Many teachers find that linking the three colors to clear statements about their understanding helps students make more meaningful choices about their responses. For example, some teachers find it particularly useful to tell students that green indicates the student is ready to explain the concept to someone else, which certainly seems to get male students to think a little more carefully before signaling green. However, as we saw in the previous chapter, students can be confident that they know something when they don't, so it remains important that teachers do not take student self-reports at face value.

Another way to anchor self-reports is to let the students use colored cups as ways of signaling for help when working individually, in pairs, or in groups. Green means "I'm okay." Yellow means "I have a question, but it's not stopping me from working," and red means "I'm stuck, and I can't make any progress until someone comes to help me." As a teacher in *The Classroom Experiment* says, "It stops them from having to keep their hand up the whole time, and it means I can get to them fast. I have noticed that they are buckling down quicker to it, so that's nice to see." This technique obviously also works well when students are working in pairs or groups.

Make Self-Reports Consequential

A variation on anchoring self-reports to a standard is to make them consequential. For example, some teachers provide each student with three colored paper or plastic cups (red, yellow, and green). At the beginning of the lesson the cups are nested so that the green cup is showing. To signal that the lesson is going too fast, a student displays the yellow cup, and to stop the lesson in order to ask a question, the student displays a red cup. Accountability is built in by the fact that as soon as one student shows a red cup, the teacher selects another student at random from among those showing green cups, and that student is expected to answer the question being posed by the student who showed the red cup.

Cautions

Don't Make Self-Reports Too Consequential!

Teachers who use the colored cups as described earlier may encounter one particular problem: the students are stopping the lesson all the time, saying that they do not understand. We think that, in general, this is a problem that a teacher should want to have. The fact that our students are telling us immediately when they don't understand may be annoying, and it may disrupt our carefully planned lessons, but this must surely be better than a student saying nothing and assuming she is the only one in the class who doesn't understand. That said, some teachers introduce an additional rule, which is that you can show a red cup only once in each lesson, and if you want to stop the lesson a second time, you have to get a neighbor to do it. Inevitably, this makes students a bit more cautious about using their one opportunity to show a red cup, and it may be more appropriate for some classrooms to give students two, or even three, opportunities to stop the lesson. The important thing to remember is that there is always a delicate balancing act in such situations; you will need to be vigilant in ensuring that students are focusing on their own understanding and providing you with the information you need to teach effectively, rather than trying to "game" the system.

Enhancements

Plus-Minus-Interesting

One particularly powerful and easily applied structure for self-assessment is to ask students, at the completion of a piece of work, to identify one thing they found easy about the task (plus), one thing they found difficult (minus), and one thing they found interesting. You can collect the students' responses in a number of ways. You can put up three flipcharts, or three sheets of butcher's paper, and have students put up their comments while the class is engaged in another activity, or you can get the students to write their three comments on self-adhesive notes and have them all place them on the board or a wall at the same time. When all students write on the same sheet of paper, they are, of course, able to see the others' responses, which has both negative and positive aspects. One negative is that students can see what others have written before they write their own, and they may be influenced by what the notes say. On the other hand, the fact that students can see what others have written may prompt them to comment on something that they had not thought to mention.

A third alternative, one that minimizes student movement, is to use three different colors of index cards and use them like exit passes. Some teachers allow students to post their responses anonymously, but most teachers find that students are, within a few weeks of beginning such activities, quite happy to have their comments attributed. Also, you will need to decide whether to insist that students write a comment for each of the three categories (plus, minus, or interesting), or allow them to comment only when they feel they have something to say.

A group of third graders in New Jersey undertakes a homework activity in which they complete a number of multi-digit subtractions. The teacher stresses to the students the importance of doing a ballpark estimate before attempting the calculation—a rough calculation that the students could use in evaluating the reasonableness of their answers. The teacher starts the following day with a reading activity but asks the class to write their comments on the three flip charts at some point during the reading activity so that the teacher could draw on the responses when reviewing the math homework later in the day. The students' responses are shown in the following three panels.

Plus

- I got that ballpark estimates are supposed to be simple. (Meaghan)
- I know that you have to look at it and say "Okay." (Frankie)
- I know that when I am adding the number I end up with must be bigger than the one I started at. (Jon)
- I get most of the problems. (Julianna)
- It was easy for me because on the first one it says 328 so I took the 2 and made it a 12. (Kelly)
- I know that we would have to regroup. (Alana)
- I know how to do plus and minus because we have been doing it for a long time. (Darel)
- I think because 4 some years we've been I think I finnaly that adding is combining the two numbers in the problem. (Trevor)
- I think I am good at the partial sums method. (Aidan)
- I get it when you cross out a number and make it a new one. (Emma)
- I know that when you can't – from both colomes you go to the third colome and take that from it. (Olivia)
- I know when my answer is right the ball park estimate is close to the answer. (Brendan)

Minus

- I am still a tiny bit confused about subtraction regrouping. (Meaghan)
- I am a little bit confused about ball park estimates. (Julianna)
- I get confused because sometimes I don't get the problem. (Frankie)
- I am confused when you subtract really big numbers like 1,000 something. (Jon)
- I'm still a little bit confused about regrouping. (Trevor)
- I am confused about a little of the subtraction regrouping. (Aidan)
- I am a little confused about the regrouping still. (Kelly)
- Minus is confusing when you have to regroup twice. (Alana)
- Minus is a little bit hard when you have to regroup. (Darel)
- I don't understand when you borrow which colome to borrow from when both are 0. (Olivia)
- I am still confused about showing what I did to solve the problem. (Brendan)
- I am a little confused about when you need to subtract. (Emma)

Interesting

- Carrying the number over to the next number. (Julianna)
- It's interesting how some people go to the nearest hundred while some go to the nearest ten. (Meaghan)
- It's interesting how some have to regroup twice. (Alana)
- It's pretty interesting about how you have to really work hard. (Frankie)
- I am interested in borrowing because I didn't just get it yet. I want to really get to know it. (Jon)
- I find it weird that you could just keep going from colome to colome when you need to borrow. (Olivia)
- On the ball park estimate it is easy but sometimes hard. (Kelly)
- I really think that regrouping is pretty amazing. (Trevor)
- It is cool how addition and subtraction regrouping is just moving numbers and you could get it right easily. (Brendan)

Such an activity has a number of immediate benefits. The teacher can quickly see whether the activity is appropriate for the group. Some students, such as Darel, clearly thinks the activity was too easy, but others are happy to admit that they are still "a tiny bit confused" about regrouping. Also, because the prompt does not channel students' responses in any particular direction, many issues are brought up that would be unlikely to be raised with more direct questioning.

Olivia's response on the "minus" flipchart is particularly interesting: "I don't understand when you borrow which colome to borrow from when both are 0." Many teachers are surprised that a third-grade student would be able to ask for help with such precision and clarity. It is far more typical for a classroom exchange to go along the following lines:

Student: I can't do it.

Teacher: What is it that you can't do?

Student: I can't do any of it.

One of the clearest benefits of getting students to engage in reflecting on work they have done, and, specifically, what they found easy and what they found difficult, is that students become much more precise in asking for help, which saves the teacher a huge amount of time. Karen Vear, a high school math teacher, sums up the change in her students like this: "My students used to say, 'I can't do quadratics.' Now they say things like, 'I can't do quadratics when there's a minus in front of the x squared.'"

Make Time to Help Students Own the Learning

As noted in Chapter 3, although it would be wonderful if our students are always motivated by the work we offer them, the simple truth is they are not. There are some teachers who fondly recall a bygone era when all students were polite and motivated; for our part, we doubt that such a time ever existed, and even if it did, as Steely Dan sang in their 1974 song "Pretzel Logic," "those days are gone forever, over a long time ago." We need to build in time to help our students develop a sense of ownership of their work.

More importantly, as has been stressed already, regardless of whatever happened in the past, we need to help our students learn without us, and this is very difficult for most teachers because we tend to believe that we are the main causes of student learning. In recent years, study after study shows that the quality of teachers is the most important influence on how much students learn in school. And, on a personal level, we see our students making progress in our lessons, so we believe that we create learning, despite the fact that, deep down, we all know that teachers do not create learning; only learners create learning. What teachers can do is create the circumstances within which learners learn.

In recent years, the work of instrumental music teachers has greatly influenced our thinking on this matter. Even where the school district strongly supports instrumental music tuition, tutors get very little time with each student. The result is that tutors know that if the only improvement that the students make is when the tutor is working with the student, the student will make little progress on the instrument. In fact, instrumental music teachers know that the greatest improvement comes through individual practice. As a result, music tutors spend a great deal of time—sometimes the majority of the instructional time they have with their students—ensuring that the students know what it means to practice productively on their own.

Tips

Make Self-Assessment a Routine Part of Classwork

Marzano, Kendall, and Gaddy (1999) report the result of a study in which they ask teachers how much time they would need to adequately address the standards their schools were required to teach each year—their answer is twenty months! The Common Core State Standards may have reduced this figure somewhat for math and English language arts, but there is still far too much content in our standards to do them justice. It therefore seems perverse to take time away from teaching to give students time for self-assessment. But, as Livingstone identifies, in the quotation at the beginning of this chapter, time getting students to reflect on their learning makes them more powerful learners, so that, ultimately, it increases achievement.

Direct empirical evidence for this comes from the King's-Medway-Oxfordshire Formative Assessment Project (KMOFAP), which worked with teachers in two counties in England to help them incorporate classroom formative assessment into their daily teaching routines. Teachers found that by building in time to generate a sense of ownership of the learning in the students, they covered the content more slowly, but they found that because the coverage was deeper, they needed to do much less reteaching. More importantly, when compared with other students in the same schools, students taught by teachers participating in the KMOFAP project gained higher scores on standardized tests and examinations (Wiliam, Lee, Harrison, & Black, 2004).

Learning Portfolios

One particularly powerful way to make self-assessment a regular part of the work of the class is to have students keep "learning portfolios." Many teachers get students to maintain a portfolio of work (e.g., for their creative writing), but this portfolio is generally the "latest and best" work. Such a portfolio has its uses, but we think it is also valuable for students to maintain a learning portfolio that records the learning journey. The idea is that when students do better work—for example, a new "personal best" in creative writing— they add it to the portfolio but do not remove earlier work. Periodically, you can ask students to review their portfolio and reflect on what has improved about their work. This process has two particular benefits. First, comparing earlier work with later work defines a trajectory of improvement that can be used to identify what kinds of changes in the future will produce further improvement. Second, by constantly reminding students of the fact that the work they are doing now is better than the work they did previously, students are more likely to develop a growth mindset (see Chapter 5).

Question Parking Lot

Sid—the student we heard from in earlier chapters—talks about how difficult it is to ask questions once "the moment has passed":

> It feels worrying when I feel like I'm left behind. The longer you leave it the harder it is. You can't walk up to a teacher and say "two lessons ago I didn't understand that."

This natural reluctance to raise a question may be the result of being aware of how busy the teacher is or of not wanting to appear foolish in front of one's peers, but whatever the cause, it is a much more significant issue than most teachers realize. That is why it can be very useful to have a "parking lot" where questions can be posted either anonymously or with attribution. As students put up questions, you can respond to the questions as appropriate, but you can also schedule "parking lot time," when students can choose to respond to issues that have been parked. Not only does this create a safe forum for students to raise their confusions, but it also sends a message that some issues are too complex to be dealt with in a single lesson and may require several "return visits" to be dealt with properly.

Cautions

Ask Students to Identify Changes, but Not Make Them

One of the reasons that students dislike self-assessment is that they often end up creating more work for themselves. As noted earlier, we think that the major purpose of peer assessment and self-assessment is not that students and their peers are able to assess their work in the same way that a teacher would. Rather, the aim is to work out what needs to be done to improve the work. The problem for students, then, is that often they undertake a self-assessment and determine what needs to be done to improve the work, and then the teacher asks the students to redraft the work or improve it along the lines of the self-assessment. The danger in this is that to avoid more work, the students include only things that are easy to fix in their self-assessment. One way around this problem is to ask the students, "If you were going to redraft this, what would you change?" This is an efficient technique because the most demanding intellectual work is actually working out what needs to be changed; actually making the indicated changes is much less useful for the student's learning.

Enhancements

Survey Students Regularly on Their Learning

It is much easier to get into a habit of surveying students on their learning regularly if you have a form for the students to complete, especially if they just have to check a box rather than write a response. Obviously the questions you ask will depend on your students and your context, but to get you started, we have designed one form that you could use, and this is shown here. This form is included as a resource you can photocopy, with two forms to a page, at the end of the handbook.

STUDENT REFLECTIONS ON LEARNING (no name please—just check a box next to each statement)

	Disagree	Sometimes	Agree
I believe that I can learn a lot.			
I learn a lot in class.			
My teacher believes that I can learn a lot.			
I find it hard when other students look at my work.			
My classmates help me learn.			
When I work hard I get smarter.			
My teacher helps me learn.			
I enjoy helping other students learn.			

Use Frameworks to Help Students See the Connections in Their Self-Assessments

One of the problems with self-assessment activities is that often they seem to be related only to the activity at hand. Students do a self-assessment on one task one day, and another on another task on another day, but make little attempt to connect the different self-assessments. There are two problems with this. First, this reduces the opportunity for students to make connections with their existing knowledge, which as we saw in Chapter 3 is helpful for long-term retention. Second, there is little progression in students' self-assessment. Each self-assessment is a kind of mini "Groundhog Day" with nothing developing from one week to the next.

The REAL framework, developed in Australia, attempts to address this by connecting student self-assessment to a developmental framework called the SOLO taxonomy, which Biggs and Collis (1982) developed. Previous taxonomies, such as those developed by Benjamin Bloom (1956), look at educational objectives. In contrast, Biggs and Collis suggest it is more helpful to look at what students actually do, and in particular, what evidence of their thinking is present in the work they do (hence the acronym SOLO—Structure of the Observed Learning Outcome).

The SOLO taxonomy identifies five different levels of structure that we might observe in students' work:

Prestructural:	The response does not address the requirements of the task.
Unistructural:	The response addresses a single aspect of the task
Multistructural:	The response addresses multiple aspects of the task, but these multiple aspects are treated independently.
Relational:	The response addresses different aspects of the task that are related to each other and therefore become an integrated whole.
Extended abstract:	The "integrated whole" is conceptualized as a higher level—for example, as an element of a more abstract structure, or applied to new relevant areas.

Although the taxonomy is presented in linear form, because concepts generated at the extended abstract level can be the building blocks for new relationships between concepts, the taxonomy can also be thought of as cyclical or spiral in nature.

In the REAL framework, the SOLO taxonomy is used to identify a number of self-assessment prompts that address the feelings, thoughts, and actions related to the work (Munns & Woodward, 2006). At each level, students are asked about five aspects of their learning:

T Thinking about achievement

L Looking for evidence

W Working with other people

O Overcoming barriers

R Reframing the task

The unistructural level is concerned with just describing feelings, thoughts, and actions.

Feelings	Thoughts	Actions	
What were the fun bits in your learning?	Write a memo to someone about the most important thing you learned today	What new things can you do now?	T
What surprised you about your learning?	What is your best hard work?	List your strengths.	L
How does working with others make you feel?	What cooperation helped your learning?	Who helped you the most?	W
How do you feel when the work gets tricky?	What was the tricky part?	What is your biggest improvement?	O

(continued)

Feelings	Thoughts	Actions	
What would make you feel better about today's work?	Name two things to make you think harder.	What would you change about today's work to help you improve?	R

At the multistructural level, students are expected to develop, justify, and analyze their feelings, thoughts, and actions.

Feelings	Thoughts	Actions	
Why were the fun bits fun?	What strategies did you use to learn something important?	What goals did you assess for yourself in this work, and how well did you achieve them?	T
Why were you surprised about your learning today?	How did you know you had learned something?	What is the evidence of your achievement in today's learning?	L
Why does cooperative learning make you feel the way you do about it?	What did you learn about working with others in doing this work?	What advice would you give to students who will be working on similar projects in the future?	W
How do you feel when you have solved a problem?	Write down two questions you could not answer.	How could we change this work next time we do something similar?	O
How could changes in today's work help you feel better about it?	Why do you think doing it differently will help you with your learning?	What would you change about it if you were to do a similar task to improve your learning?	R

At the relational level, students are asked to relate their feelings, thoughts, ideas, and actions to other aspects of their work.

Feelings	Thoughts	Actions	
How do you feel when you achieve your goals?	Connect this knowledge to something you already know or can do.	Think of a way to use . . . since we practiced it in class.	T
What other feelings do you have about this work?	How does this work relate to something you already know?	Reflect on the strategy we used and why we used it.	L

(continued)

Feelings	Thoughts	Actions	
How can you ensure your group has positive feelings about your work together?	Who do you know that would find this approach helpful?	How could your involvement in teamwork next time be different from this time?	W
What problems do you have to solve about how you feel when the work gets tough?	Find three situations where this new knowledge could be useful.	List five places you could use the skills you have learned in doing this work.	O
How can you feel more "in control" in your work at school?	When and where else could you use this information?	What would you do differently in your next project now that you know what you know?	R

Finally, at the extended abstract level, students are expected to translate their feelings, thoughts, and actions into concepts that they can use in guiding their future work.

Feelings	Thoughts	Actions	
Think about the many feelings you have about your work. Use colors or drawings to represent at least one of these feelings.	Explain how your thinking was different from yesterday, and how it could be different tomorrow.	How is what you have learned important for you as a person?	T
How can you generate some specific feelings about your word, such as empathy or curiosity?	Why is it important for you to know or understand or be able to do this?	Identify three ways the skills you have learned could be used elsewhere.	L
Compare the feelings of other members of your group with your own.	Reflect on a conversation you had with someone else that moved your thinking forward.	How would you help someone else to learn something you discovered today?	W
What was the most difficult part of discussing your feelings about the task, and how did you deal with this?	How could you broaden your thinking and learn more about what you did today?	What did you find out about your own problem-solving skills while doing this work?	O

(continued)

Feelings	Thoughts	Actions	
What other positive feelings would you like to generate in future work?	Represent what you think with a drawing, a matrix, a concept map, or in some other way.	What advice could you give your teacher before continuing the lesson?	R

Inevitably, some of the entries in the table are a little "forced," and in many cases, the distinction between the columns and the rows is not always clear. However, we have included the four tables in their entirety (with some slight changes in wording) because we feel that the three dimensions in the framework provide a useful framework for thinking about the way we use self-assessment. First, there are the three aspects of learning: feelings, thoughts, and actions. Each of these is important and interacts in complex ways with the others, as is clear from the work of Monique Boekaerts (2006) discussed earlier. Second, there are the five categories of probes: thinking about achievement, looking for evidence, working with other people, overcoming barriers, and reframing the task. These help ensure that the self-assessment remains broadly focused on different kinds of processes in learning. Third, using the developmental levels of the SOLO taxonomy allows students and teachers to identify progression in self-assessment but more importantly, also provides a model for students to see "what's next?" At the end of the book, we include the tables in a different format, focusing on the progression within each of the three aspects of learning (feelings, thoughts, and actions). These sheets can be used in a variety of ways, but one obvious way is to use them as an extension of the learning logs described in Chapter 4 that supports differentiation. Once students understand that the prompts toward the right are more challenging, they can respond to whichever prompts are most appropriate for them at that time. For more details of the work of the "Fair Go" project, see Munns, Sawyer, and Cole (2013) and the project website at http://socialventures.com.au/case-studies/uws-fair-go-project/.

Student-Led Parent-Teacher Conferences

One natural consequence of "activating students as owners of their own learning" in many of the schools with which we have worked over recent years is that students come to play a more prominent role in parents' meetings. Some schools go so far as to insist that students lead all parent-teacher conferences. Obviously, there are many ways this can be done, but whatever the approach taken, successful student-led parent teacher conferences require detailed planning.

Before the meeting, students need time to plan what they will discuss with their parents or guardians and teachers. The following list, while not exhaustive, will give you some ideas to get you started.

1. What have I enjoyed most so far this year?
2. In what subjects am I doing particularly well? Why?

3. What subjects am I finding most difficult and why?

4. What have I got to do to make improvements in this subject?

5. Have I had full attendance this term? Have I made up any work missed? Are there gaps in my work? Do I need support to catch up and if so, from whom?

6. How well do I cope with homework? How long am I spending on homework each day? Have I met all homework/coursework deadlines?

7. What one thing am I going to do this term to improve my learning?

8. What help do I need from my parents?

9. What help do I need from my teachers?

We have also found it helpful to provide students with a laminated "reminder sheet" that, during the conference, helps them focus on the important issues.

Am I where I thought I would be?
Was the data what was expected?
Was it fair and accurate?

Did I meet my targets?
What were the barriers to achieving all targets?
What support did I seek to achieve all targets?

Review of Target
Set SMART targets to raise achievement.
What I plan to do—how to achieve targets
How am I going to do this? How it will be measured?
Will I report back?
Who can help me?

As stated earlier, different schools will structure these events differently, but what we find most interesting is that once schools discover the power of really listening to students, it changes the entire work of the school.

Nurture Both Intrinsic and Extrinsic Motivation

In education, it is routinely assumed that intrinsic motivation is better than extrinsic motivation—indeed, extrinsic motivation is routinely equated with punishments, blandishments, and rewards, while intrinsic motivation is portrayed as pure and unsullied. As we will see, things are a little more complicated than that, and we believe that there is a clear and important role for both intrinsic and extrinsic motivation in helping students become owners of their own learning.

As Ryan and Deci (2000) point out, "To be motivated means *to be moved* to do something" (p. 54). Of course, there are different *levels* of motivation—people differ in how much they want to do something—and *kinds* of motivation. Psychologists routinely draw a distinction between intrinsic and extrinsic motivation, although different psychologists have slightly different definitions of the two kinds. The most common way of distinguishing between the two main kinds of motivation is to use intrinsic motivation to refer to situations where an individual does something because it is inherently interesting or enjoyable, and to use extrinsic motivation to describe those situations where something is done because it leads to an outcome that is separate from the actual activity.

Intrinsic motivation is, of course, a powerful force in learning. Winner (1996) describes children who have to be dragged away from playing the guitar, watching chess games, drawing, or other activities—students who have what she calls a "rage to master." There is no doubt that if students are intrinsically motivated to do something, then we should do all we can to sustain that motivation. Intrinsic motivation is enhanced by feelings of competence—most people like doing things they are good at—and feelings of competence are enhanced by activities that are challenging, but achievable, and by feedback that encourages further exploration. Feelings of competence tend to be undermined by demeaning evaluations, and activities that are too easy or too hard (Deci & Ryan, 1985). However, feelings of competence sustain intrinsic motivation only when individuals also have a sense of autonomy. In other words, doing something well when you don't feel in control of it—for example, when too much support is provided—actually undermines intrinsic motivation, because proving competences becomes more important than getting better (as was discussed in the Chapter 5).

However, if our students do only what they are intrinsically motivated to do, they will not achieve very much. We therefore need to use extrinsic motivation as well. The challenge, of course, is to get the benefits of extrinsic motivation without the disadvantages, and to do this, we need to understand which kinds of extrinsic motivation promote learning and which do not.

One way to do this is to consider four high school students, Arjan, Bettina, Cameron, and Destiny, and their different motivations for working hard in school. Arjan wants to major in journalism but studies hard in all his courses, including the ones he doesn't find interesting, because he wants to attend an elite college and believes that a good GPA across all his studies is the best way to achieve this. Bettina studies hard because she believes that since her parents both went to college and her friends are planning to go to college, she will feel like a failure if she doesn't go to college. Cameron isn't sure whether he wants to go to college but works hard because his parents pressure him to do so. Destiny works hard because she really wants to be an engineer and knows that academic success in high school is necessary to achieve this goal. She works especially hard in math because although she doesn't enjoy a lot of it, she knows that a high level of mathematical fluency is essential in engineering.

Each of these four students is extrinsically motivated but in different ways. For Arjan, the motivation to study subjects he doesn't enjoy comes from outside—he doesn't see algebra as particularly important to his chosen field of journalism—but he accepts that success in algebra will help him achieve personally important things. In other words, the "locus of motivation" comes from outside—he didn't make the state policy that passing Algebra I is a requirement for graduating high school—but the values are his—and he accepts that success in algebra will help him do what he wants to do.

Bettina is in some ways the opposite of Arjan. The motivation comes from inside—her belief that she will feel like a failure if she doesn't go to college—but the value system is not her own, but rather a set of societal expectations. She is going along with what others regard as important.

For Cameron, both the locus of motivation and the values are external. He is working hard because his parents make it very clear that this is what is expected of him, so the values are his parents', not his; the motivation also comes from the parents—they "make" him work.

Finally, for Destiny, both locus of motivation and the value system are internal. She wants to be an engineer and knows that being good at math is part of the package. She works hard at math *not* because she is intrinsically motivated—indeed she finds a lot of the math she has to study tedious—but she wants to be good at math so she can be a better engineer.

These four different kinds of motivation can be portrayed diagrammatically, as shown in Table 7.1, using labels for each of the four kinds of motivation Deci and Ryan (1994) propose.

Table 7.1: Kinds of Extrinsic Motivation (after Deci & Ryan, 1994)

		Value System	
		External	Internal
Locus of motivation	External	External (Cameron)	Identified (Arjan)
	Internal	Introjected (Bettina)	Integrated (Destiny)

While it might be obvious that Destiny is the most autonomous of the four students and Cameron is the least, what is less obvious is that in terms of autonomy, the value system matters more than the locus of motivation (Ryan & Connell, 1989). What this means is that trying to motivate students through making them feel bad about failure is likely to be less effective than getting them to value the goals by making them personally relevant, through making them either interesting or personally significant.

Go to www.learningsciences.com/bookresources to download figures and tables.

The difficulty in all this is that while we are interested in the student's own authentic voice, we also have to ensure that our students satisfy society's demands for achievement defined in traditional terms, and this is a difficult balancing act to pull off.

We close this section with a piece written by Sibani Raychaudhuri (1988), a British poet of Asian heritage, who writes in both Bengali and English. In the poem, she reflects on her experience during her fourth year at an English secondary school (i.e., ninth grade).

Self-Assessment

My red folder
in the fourth year
wants me to be clear
and positive
about what I achieve
in school
"in my own words"
which are foreign to me.

In my own words
in my own language
(which has no place here)
how can I feel clear
and positive?

My red folder
in the fourth year
wants me to be positive
about my grade E
in English History:
the heritage and glory
of the British Empire
"in my own words."

My red folder
in the fourth year
suddenly
out of nowhere
wants me to assert
what I achieve
in school
"in my own words."
How can I blow the trumpet
they've taken from me?

Engage Students as Lesson Observers

Sid—one of the students in *The Classroom Experiment*—describes the beginning of a typical day at school like this:

> At the beginning of the day I feel a bit worried about coming into school, and I dread it because it's just another five hours of the day which I think is wasted, and you'll only learn like one thing a week really that you'll actually remember.

Of course, teachers don't often hear such views from their students, because we rarely make a point of listening to our students as a key lever for improving education; this is why formative assessment is so important. One teacher describes the essence of formative assessment as "making the teacher's hearing better and making the students' voices louder." Many teachers tell us that as they develop their practice of classroom formative assessment, they become increasingly aware of how they give little attention to the views of the students. Schools regularly consult students about cafeterias and restrooms but rarely do they ask students about the central function of the school—student learning.

The traditional defense of this stance is that teachers are the experts about education—they have, after all, in most cases received extensive training for their role—while students don't know enough about the subtleties of teaching to provide useful insights. However, what has struck us as we worked with schools, teachers, and students over the past twenty years is the profound insights that students have into what happens in classrooms and how instruction could be improved, and which are currently being ignored.

Katie, one of the students who participates in the TV show *The Classroom Experiment*, says, "I don't think a teacher has ever asked me what I thought of the lesson, unless it was another teacher asking how it went or how I behaved, but not the actual teacher who was teaching the lesson." Another student, Sidney, is even more forthright:

> Teachers never ask me what I thought of a lesson, and I think that's quite bad really because we are students and the only people who know about how good a lesson was is us. Not people who write books about how to make lessons, not the government; it's just the students.

As a result, in the *Embedding Formative Assessment Professional Development Pack*, we encourage teachers to invite students to the initial segment of at least some of their teacher learning community (TLC) meetings. After one such meeting, a teacher says, "I've been teaching twenty years, and that's the first time I've had structured feedback from the client." Any commercial organization that makes no effort to get feedback on its core operations from its clients would probably go out of business rather quickly, and we think that any school that is serious about improvement needs to listen to the views of students about how to improve instruction.

For the teachers working on their own—the main audience for this book—obviously inviting students to meetings is not an option. However, what you can do is invite students to give you feedback on your teaching.

This may sound intimidating at first, probably because it is, both for the teacher and the students. As Emily, another student who participates in the TV show *The Classroom*

Experiment, says, "I never really tell the teacher what I thought of the lesson, because they might consider it quite rude if I were to comment on their teaching styles."

But that is often because we have a fixed mindset ourselves about our abilities as teachers. When we embrace the idea that we can continue to improve our abilities as teachers, feedback—whoever it is from—is the fuel for that improvement, or, as Rick Tate says, "Feedback is the breakfast of champions" (Blanchard, 2009).

The three key phases for introducing "students as learning partners" in a school are initial training, organizing the observation, and the actual observation/feedback session itself.

Initial Training

There are obviously many ways in which you can train students for their role as lesson observers. Ahead, we outline one model that we believe will provide a useful starting point for you, based on the work of Michael Fielding and his colleagues on "mutual support and observation" (Fielding, 1989) and developed further by Gill Mullis and others at the Specialist Schools and Academies Trust in the United Kingdom (Mullis, 2011). However, it is highly likely that this model will need to be adapted to take into account the particular circumstances of your school. You will also need to make sure that you have the consent of the relevant authorities in the school and district, and, depending on the agreements in place, the parents or guardians of the students participating.

Group size: Our experience is that training students as lesson observers is best done with a reasonably large group—say ten to fifteen students—even if you plan to ask only a few students to engage in the process. Some teachers find it easier to get appropriate feedback from students they do not teach, but this obviously takes more organization and coordination to get students released from other teachers' classrooms.

Selection of students: In general, it is likely that the older students are, the more likely they are able to provide good insights into your teaching. However, even in elementary school, students have quite deep insights into their own learning, so as long as you accept that the observation will be different depending on the age of the students involved, we do not see any clear lower age limit for students to participate in lesson observation. In order to avoid isolating students, we find it useful to have students observing in mixed-sex pairs (i.e., one male and one female). Some students may be reluctant to take on this role, but our experience is that students regard it as an honor and a privilege:

Katie:	It is a responsibility, but then it is a privilege, as well, for us to be chosen out of the whole group.
Sid:	For a teacher to allow you into the classroom and give feedback, I think there's got to be some trust really. So I think that it's quite a big privilege to be able to be put in that position.

Training time: We recommend that training the students for their role as observers of teaching takes at least two to three hours, which, in most schools, needs to be broken up into several sessions. We recommend that any session starts with some kind of ice-breaker activity to get the students talking and used to working with each other, and if the training is broken up over a number of sessions, it is probably a good idea to begin each session with some kind of warm-up activity.

Format: Obviously, there are many different possible formats for the training, but our experience suggests that a training session needs to include the following elements:

- Characteristics of good lessons and associated evidence
- Practice video observation and debrief
- A "code of conduct"
- Lesson observation forms designs
- Lesson observation forms trials
- Practice feedback sessions

Each of these elements is discussed briefly ahead.

Characteristics of Good Lessons and Associated Evidence

Once the group completes the warm-up activity, a good starting point for the training is to get students to discuss what makes a good lesson—the Kagan structures mentioned in Chapter 6 are particularly useful here. Once the group shares its ideas about the characteristics of a good lesson, students can work in pairs or groups to prioritize the characteristics of a good lesson and decide on a small number (four to six, and certainly no more than ten) that they regard as the most important.

Then, for each of the characteristics of a good lesson, you can ask students to think about what they would want to see as evidence of that characteristic. For example, if the students agree that a good lesson is one in which the teacher connects the content of the lesson to the students' experiences, students could record evidence of any such connections.

Practicing Video Observation and Debrief

This agreed list of characteristics of good lessons, together with the evidence they would expect to see if that characteristic were present, provides the basis for the framework that students will use for observing lessons. Recall that in Chapter 6, we recommended that peer assessment should start with the work of anonymous peers. For the same reason, we suggest that the next step is to give the students the chance to use the observation framework on a piece of video from another school. Students can watch the video and then work in pairs and agree on the evidence they think they should record, and then, along the lines of the German case study in Chapter 3, ask them to suggest feedback they might give to the teacher in the video.

One way to structure the feedback is to ask the students to begin by identifying questions they might ask the teacher, either as prompts for reflection by the teacher or to clarify any issues that the students do not understand. Some possible prompts for this are:

Could you say a little more about why you . . . ?

What did you learn in teaching that lesson?

What would you do differently next time you teach that lesson?

Of course, in this training session, there is no teacher to respond to these questions, but giving the students the chance to practice asking such questions will help them frame such questions when they are providing feedback to you. Students can then practice the formal feedback session, taking into account the characteristics of effective feedback discussed in Chapter 5.

Adopting a Code of Conduct

After the feedback is given, the group can then discuss the feedback suggested by the members of the group and can draw up a list of "dos" and "don'ts" for feedback. In drawing up such a list it can be especially helpful to focus on the kinds of words or phrases that are helpful to use and words or phrases that are particularly unhelpful. These can then be formalized into a code of conduct for students observing teachers. Whatever else it contains, the code of conduct must include clear policies regarding confidentiality of the evidence collected during the observations.

Designing Lesson Observation Forms

After they complete the feedback session, students should then look at the evidence they collected during the video observation and decide how they would like to collect information when they are actually observing a lesson. Some students develop forms that can be filled in during the observation, while others prefer a less structured format, and others prefer a blank sheet of paper accompanied by a prompt sheet to remind students about the things they could be looking for. There are no right answers here. The important thing is that students understand the need to undertake some formal recording of what they observe in order to provide feedback. People always think they are going to remember important things that happen in the lesson, but they don't!

Trialing the Lesson Observation Forms

Once students finalize their system for recording lesson observations, they can be trialed out. Some schools try doing this in role-play exercises, but others find such exercises rather artificial. In particular, when students are role-playing, the things they do will not as a rule be similar to what happens in real classrooms, so the value of such observations is limited. Videos of classroom practice, for all their imperfections, are likely to be most useful here. At the end of the trialing of the lesson observation forms, the students should discuss whether their chosen means of recording the lesson observation works, and make any adjustments needed.

Practice Feedback Sessions

The final part of the training is for students to practice giving feedback to a teacher on the basis of the observed lesson. One particularly useful way of doing this is as a "fish-bowl" activity involving students in groups of six. The session begins with two students working as a pair, who practice giving feedback to a third student, who plays the part of the teacher in the video they have watched as a group. Three other students observe the process (hence the idea of a fish bowl), and at the end of the process, the second and then the third pair each take a turn giving feedback. At the end, the students discuss their experience, and make any necessary changes to the observation forms or the code of conduct.

Planning the Observation

At least in the initial stages, it is essential that you choose a clear focus for the observation—what exactly you would like to get feedback on—and ideally, find some time to sit down with the student observers to be clear about their roles and responsibilities, and what it is you want to get out of the lesson. Obviously setting the time for the observation will take some negotiation, especially if the students undertaking the observation are not students you teach. It is also important to allow enough time (at least thirty minutes) for the feedback to take place as soon as possible after the lesson, partly because you will want to know what the students think but also because the feedback the students are able to provide is likely to be more focused and relevant if it is given shortly after the lesson. If students have any other ideas that occur to them afterward, they can always tell you about this at a later time.

Observation and Feedback

In general, the more time that is taken with the training and preparation, the more smoothly the observation and feedback sessions run. If the student observers are not students from the class that is the focus of the observation, your students will probably want to know who the visitors are and why they are there. Our advice would be to be open and honest with the students and tell them that the observers are there at your invitation to help you improve specific aspects of your practice.

Perhaps the most important benefit of involving students as lesson observers is the sense of partnership it creates between the students and the teacher—the idea that teaching is not something that teachers do to students but something that teachers and students do together, with teachers and students playing different roles, but with a common purpose. As Katie says, "It feels nice to think that a teacher is finally listening to our opinions on maybe how to do something different in the lesson."

One specific benefit of involving students as observers of lessons is the way that it actually makes the students more appreciative of the complexity of teaching:

| Sid: | I think it must be quite hard to be a teacher because you've got all these things that you've got to keep on top of, like, do people not understand the work? Are you praising enough people? Are people being silly? Are they doing it all [the work]? |

An unexpected bonus is that it makes one of the participating students more aware of the impact of her behavior:

| Katie: | Now I have realized how hard it is, how much work Miss goes through to do all the lessons, plus deal with all the students. So I will think twice about my behavior now. |

Tips

Have Students Develop Specialisms

Many schools find it useful to encourage students to identify specialisms in their observation. After all, as the expertise research shows, the more you practice something, the better you get. At Seven Kings High School in Greater London, student observers produced brochures of the services they offer (e.g., questioning), so teachers can choose which students to ask to observe them when they have a particular aspect of their practice that they want to develop.

Cautions

Start Focused, and Then Open Out

One of the central principles of students acting as lesson observers is that the teacher chooses a focus for the observation. This creates something of a tension because a key goal of having students acting as observers is to get the student perspective on what happens in classrooms. At the beginning, it may be appropriate to ask the students to provide feedback on very specific aspects of the lesson. However, over time, as they develop expertise and the trust grows, you can open up the process to include the students' own ideas about how you could improve your teaching.

Enhancements

Students as Videographers

Some schools take the idea of students observing lessons one stage further, and that is to get students to create video recordings of lessons. Our work to date suggests that this is best done in teams of three, with one person playing the role of camera operator, one as sound engineer, and one as director. Most schools have video cameras available, but sound quality is usually more of a problem in schools, because classrooms are noisy places, and people usually spend much more money on the video equipment than on the sound equipment. Over the years, we have tried a number of setups, and we now think the best compromise between sound quality and manageability is to have a cordless lapel microphone on the teacher and a highly directional boom microphone (again, ideally, cordless) for recording the contributions of the students.

Obviously students will need some training in the use of the equipment, but more important is getting students to understand the goal of the videoing, which is to capture video material that helps teachers understand their work better. Students have to understand the need for the video recording to "show" rather than "tell"—in other words, the videographer should be a neutral observer (e.g., a "fly on the wall") rather than seeking to highlight particular aspects of the lesson being videoed. In general, the less obtrusive the crew, the more useful the resulting recording is to the teacher.

So far, we have seen sixth- and seventh-grade students produce quite compelling videos of classrooms, showing real insight into what is going on and providing useful perspectives for teachers to aid reflection on practice.

As with the previous chapters, we end the chapter with a recap, followed by a reflection checklist you might find useful to complete, a planning sheet for using a technique with a class, and a peer observation sheet (so that you can ask a colleague to give you feedback).

There is a copy of the each of the sheets at the back of the handbook for you to copy if needed, so feel free to write all over the following sheets!

RECAP

Teachers do not create learning; only learners create learning. What teachers can do is create the circumstances within which learners learn.

- Self-regulated learning
  - Metacognition
  - Emotions
  - Protection of well-being versus effort to increase capability
  - Fixed versus growth mindset
  - Challenging tasks = failure at first

- Self-reports
  - Unreliable
    - Social pressure
  - Can be useful if something happens as a result
  - Focus on improvement, not standards
  - Anchor to a clear standard
  - Make them consequential
    - But not too consequential!
  - Plus-minus-interesting
- Make time to help students own the learning
  - Make self-assessment a routine part of classwork
  - Learning portfolios
  - Ask students to identify changes but not make them
  - Use frameworks to help students see the connections
    - REAL framework
- Nurture both intrinsic and extrinsic motivation
  - Intrinsic: competence, challenging but achievable, encouraging feedback, autonomy
  - Extrinsic: motivation from outside or inside, values are internal or external (and more important than motivation)
- Engage students as lesson observers
  - Training
  - Organizing
  - Observation/feedback
  - Student videographers

REFLECTION CHECKLIST FOR STRATEGY 5:
Activating Students as Owners of Their Own Learning

	I don't do this	I do this sometimes	This is embedded in my practice	I could support someone else
I use student self-reports but am careful to check on the accuracy of the reporting.				
Student self-assessment is a routine part of my work.				
Students have learning portfolios that focus on their progress.				
I give students challenging tasks that are achievable with effort, and make it clear that failure is not only acceptable but also expected (otherwise the work is too easy).				
I use a framework to help my students see connections.				
I use both intrinsic and extrinsic orientations to motivate my students.				
I use trained students to observe some of my lessons.				
I use trained students to videotape parts of my lessons.				
Other techniques for this strategy that I use to improve student learning:				

LESSON PLANNING SHEET

The technique I am going to use:
Why I am planning to use it and the results I am hoping for:
Class and date:
Preparation for the lesson:
What I am going to do less of:
Reflecting on how the technique worked, including evidence to support my claims:
What I am going to do next:

PEER OBSERVATION SHEET

Class to be observed:
Peer's name:
Technique to be observed:
What I want my peer to comment on:
Peer's comments:
Reflections after reading peer's comments and/or talking through the observation:
What I will do next:

Go to www.learningsciences.com/bookresources to download this page.

Embedding Formative Assessment © 2015 Learning Sciences International

CONCLUSION

We never intended for you to read this book from cover to cover—we envisaged it as a resource from which you could get some ideas about how to improve your practice, starting with the strategies that you could most easily incorporate into your teaching, and then, hopefully, moving on to those that present greater challenges. As a result, we have no idea how much—or indeed how little—of the book you have read by the time you reach this concluding chapter.

The basic premise of this book is that there is now substantial—many researchers would say overwhelming—evidence that developing classroom formative assessment is one of the most, if not *the* most, powerful ways of improving student achievement in schools. While different writers emphasize different aspects of the process, three ideas seem central to most of what has been written about formative assessment.

The first is that the relationship between what we do as teachers, and what our students learn as a result, is far from straightforward. However, many teachers still believe that if they have taught something their students must have learned it. We often plan our teaching precisely on this basis. This is rather paradoxical. Every teacher we have ever met knows that no lesson plan survives the first contact with real children, and yet the vast majority of teachers design their lessons as if they will work perfectly. This is why we think that we should incorporate what we know about student learning into the way we plan teaching—we build "plan B" into "plan A." In other words, we design our instruction on the assumption that students may not have learned what we wanted them to learn, and build frequent "checks for understanding" into our lessons.

Now, of course, there is nothing new in this. Over thirty years ago, Madeline Hunter (1982) stressed the importance of "checking for understanding." However, when we use an "assessment lens" to look at classrooms, we think about the quality of the evidence we are getting. Who are we hearing from? Who are we not hearing from? Can we assume that those who respond are representative of those who do not? In particular, as soon as we realize that the answer to the last of these questions is generally "No," we are forced to reexamine many of our standard practices.

The second key idea is that the most effective instructional adjustments occur over very short timescales. In this book, we have discussed some of the different views about what, exactly, constitutes formative assessment, and we suggested that this isn't a very important issue. People will use words in ways that suit them, and there is nothing that we—or indeed anyone else—can do to stop it. What is important is that we examine which kinds of instructional adjustments have the biggest impact on our students' learning, and the research indicates pretty clearly that the most effective formative assessment is short-cycle formative assessment—something that happens minute-by-minute and day-by-day, not week-by-week or month-by-month.

The third key idea is that, unfortunately, the kind of formative assessment that has the greatest impact on student achievement is also the most difficult to implement because it involves changing what teachers do in classrooms. In our experience of working with teachers, we have found that it is quite easy to change what teachers do when students are not present, but rather more difficult to change what teachers do when students are present. What this means is that helping teachers develop their practice is largely a matter of habit change, which is very difficult, as Sid, one of the students in *The Classroom Experiment* TV show, realizes:

> What needs to happen is, to stop the teachers forgetting to use things, they need to be doing it all the time. The only way you can do that is if it's the whole school. So the sticks and the whiteboards are out all the time, and they do it for every lesson.

Accordingly, in this book, as well as providing a number of techniques for you to adapt and try out in your practice, we have provided sheets and grids that are intended to make the whole process very practical and grounded in your day-to-day teaching.

Some of you will be the only teacher in your building interested in taking this work forward. It will be lonely, difficult, and challenging work, but we have seen many cases where teachers made real progress even though no one else in their building is working this way. What is most interesting in such cases is that often students become agents for change. When students come to see the power of feedback that is intended to move learning forward rather than evaluate previous learning, they begin to ask why such feedback is the exception rather than the norm. We have seen students saying to teachers, "What's the point of giving me a score or a grade? How is that going to help me improve?"

As you begin to experience success, you may well find other teachers approaching you about what you are doing, asking questions such as, "Why are your students so positive about social studies this semester?" Obviously any such interest is to be welcomed, and you can then build up a group of like-minded teachers in your building who work on exploring these ideas together.

Ultimately, the aim will always be to get all teachers in a building participating in this process, through the creation of building-based teacher learning communities as described in the chapter "Your Professional Learning." Depending on your role, that may or may not be your responsibility. However, what *is* every teacher's responsibility is to improve classroom practice, not because you are not good enough but because you can be even better, and when you do your job better, your students will live longer, be healthier, and contribute more to society. For that reason, we end this book by asking you to reflect on your professional learning about classroom formative assessment by once again completing the following form—on the assumption you have tried out at least one of the techniques in this book—and also ask your students to complete the **student reflections on learning survey** and/or **student feedback to teacher survey**.

THE TECHNIQUES I NOW REGULARLY USE

Clarifying, sharing, and understanding learning intentions and success criteria:

Engineering effective discussion, tasks, and activities that elicit evidence of learning:

Providing feedback that moves learning forward:

Activating students as learning resources for one another:

Activating students as owners of their own learning:

Other techniques:

Resources

REFLECTION CHECKLIST FOR STRATEGY 1:
Clarifying, Sharing, and Understanding Learning Intentions and Success Criteria

	I don't do this	I do this sometimes	This is embedded in my practice	I could support someone else
I know what the learning intention of the lesson is, although sometimes I do not tell the students at the start of the lesson.				
I keep the learning intention and success criteria for a lesson context free.				
I communicate quality by using at least two pieces of anonymous work.				
At the end of a lesson I sometimes ask my students what they have learned.				
I use rubrics to discuss quality with my students.				
Other techniques for this strategy that I use to improve student learning:				

REFLECTION CHECKLIST FOR STRATEGY 2:
Engineering Effective Discussion, Tasks, and Activities That Elicit Evidence of Learning

	I don't do this	I do this sometimes	This is embedded in my practice	I could support someone else
I find out what every student knows at least once a lesson, by using an all-student response system.				
I ensure that all students have time to think about an answer to a question I pose before I choose who answers.				
I give a student a way out if unable to answer my question, but then I come back to that student.				
I ask a hinge question during a lesson when I need to decide whether I could move on.				
Students pose their own questions, which other students answer.				
I make "no hands up" a standard classroom policy.				
I use statements rather than questions to encourage more thoughtful answers.				
I use learning logs, exit cards, or another way of collecting extended responses from students.				
I test students, look at their answers, and then teach the areas that students have problems with before I move on.				
Other techniques for this strategy that I use to improve student learning:				

REFLECTION CHECKLIST FOR STRATEGY 3:
Providing Feedback That Moves Learning Forward

	I don't do this	I do this sometimes	This is embedded in my practice	I could support someone else
I focus on student response to my feedback rather than the feedback itself.				
I praise students for effort rather than ability.				
I give students task-involving feedback rather than ego-involving feedback.				
I limit the written feedback I give to students, and give class time for students to respond.				
I give "balanced" written feedback.				
I make feedback into detective work for my students.				
I use comment-only grading.				
Other techniques for this strategy that I use to improve student learning:				

REFLECTION CHECKLIST FOR STRATEGY 4:
Activating Students as Learning Resources for One Another

	I don't do this	I do this sometimes	This is embedded in my practice	I could support someone else
I have groups of students working cooperatively at times.				
Pairs of students look at anonymous work to comment on.				
My students use "two stars and a wish," or another technique, to give feedback to each other.				
I support some students with sentence starters.				
I discuss ground rules of peer feedback with students.				
I use a structured protocol to ensure well-paced feedback and response between pairs of students.				
I get peers to mediate my feedback to students.				
I use group goals.				
I prioritize individual accountability in peer and group work.				
Other techniques for this strategy that I use to improve student learning:				

REFLECTION CHECKLIST FOR STRATEGY 5:
Activating Students as Owners of Their Own Learning

	I don't do this	I do this sometimes	This is embedded in my practice	I could support someone else
I use student self-reports but am careful to check on the accuracy of the reporting.				
Student self-assessment is a routine part of my work.				
Students have learning portfolios that focus on their progress.				
I give students challenging tasks that are achievable with effort, and make it clear that failure is not only acceptable but also expected (otherwise the work is too easy).				
I use a framework to help my students see connections.				
I use both intrinsic and extrinsic orientations to motivate my students.				
I use trained students to observe some of my lessons.				
I use trained students to videotape parts of my lessons.				
Other techniques for this strategy that I use to improve student learning:				

LESSON PLANNING SHEET

The technique I am going to use:
Why I am planning to use it and the results I am hoping for:
Class and date:
Preparation for the lesson:
What I am going to do less of:
Reflecting on how the technique worked, including evidence to support my claims:
What I am going to do next:

PEER OBSERVATION SHEET

Class to be observed:
Peer's name:
Technique to be observed:
What I want my peer to comment on:
Peer's comments:
Reflections after reading peer's comments and/or talking through the observation:
What I will do next:

STUDENT SURVEY

Name: Date:

Circle one number for each line to show me what you felt about this lesson:

The pace	Slow	1	2	3	4	5	Fast
The difficulty	Easy	1	2	3	4	5	Difficult
My interest	Low	1	2	3	4	5	High
My understanding	Low	1	2	3	4	5	High
My learning	Poor	1	2	3	4	5	Good

STUDENT SURVEY

Name: Date:

Circle one number for each line to show me what you felt about this lesson:

The pace	Slow	1	2	3	4	5	Fast
The difficulty	Easy	1	2	3	4	5	Difficult
My interest	Low	1	2	3	4	5	High
My understanding	Low	1	2	3	4	5	High
My learning	Poor	1	2	3	4	5	Good

STUDENT SURVEY

Name: Date:

Circle one number for each line to show me what you felt about this lesson:

The pace	Slow	1	2	3	4	5	Fast
The difficulty	Easy	1	2	3	4	5	Difficult
My interest	Low	1	2	3	4	5	High
My understanding	Low	1	2	3	4	5	High
My learning	Poor	1	2	3	4	5	Good

STUDENT FEEDBACK TO TEACHER (no name please—just check one box next to each statement)

	Never	Sometimes	Often
Does your teacher tell you what is expected before you start an assignment?			
Do you compare anonymous pieces of work to understand what makes a good assignment?			
Does your teacher ask what you have learned at the end of a lesson?			
Does your teacher choose students at random to answer questions?			
Does your teacher wait three seconds after asking a question to give everyone a chance to think?			
Does your teacher wait three seconds after a student answers a question to allow that student to give a fuller answer?			
Does your teacher ask all students to answer a question at the same time?			
When your teacher grades an assignment, do you get comments that help you improve?			
Do you give feedback to other students?			
Do you work with others in a group to try to help everyone improve?			

MY LEARNING LOG

Name: _____   **Date:** _____

I might have learned more if

I was surprised by

I was particularly interested in

One thing I learned is

The most useful thing I will take from this lesson is

I want to find out more about

I'm not sure about

What I most liked about the lesson was

STUDENT REFLECTIONS ON LEARNING (no name please—just check a box next to each statement)

	Disagree	Sometimes	Agree
I believe that I can learn a lot.			
I learn a lot in class.			
My teacher believes that I can learn a lot.			
I find it hard when other students look at my work.			
My classmates help me learn.			
When I work hard I get smarter.			
My teacher helps me learn.			
I enjoy helping other students learn.			

STUDENT REFLECTIONS ON LEARNING (no name please—just check a box next to each statement)

	Disagree	Sometimes	Agree
I believe that I can learn a lot.			
I learn a lot in class.			
My teacher believes that I can learn a lot.			
I find it hard when other students look at my work.			
My classmates help me learn.			
When I work hard I get smarter.			
My teacher helps me learn.			
I enjoy helping other students learn.			

EXAMPLE LETTER FROM CLASS TEACHER TO PARENTS

Dear Parent,

NO HANDS UP—EXCEPT TO ASK A QUESTION!

I am going to try to make some improvements to the teaching and learning in my classroom.

Research shows that many students say very little in classrooms, while others are desperate to answer the teacher's questions. And importantly, students learn more when the teacher chooses students randomly to answer questions.

I have explained this to the class, and told them that I am going to try to choose them at random, so that all of them must think about the answers—not just a few. It will be difficult for me to change my style of questioning, and I realize that my students may not be keen on the change at the start, but I would like you to give me a month to show that I can get all students in the class more engaged.

The school leaders know that we are always trying to improve as teachers and are encouraging us to try out techniques that are now being used successfully in many schools.

Please contact me if you have a pressing question about this.

Yours sincerely,

SELF-ASSESSMENT PROMPTS THAT ADDRESS YOUR FEELINGS ABOUT THE WORK

	Describe	Develop, Justify, and Analyze	Relate to Other Aspects of Your Work	Translate Into Concepts
Thinking about achievement	What were the fun bits in your learning?	Why were the fun bits fun?	How do you feel when you achieve your goals?	Think about the many feelings you have about your work. Use colors or drawings to represent at least one of these feelings.
Looking for evidence	What surprised you about your learning?	Why were you surprised about your learning today?	What other feelings do you have about this work?	How can you generate some specific feelings about your word, such as empathy or curiosity?
Working with other people	How does working with others make you feel?	Why does cooperative learning make you feel the way you do about it?	How can you ensure your group has positive feelings about your work together?	Compare the feelings of other members of your group with your own.
Overcoming barriers	How do you feel when the work gets tricky?	How do you feel when you have solved a problem?	What problems do you have to solve about how you feel when the work gets tough?	What was the most difficult part of discussing your feelings about the task, and how did you deal with this?
Reframing the task	What would make you feel better about today's work?	How could changes in today's work help you feel better about it?	How can you feel more in control in your work at school?	What other positive feelings would you like to generate in future work?

SELF-ASSESSMENT PROMPTS THAT ADDRESS YOUR THOUGHTS ABOUT THE WORK

	Describe	Develop, Justify, and Analyze	Relate to Other Aspects of Your Work	Translate Into Concepts
Thinking about achievement	Write a memo to someone about the most important thing you learned today.	What strategies did you use to learn something important?	Connect this knowledge to something you already know or can do.	Explain how your thinking was different from yesterday, and how it could be different tomorrow.
Looking for evidence	What is your best hard work?	How did you know you had learned something?	How does this work relate to something you already know?	Why is it important for you to know or understand or be able to do this?
Working with other people	What cooperation helped your learning?	What did you learn about working with others in doing this work?	Who do you know that would find this approach helpful?	Reflect on a conversation you had with someone else that moved your thinking forward.
Overcoming barriers	What was the tricky part?	Write down two questions you could not answer.	Find three situations where this new knowledge could be useful.	How could you broaden your thinking and learn more about what you did today?
Reframing the task	Name two things to make you think harder.	Why do you think doing it differently will help you with your learning?	When and where else could you use this information?	Represent what you think with a drawing, a matrix, a concept map, or in some other way.

SELF-ASSESSMENT PROMPTS THAT ADDRESS YOUR ACTIONS IN THE WORK

	Describe	Develop, Justify, and Analyze	Relate to Other Aspects of Your Work	Translate Into Concepts
Thinking about achievement	What new things can you do now?	What goals did you assess for yourself in this work, and how well did you achieve them?	Think of a way to use . . . since we practiced it in class	How is what you have learned important for you as a person?
Looking for evidence	List your strengths.	What is the evidence of your achievement in today's learning?	Reflect on the strategy we used and why we used it.	Identify three ways the skills you have learned could be used elsewhere.
Working with other people	Who helped you the most?	What advice would you give to students who will be working on similar projects in the future?	How could you become more involved in teamwork next time that would be different from this time?	How would you help someone else to learn something you discovered today?
Overcoming barriers	What is your biggest improvement?	How could we change this work next time we do something similar?	List five places you could use the skills you have learned in doing this work.	What did you find out about your own problem-solving skills while doing this work?
Reframing the task	What would you change about today's work to help you improve?	What would you change about if you were to do a similar task to improve your learning?	What would you do differently in your next project now that you know what you know?	What advice could you give your teacher before continuing the lesson?

Appendix
A BRIEF GUIDE TO EFFECT SIZES

In education, we often want to compare the results of studies where student achievement is measured in different ways. For example, if we are measuring the impact of different policies to increase student attendance in high school, one study might report the impact on SAT scores, another might report impact on ACT scores, and another might report scores on the Advanced Placement examinations. If we find that the average scores are one point higher in the schools where the policy has been implemented, that would be a disappointing result if the measure is SAT scores (which range from 200 to 800), an important effect if the measure is an ACT score (range from 1 to 36), and an implausibly large effect for AP (where the scores range from just 1 to 5).

To make outcome measures from different studies comparable, researchers therefore often standardize their results by dividing the difference between the experimental group and the control group by a measure of how spread out the data are. The range in the data (i.e., the difference between the largest score and the smallest score) is not a particularly useful measure, because changes at the extremes (e.g., one particularly high-achieving student turning up or not) can have a big effect on the range. That is why researchers in education and psychology tend to use the standard deviation, which is a measure of how far, on average, the data in the set are from the mean.[1] Formally, Jacob Cohen (1988) proposes that the *standardized effect size*—often called "Cohen's *d*"—be defined as:

$$\frac{\text{experimental group mean} - \text{control group mean}}{\text{standard deviation}}$$

Ideally, we would use the standard deviation of the whole population, but of course we don't usually know that, so researchers use the standard deviation of both the control group and the experimental group pooled together, or just the control group— whichever the researchers believe will give the best estimate of the population standard deviation.

---

[1]To find the standard deviation of a set of numbers, we calculate the mean of the set, subtract each number from the mean, square each of the results to get rid of the minus signs, take the mean of the resulting numbers, and then square root.

Jacob Cohen suggests that effect sizes of up to 0.3 might be regarded as small, those from 0.4 to 0.7 as medium, and those more than 0.8 as large. In doing so, he is aware that there is "a certain risk inherent in offering conventional operational definitions for these terms" (Cohen, 1988, p. 25), but he thinks the risk is justified because "more is to be gained than lost by supplying a common conventional frame of reference which is recommended for use only when no better basis for estimating the ES [effect size] index is available" (p. 25). Unfortunately, these days very few people actually take the time to read what Cohen says and routinely interpret effect sizes according to Cohen's suggestion, whatever the context—a practice that Russell Lenth (2006) derides as "T-shirt effect sizes" (i.e., small, medium, and large).

The problem with using Cohen's recommendation is that in education, relatively small effect sizes can be educationally important. The average annual progress of a student in middle school or high school is around 0.3 to 0.4 standard deviations. An effect size of 0.1, which, according to Cohen, would be regarded as "small," would equate to an increase in the rate of learning of 25 to 33 percent, so students would be taking nine to ten months to learn what they used to learn in twelve. Such an improvement would be hugely significant, worth billions of dollars every year, so it seems odd to describe the effect as small.

There are a number of other problems with using effect sizes in educational research, many of which are described in more detail in Dylan's forthcoming book, *Leadership for Teacher Learning*, but the big takeaway is that there are no hard-and-fast rules for interpreting effect sizes. Your own judgment will always be important.

References

Agarwal, P. K., D'Antonio, L., Roediger III, H. L., McDermott, K. B., & McDaniel, M. A. (2014). Classroom-based programs of retrieval practice reduce middle school and high school students' test anxiety. *Journal of Applied Research in Memory and Cognition, 3*(3), 131–139. doi:10.1016/j.jarmac.2014.07.002

Alderson, J. (Writer), & J. Chard (Director). (2007). *Formative assessment and personalised learning—secondary* [Video]. In Available Light (Producer). London, UK: Teachers' TV.

Allal, L., & Lopez, L. M. (2005). Formative assessment of learning: A review of publications in French. In J. Looney (Ed.), *Formative assessment: Improving learning in secondary classrooms* (pp. 241–264). Paris, France: Organisation for Economic Cooperation and Development.

Anderson, J. R., Reder, L. M., & Simon, H. A. (1996). Situated learning and education. *Educational Researcher, 25*(4), 5–11.

Andrade, H. G. (2000). Using rubrics to promote thinking and learning. *Educational Leadership, 57*(5), 13–18.

Andrade, H. L., & Cizek, G. J. (Eds.). (2010). *Handbook of formative assessment.* New York, NY: Taylor & Francis.

Aronson, J., Fried, C. B., & Good, C. (2002). Reducing the effects of stereotype threat on African American college students by shaping theories of intelligence. *Journal of Experimental Social Psychology, 38*(2), 113–125.

Arter, J. A., & McTighe, J. (2001). *Scoring rubrics in the classroom.* Thousand Oaks, CA: Corwin Press.

Bandura, A. (1977). Self-efficacy: Towards a unifying theory of behavioral change. *Psychological Review, 84*(2), 191–215.

Bangert-Drowns, R. L., Kulik, C.-L. C., Kulik, J. A., & Morgan, M. (1991). The instructional effect of feedback in test-like events. *Review of Educational Research, 61*(2), 213–238.

Barkat, J. C. G. (2014). *Handing over the baton: An intervention study looking at improving students' motivational attitudes towards taking greater ownership of their learning at*

KS4 (Unpublished doctoral dissertation). Institute of Education, University of London, London, UK.

Barry, D., & Wiliam, D. (Writers) & E. Hardy (Director). (2010). The classroom experiment (part 2) [TV]. In D. Barry (Producer), *The classroom experiment.* London, England: BBC TV.

Berliner, D. C. (1994). Expertise: The wonder of exemplary performances. In J. N. Mangieri & C. C. Block (Eds.), *Creating powerful thinking in teachers and students: Diverse perspectives* (pp. 161–186). Fort Worth, TX: Harcourt Brace College.

Biggs, J. B., & Collis, K. F. (1982). *Evaluating the quality of learning: The SOLO taxonomy (structure of the observed learning outcome).* London, UK: Academic Press.

Bjork, R. A., & Richardson-Klavehn, A. (1989). On the puzzling relationship between environment context and human memory. In C. Izawa (Ed.), *Current issues in cognitive processes: The Tulane Flowerree Symposium on Cognition* (pp. 313–344). Hillsdale, NJ: Erlbaum.

Black, P., Harrison, C., Lee, C., Marshall, B., & Wiliam, D. (2003). *Assessment for learning: Putting it into practice.* Buckingham, UK: Open University Press.

Black, P., Harrison, C., Lee, C., Marshall, B., & Wiliam, D. (2004). Working inside the black box: Assessment for learning in the classroom. *Phi Delta Kappan, 86*(1), 8–21.

Black, P. J., & Wiliam, D. (1998a). Assessment and classroom learning. *Assessment in Education: Principles, Policy and Practice, 5*(1), 7–74.

Black, P. J., & Wiliam, D. (1998b). Inside the black box: Raising standards through classroom assessment. *Phi Delta Kappan, 80*(2), 139–148.

Black, P. J., & Wiliam, D. (2009). Developing the theory of formative assessment. *Educational Assessment, Evaluation and Accountability, 21*(1), 5–31.

Blackwell, L. S., Dweck, C. S., & Trzesniewski, K. (2007). Implicit theories of intelligence predict achievement across an adolescent transition: A longitudinal study and an intervention. *Child Development, 78*(1), 246–263.

Blanchard, K. H. (2009, August 17). *Feedback is the breakfast of champions.* Retrieved January 17, 2015, from http://howwelead.org/2009/08/17/feedback-is-the-breakfast-of-champions/

Bloom, B. S. (Ed.). (1956). *Taxonomy of educational objectives: The classification of educational goals: Handbook 1. Cognitive domain.* New York, NY: Longman.

Bloom, B. S. (1984). The search for methods of instruction as effective as one-to-one tutoring. *Educational Leadership, 41*(8), 4–17.

Boekaerts, M. (1996). Self-regulated learning at the junction of cognition and motivation. *European Psychologist, 1*(2), 100–112.

Boekaerts, M. (2006). Self-regulation and effort investment. In K. A. Renninger, I. E. Sigel, & R. M. Lerner (Eds.), *Handbook of child psychology: Vol. 4. Child psychology in practice* (6th ed., pp. 345–377). Hoboken, NJ: Wiley.

Boekaerts, M., Maes, S., & Karoly, P. (2005). Self-regulation across domains of applied psychology: Is there an emerging consensus? *Applied Psychology: An International Review, 54*(2), 149–154.

Broadfoot, P. M., Daugherty, R., Gardner, J., Gipps, C. V., Harlen, W., James, M., & Stobart, G. (1999). *Assessment for learning: Beyond the black box.* Cambridge, UK: University of Cambridge School of Education.

Brookhart, S. M. (2004). Classroom assessment: Tensions and intersections in theory and practice. *Teachers College Record, 106*(3), 429–458.

Brookhart, S. M. (2007). Expanding views about formative classroom assessment: A review of the literature. In J. H. McMillan (Ed.), *Formative classroom assessment: Theory into practice* (pp. 43–62). New York, NY: Teachers College Press.

Brophy, J. (1981). Teacher praise: A functional analysis. *Review of Educational Research, 51*(1), 5–32.

Brown, A. L., & Campione, J. C. (1996). Psychological theory and the design of innovative learning environments: On procedures, principles, and systems. In L. Schauble & R. Glaser (Eds.), *Innovations in learning: New environments for education* (pp. 291–292). Hillsdale, NJ: Erlbaum.

Brown, G., & Wragg, E. C. (1993). *Questioning.* London, UK: Routledge.

Brown, P. C., Roediger, H. L., III, & McDaniel, M. A. (2014). *Make it stick: The science of successful learning.* Cambridge, MA: Belknap Press.

Burgess, J. P. (1992). Synthetic physics and nominalist realism. In C. W. Savage & P. Ehrlich (Eds.), *Philosophical and foundational issues in measurement theory* (pp. 119–138). Hillsdale, NJ: Erlbaum.

Butler, R. (1987). Task-involving and ego-involving properties of evaluation: Effects of different feedback conditions on motivational perceptions, interest and performance. *Journal of Educational Psychology, 79*(4), 474–482.

Butler, R. (1988). Enhancing and undermining intrinsic motivation: The effects of task-involving and ego-involving evaluation on interest and performance. *British Journal of Educational Psychology, 58*(1), 1–14.

Butterfield, B., & Metcalfe, J. (2001). Errors committed with high confidence are hypercorrected. *Journal of Experimental Psychology: Learning, Memory, and Cognition, 27*(6), 1491–1494.

Campbell, J. (1949/2004). *The hero with a thousand faces.* Princeton, NJ: Princeton University Press.

Chickering, A. W. (1983). Grades: One more tilt at the windmill. *American Association for Higher Education Bulletin, 35*(8), 10–13.

Cimpian, A., Arce, H.-M. C., Markman, E. M., & Dweck, C. S. (2007). Subtle linguistic cues affect children's motivation. *Psychological Science, 18*(4), 314–316. doi:10.1111/j.1467-9280.2007.01896.x

Ciofalo, J., & Leahy, S. (2006). *Personal action plans: Helping to adapt and modify techniques*. Paper presented at the annual meeting of the American Educational Research Association, San Francisco, CA.

Clarke, S. (2001). *Unlocking formative assessment*. London, UK: Hodder & Stoughton.

Clarke, S. (2003). *Enriching feedback in the primary classroom*. London, UK: Hodder & Stoughton.

Clarke, S. (2005). *Formative assessment in the secondary classroom*. London, UK: Hodder & Stoughton.

Claxton, G. L. (1995). What kind of learning does self-assessment drive? Developing a "nose" for quality: Comments on Klenowski. *Assessment in Education: Principles, Policy and Practice, 2*(3), 339–343.

Clifford, M. M. (1988). Failure tolerance and academic risk-taking in ten- to twelve-year-old students. *British Journal of Educational Psychology, 58*(1), 15–27. doi: 10.1111/j.2044-8279.1988.tb00875.x

Cohen, J. (1988). *Statistical power analysis for the behavioral sciences* (2nd ed.). Hillsdale, NJ: Erlbaum.

Condry, J., & Chambers, J. (1978). Intrinsic motivation and the process of learning. In M. R. Lepper & D. Greene (Eds.), *The hidden costs of rewards: New perspectives on the psychology of human motivation* (pp. 61–84). Hillsdale, NJ: Erlbaum.

Corcoran, T., Mosher, F. A., & Rogat, A. (2009). *Learning progressions in science: An evidence-based approach to reform* (Vol. RR-63). Philadelphia: University of Pennsylvania Consortium for Policy Research in Education.

Covey, S. R. (1989). *The seven habits of highly effective people: Restoring the character ethic*. New York, NY: Simon & Schuster.

Crooks, T. J. (1988). The impact of classroom evaluation practices on students. *Review of Educational Research, 58*(4), 438–481.

Daro, P., Mosher, F. A., & Corcoran, T. (2011). *Learning trajectories in mathematics: A foundation for standards, curriculum, assessment, and instruction*. Philadelphia, PA: Centre for Policy Research in Education.

Davis, B. (1997). Listening for differences: An evolving conception of mathematics teaching. *Journal for Research in Mathematics Education, 28*(3), 355–376.

Deci, E. L., & Ryan, R. M. (1985). *Intrinsic motivation and self-determination in human behavior*. New York, NY: Plenum Press.

Deci, E. L., & Ryan, R. M. (1994). Promoting self-determined education. *Scandinavian Journal of Educational Research, 38*(1), 3–14.

Deevers, M. (2006). *Linking classroom assessment practices with student motivation in mathematics*. Paper presented at the Annual meeting of the American Educational Research Association, San Francisco, CA.

Dempster, F. N. (1991). Synthesis of research on reviews and tests. *Educational Leadership, 48*(7), 71–76.

Dempster, F. N. (1992). Using tests to promote learning: A neglected classroom resource. *Journal of Research and Development in Education, 25*(4), 213–217.

Denvir, B., & Brown, M. L. (1986). Understanding of number concepts in low-attaining 7–9 year olds: Part 1. Development of descriptive framework and diagnostic instrument. *Educational Studies in Mathematics, 17*(1), 15–36.

Dillon, J. T. (1988). *Questioning and teaching: A manual of practice.* London, UK: Croom Helm.

Driver, R., & Easley, J. (1978). Pupils and paradigms: A review of literature related to concept development in adolescent science students. *Studies in Science Education, 5*(1), 61–84. doi: 10.1080/03057267808559857

Duffy, C. A. (1987). Stealing. In C. A. Duffy (Ed.), *Selling Manhattan.* Greenwich, UK: Anvil Press Poetry.

Dukes, R. L., & Albanesi, H. (2013). Seeing red: Quality of an essay, color of the grading pen, and student reactions to the grading process. *Social Science Journal, 50*(1), 96–100. doi:10.1016/j.soscij.2012.07.005

Dweck, C. S. (2000). *Self-theories: Their role in motivation, personality and development.* Philadelphia, PA: Psychology Press.

Dweck, C. S. (2006). *Mindset: The new psychology of success.* New York, NY: Random House.

Dweck, C. S., & Leggett, E. L. (1988). A social cognitive approach to motivation and personality. *Psychological Review, 95*(2), 256–273.

Elshout-Mohr, M. (1994). Feedback in self-instruction. *European Education, 26*(2), 58–73.

Epstein, D. (2013). *The sports gene: Inside the science of extraordinary athletic performance.* New York, NY: Penguin.

Exley, K., & Linton, K. (2014). *FA and spellings.* Enfield, UK: Southbury Primary School.

Ferri, D. (2005). Trying to make sure girls in class get as many chances to participate as the boys [Radio]. *All Things Considered.* Washington, DC: American Public Media.

Fielding, M. (1989). The fraternal foundations of democracy: Towards emancipatory practice in school-based INSET. In C. Harber & R. Meighan (Eds.), *The democratic school: Educational management and the practice of democracy* (pp. 133–145). Ticknall, UK: Education Now.

Flavell, J. H. (1976). Metacognitive aspects of problem solving. In L. B. Resnick (Ed.), *The nature of intelligence* (pp. 231–235). Hillsdale, NJ: Erlbaum.

Flavell, J. H. (1981). Cognitive monitoring. In W. P. Dickson (Ed.), *Children's oral communication skills* (pp. 35–60). New York, NY: Academic Press.

Foos, P. W., Mora, J. J., & Tkacz, S. (1994). Student study techniques and the generation effect. *Journal of Educational Psychology, 86*(4), 567–576.

Fry, E. (1980). The new instant word list. *Reading Teacher, 34*(3), 284–289.

Fuchs, L. S., & Fuchs, D. (1986). Effects of systematic formative evaluation—a meta-analysis. *Exceptional Children, 53*(3), 199–208.

Fullan, M., & Stiegelbauer, S. (1991). *The new meaning of educational change.* London, UK: Cassell.

Gallimore, R., Ermeling, B. A., Saunders, W. M., & Goldenberg, C. N. (2009). Moving the learning of teaching closer to practice: Teacher education implications of school-based inquiry teams. *Elementary School Journal, 109*(5), 537–553.

Gilbert, J. K., Osborne, R. J., & Fensham, P. J. (1982). Children's science and its consequences for teaching. *Science Education, 66*(4), 623–663.

Ginsburg, H. P. (2001). *The Mellon Literacy Project: What does it teach us about educational research, practice, and sustainability?* New York, NY: Russell Sage Foundation.

Godden, D. R., & Baddeley, A. D. (1975). Context-dependent memory in two natural environments: On land and underwater. *British Journal of Psychology, 66*(3), 325–331.

Grossman, P., Wineburg, S. S., & Woolworth, S. (2000). *What makes teacher community different from a gathering of teachers?* Seattle: University of Washington Center for the Study of Teaching and Policy.

Gunderson, E. A., Gripshover, S. J., Romero, C., Dweck, C. S., Goldin-Meadow, S., & Levine, S. C. (2013). Parent praise to 1- to 3-year-olds predicts children's motivational frameworks 5 years later. *Child Development, 84*(5), 1526–1541. doi: 10.1111/cdev.12064

Guthrie, J. T., Seifert, M., Burnham, N. A., & Caplan, R. I. (1974). The maze technique to assess, monitor reading comprehension. *Reading Teacher, 28*(2), 161–168.

Haidt, J. (2005). *The happiness hypothesis: Finding modern truth in ancient wisdom.* New York, NY: Basic Books.

Hansford, B. C., & Hattie, J. A. (1982). The relationship between self and achievement/performance measures. *Review of Educational Research, 52*(1), 123–142. doi:10.3102/00346543052001123

Harlen, W. (Ed.). (2010). *Principles and big ideas of science education.* Hatfield, UK: Association for Science Education.

Hartley, L. P. (1953). *The go-between.* London, UK: Hamish Hamilton.

Hattie, J., & Timperley, H. (2007). The power of feedback. *Review of Educational Research, 77*(1), 81–112.

Hemery, D. (1986). *The pursuit of sporting excellence: A study of sport's highest achievers.* Champaign, IL: Human Kinetics Books.

Herbst, S., & Davies, A. (2014, April 23). To quote the experts. Retrieved January 18, 2015, from http://sandraherbst.blogspot.com/2014/04/to-quote-experts.html

Hodgen, J., & Wiliam, D. (2006). *Mathematics inside the black box: Assessment for learning in the mathematics classroom.* London, UK: NFER-Nelson.

Hong, Y.-y., Chiu, C.-y., Dweck, C. S., Lin, D. M. S., & Wan, W. (1999). Implicit theories, attributions, and coping: A meaning system approach. *Journal of Personality and Social Psychology, 77*(3), 588–599. doi:10.1037/0022-3514.77.3.588

Howard, J. (1991). *Getting smart: The social construction of intelligence.* Waltham, MA: Efficacy Institute.

Howard-Jones, P. (2014). *Neuroscience and education: A review of educational interventions and approaches informed by neuroscience.* London, UK: Education Endowment Foundation.

Hunter, M. (1982). *Mastery teaching.* El Segundo, CA: Tip.

Jackson, R. R. (2009). *Never work harder than your students, and other principles of great teaching.* Alexandria, VA: ASCD.

Johnson, D. W., Johnson, R. T., & Smith, K. A. (1998). Cooperative learning returns to college: What evidence is there that it works? *Change: The Magazine of Higher Learning, 30*(4), 26–35. doi:10.1080/00091389809602629

Johnson, R. T., & Johnson, D. W. (1994). An overview of cooperative learning. In J. S. Thousand, R. A. Villa, & A. I. Nevin (Eds.), *Creativity and collaborative learning: A practical guide to empowering students and teachers* (pp. 31–44). Baltimore, MD: Paul H. Brookes.

Kagan, S., & Kagan, M. (2009). *Kagan cooperative learning.* San Clemente, CA: Kagan.

Keeley, P. (2012). *Science formative assessment: 75 practical strategies for linking assessment, instruction, and learning.* Thousand Oaks, CA: Corwin.

Kerr, R., & Booth, B. (1978). Specific and varied practice of motor skill. *Perceptual and Motor Skills, 46*(2), 395– 401.

Kluger, A. N., & DeNisi, A. (1996). The effects of feedback interventions on performance: A historical review, a meta-analysis, and a preliminary feedback intervention theory. *Psychological Bulletin, 119*(2), 254–284.

Kobrin, J. L., Camara, W. J., & Milewski, G. B. (2002). *The utility of the SAT-I and SAT-II for admissions decisions in California and the nation.* New York, NY: College Board.

Kohn, A. (1994). Grading: The issue is not how but why. *Educational Leadership, 52*(2), 38–41.

Kohn, A. (2006). The trouble with rubrics. *English Journal, 95*(4), 12–15.

Köller, O. (2005). Formative assessment in classrooms: A review of the empirical German literature. In J. Looney (Ed.), *Formative assessment: Improving learning in secondary classrooms* (pp. 265–279). Paris, France: Organisation for Economic Co-operation and Development.

Kulhavy, R. W. (1977). Feedback in written instruction. *Review of Educational Research, 47*(2), 211–232.

Lave, J. (1988). *Cognition in practice: Mind, mathematics and culture in everyday life.* Cambridge, UK: Cambridge University Press.

Leahy, S., Lyon, C., Thompson, M., & Wiliam, D. (2005). Classroom assessment: Minute-by-minute and day-by-day. *Educational Leadership, 63*(3), 18–24.

Leahy, S., & Wiliam, D. (2011). *Devising learning progressions.* Paper presented at the Annual meeting of the American Educational Research Association, San Francisco, CA.

Lee, T. D., & Carnahan, H. (1990). Bandwidth knowledge of results and motor learning: More than just a relative frequency effect. *Quarterly Journal of Experimental Psychology Section A, 42*(4), 777–789. doi:10.1080/14640749008401249

Lemov, D. (2010). *Teach like a champion: 49 techniques that put students on the path to college.* San Francisco, CA: Jossey-Bass.

Lemov, D., Woolway, E., & Yezzi, K. (2012). *Practice perfect: 42 rules for getting better at getting better.* San Francisco, CA: Jossey-Bass.

Lenth, R. V. (2006, August 14). Java applets for power and sample size. Retrieved April 20, 2015, from http://homepage.stat.uiowa.edu/~rlenth/Power/

Liem, G. A. D., Ginns, P., Martin, A. J., & Stone, B. (2012). Personal best goals and academic and social functioning: A longitudinal perspective. *Learning and Instruction, 22*(3), 222–230.

Linnenbrink, E. A. (2005). The dilemma of performance-approach goals: The use of multiple goal contexts to promote students' motivation and learning. *Journal of Educational Psychology, 97*(2), 197–213.

Livingstone, R. W. (1941). *The future in education.* Cambridge, UK: Cambridge University Press.

Longhurst, N., & Norton, L. S. (1997). Self-assessment in coursework essays. *Studies in Educational Evaluation, 23*(4), 319–330. doi:10.1016/S0191-491X(97)86213-X

Lowe, G. (1980). State-dependent recall decrements with moderate doses of alcohol. *Current Psychological Research, 1*(1), 3–8.

Lyon, C. J., Wylie, E. C., & Goe, L. (2006). *Changing teachers, changing schools.* Paper presented at the annual meeting of the American Educational Research Association, San Francisco, CA.

Maher, J., & Wiliam, D. (2007, April). *Keeping learning on track in new teacher induction.* Paper presented at the Annual meeting of the American Educational Research Association, Chicago, IL.

Marzano, R. J., Kendall, J. S., & Gaddy, B. B. (1999). *Essential knowledge: The debate over what American students should know.* Denver, CO: McREL.

Matthews, R. S., Cooper, J. L., Davidson, N., & Hawkes, P. (1995). Building bridges between cooperative and collaborative learning. *Change: The Magazine of Higher Learning, 27*(4), 35–40. doi:10.1080/00091389809602629

McMillan, J. H. (Ed.). (2013). *SAGE handbook of research on classroom assessment* (2nd ed.). Thousand Oaks, CA: SAGE.

Mehan, H. (1979). "What time is it, Denise?": Asking known information questions in classroom discourse. *Theory into Practice, 28*(4), 285–294.

Mehta, R., & Zhu, R. J. (2009). Blue or red? Exploring the effect of color on cognitive performance. In A. L. McGill & S. Shavitt (Eds.), *North American Advances in Consumer Research* (Vol. 36, pp. 1045–1046). Duluth, MN: Association for Consumer Research.

Mercer, N., Dawes, L., Wegerif, R., & Sams, C. (2004). Reasoning as a scientist: Ways of helping children to use language to learn science. *British Educational Research Journal, 30*(3), 359–377.

Meyer, J., & Land, R. (2003). *Threshold concepts and troublesome knowledge: Linkages to ways of thinking and practising within the disciplines.* Edinburgh, UK: University of Edinburgh School of Education.

Minstrell, J. (1992). Facets of students' knowledge and relevant instruction. In R. Duit, F. M. Goldberg, & H. Niedderer (Eds.), *Research in physics learning: Theoretical issues and empirical studies (Proceedings of an international workshop held at the University of Bremen, March 4–8, 1991)* (pp. 110–128). Kiel, Germany: Institut für die Pädagogik der Naturwissenschaften an der Universität Kiel.

Mullet, H. G., Butler, A. C., Verdin, B., von Borries, R., & Marsh, E. J. (2014). Delaying feedback promotes transfer of knowledge despite student preferences to receive feedback immediately. *Journal of Applied Research in Memory and Cognition, 3*(3), 222–229. doi:10.1016/j.jarmac.2014.05.001

Mullis, G. (Ed.). (2011). *Students as lesson observers and learning partners: CD resource pack.* London, UK: Specialist Schools and Academies Trust.

Munns, G., Sawyer, W., & Cole, B. (Eds.). (2013). *Exemplary teachers of students in poverty.* Abingdon, UK: Routledge.

Munns, G., & Woodward, H. (2006). Student engagement and student self assessment: The REAL framework. *Assessment in Education: Principles, Policy & Practice, 13*(2), 193–213. doi:10.1080/09695940600703969

National Curriculum History Working Group. (1990). *Final report.* London, UK: Her Majesty's Stationery Office.

Natriello, G. (1987). The impact of evaluation processes on students. *Educational Psychologist, 22*(2), 155–175.

Naylor, S., & Naylor, B. (2000). *Concept cartoons in science education.* Sandbach, UK: Millgate House Education.

Novak, J. D. (1977). *A theory of education.* Ithaca, NY: Cornell University Press.

NTI Social Studies. (2014). The five big ideas of social studies. *Wikispaces.* Retrieved October 15, 2014, from http://ntisocialstudies.wikispaces.com/The+Five+Big+Ideas+of+Social+Studies

Nunes, T., Carraher, D. W., & Schliemann, A. D. (1993). *Street mathematics and school mathematics*. Cambridge, UK: Cambridge University Press.

Nyquist, J. B. (2003). *The benefits of reconstructing feedback as a larger system of formative assessment: A meta-analysis* (Unpublished master's thesis). Vanderbilt University, Nashville, TN.

Osborne, J. (2011). *Why assessment matters*. Paper presented at the Annual conference of the Science Community Representing Education, London, UK. www.score-education.org/media/6606/purposejo.pdf

Paixao, L. (2014, October 29). *Embedded formative assessment: Great book!* October 29. Retrieved November 3, 2013, from http://lianepaixao.wordpress.com/2013/10/29/embedded-formative-assessment-great-book/

Panitz, T. (1999). *Collaborative versus cooperative learning: A comparison of the two concepts which will help us understand the underlying nature of interactive learning*. Retrieved October 24, 2014, from http://files.eric.ed.gov/fulltext/ED448443.pdf

Perkins, D. (1999). The many faces of constructivism. *Educational Leadership, 57*(3), 6–11.

Popham, W. J., Keller, T., Moulding, B., Pellegrino, J. W., & Sandifer, P. (2005). Instructionally supportive accountability tests in science: A viable assessment option? *Measurement: Interdisciplinary Research and Perspectives, 3*(3), 121–179.

Propel. (n.d.). *Social studies big ideas*. Retrieved October 15, 2014, from www.coedu.usf.edu/main/departments/seced/Propel/PROPELSSE/PropelSSEBigIdeas.htm

Raychaudhuri, S. (1988). Self assessment. *English in Education, 22*(3), 12.

Reeves, J., McCall, J., & MacGilchrist, B. (2001). Change leadership: Planning, conceptualization and perception. In J. MacBeath & P. Mortimore (Eds.), *Improving school effectiveness* (pp. 122–137). Buckingham, UK: Open University Press.

Ritchhart, R., & Perkins, D. (2008). Making thinking visible. *Educational Leadership, 65*(5), 57–61.

Roberts, R. (Producer). (2014, September 15). *Elizabeth Green on education and building a better teacher*. EconTalk Episode with Elizabeth Green. Retrieved from www.econtalk.org/archives/2014/09/elizabeth_green.html

Robins, R. W., & Pals, J. L. (2002). Implicit self-theories in the academic domain: Implications for goal orientation, attributions, affect, and self-esteem change. *Self and Identity, 1*(4), 313–336.

Rolland, R. G. (2012). Synthesizing the evidence on classroom goal structures in middle and secondary schools: A meta-analysis and narrative review. *Review of Educational Research, 82*(4), 396–435. doi: 10.3102/0034654312464909

Ross, S. (1998). Self-assessment in second language testing: A meta-analysis and analysis of experiential factors. *Language Testing, 15*(1), 1–20. doi:10.1177/026553229801500101

Rowe, M. B. (1974a). Wait time and rewards as instructional variables, their influence on language, learning and fate control. *Journal of Research in Science Teaching, 11*(2), 81–94.

Rowe, M. B. (1974b). Wait time and rewards as instructional variables, their influence on language, learning and fate control: Part II, Rewards. *Journal of Research in Science Teaching, 11*(4), 291–308.

Ruiz-Primo, M. A., & Li, M. (2013). Examining formative feedback in the classroom context: New research perspectives. In J. H. McMillan (Ed.), *SAGE handbook of research on classroom assessment* (2nd ed., pp. 215–232). Thousand Oaks, CA: SAGE.

Ryan, R. M., & Connell, J. P. (1989). Perceived locus of causality and internalization: Examining reasons for acting in two domains. *Journal of Personality and Social Psychology, 57*(5), 749–761.

Ryan, R. M., & Deci, E. L. (2000). Intrinsic and extrinsic motivations: Classic definitions and new directions. *Contemporary Educational Psychology, 25*, 54–67.

Sadler, P. M. (1998). Psychometric models of student conceptions in science: Reconciling qualitative studies and distractor-driven assessment instruments. *Journal of Research in Science Teaching, 35*(3), 265–296. doi:10.1002/(SICI) 1098-2736(199803)35:3<265::AID-TEA3>3.0.CO;2-P

Saunders, W. M., Goldenberg, C. N., & Gallimore, R. (2009). Increasing achievement by focusing grade level teams on improving classroom learning: A prospective, quasi-experimental study of Title 1 schools. *American Educational Research Journal, 46*(4), 1006–1033.

Senko, C., Durik, A. M., Patel, L., Lovejoy, C. M., & Valentiner, D. (2013). Performance-approach goal effects on achievement under low versus high challenge conditions. *Learning and Instruction, 23*(1), 60–68. doi:10.1016/j.learninstruc.2012.05.006

Shulman, L. S. (2005, February). The signature pedagogies of the professions of law, medicine, engineering, and the clergy: Potential lessons for the education of teachers. In the Math Science Partnerships (MSP) Workshop, *Teacher education for effective teaching and learning.* National Research Council Center for Education, Irvine, CA.

Shute, V. J. (2008). Focus on formative feedback. *Review of Educational Research, 78*(1), 153–189.

Skipper, Y., & Douglas, K. (2012). Is no praise good praise? Effects of positive feedback on children's and university students' responses to subsequent failures. *British Journal of Educational Psychology, 82*(4), 327–339. doi:10.1111/j.2044-8279.2011.02028.x

Slamecka, N., & Graf, P. (1978). The generation effect: Delineation of a phenomenon. *Journal of Experimental Psychology: Learning, Memory, and Cognition, 14*, 592–604.

Slavin, R. E., Hurley, E. A., & Chamberlain, A. M. (2003). Cooperative learning and achievement. In W. M. Reynolds & G. J. Miller (Eds.), *Handbook of psychology: Vol. 7. Educational psychology* (pp. 177–198). Hoboken, NJ: Wiley.

Smith, P. J. K., Taylor, S. J., & Withers, K. (1997). Applying bandwidth feedback scheduling to a golf shot. *Research Quarterly for Exercise and Sport, 68*(3), 215–221.

Smith, S. M., Glenberg, A. M., & Bjork, R. A. (1978). Environmental context and human memory. *Memory and Cognition, 6*(4), 342–353.

Spendlove, D. (2009). *Putting assessment for learning into practice.* London, UK: Continuum.

Spradbery, J. (1976). Conservative pupils? Pupil resistance to curriculum innovation in mathematics. In M. F. D. Young & G. Whitty (Eds.), *Explorations into the politics of school knowledge* (pp. 236–243). Driffield, UK: Nafferton.

Springer, M. G., Ballou, D., Hamilton, L., Le, V.-N., Lockwood, J. R., McCaffrey, D., . . . Stecher, B. M. (2010). *Teacher pay for performance: Experimental evidence from the project on incentives in teaching.* Nashville, TN: National Center on Performance Incentives at Vanderbilt University.

Stone, D., & Heen, S. (2014). *Thanks for the feedback: The science and art of receiving feedback.* New York, NY: Penguin.

Svenson, O. (1981). Are we all less risky and more skillful than our fellow drivers? *Acta Psychologica, 47*(2), 143–148.

Swan, M. (1978). *The language of graphs: A collection of teaching materials.* Nottingham, UK: University of Nottingham Shell Centre for Mathematical Education.

Thomas, T., & Wiliam, D. (Writers), & E. Hardy (Director). (2010). The classroom experiment (part 1) [TV]. In D. Barry (Producer), *The classroom experiment.* London, England: BBC TV.

Thompson, M., & Goe, L. (2008). *Models of effective and scalable teacher professional development* (Vol. RR-09-07). Princeton, NJ: Educational Testing Service.

Tversky, A. (1964). On the optimal number of alternatives at a choice point. *Journal of Mathematical Psychology, 1*(2), 386–391.

Tyler, R. W. (1949). *Basic principles of curriculum and instruction.* Chicago, IL: University of Chicago Press.

van Yperen, N. W., Elliot, A. J., & Anseel, F. (2009). The influence of mastery-avoidance goals on performance improvement. *European Journal of Social Psychology, 39*(6), 932–943. doi:10.1002/ejsp.590

Wagner, L. (1990). Social and historical perspectives on peer teaching in education. In H. C. Foot, M. J. Morgan, & R. H. Shute (Eds.), *Children helping children* (pp. 21–42). Chichester, UK: Wiley.

Wainer, H. (2011). *Uneducated guesses: Using evidence to uncover misguided education policies.* Princeton, NJ: Princeton University Press.

Walsh, J. A., & Sattes, B. D. (2011). *Thinking through quality questions: Deepening student engagement.* Thousand Oaks, CA: Corwin.

Wiggins, G., & McTighe, J. (2000). *Understanding by design.* New York, NY: Prentice Hall.

Wiliam, D. (2006a). Assessment: Learning communities can use it to engineer a bridge connecting teaching and learning. *Journal of Staff Development, 27*(1), 16–20.

Wiliam, D. (2006b). The half-second delay: What follows? *Pedagogy, Culture and Society, 14*(1), 71–81.

Wiliam, D. (2007a). Content then process: Teacher learning communities in the service of formative assessment. In D. B. Reeves (Ed.), *Ahead of the curve: The power of assessment to transform teaching and learning* (pp. 183–204). Bloomington, IN: Solution Tree.

Wiliam, D. (2007b). Keeping learning on track: Classroom assessment and the regulation of learning. In F. K. Lester Jr. (Ed.), *Second handbook of mathematics teaching and learning* (pp. 1053–1098). Greenwich, CT: Information Age.

Wiliam, D. (2011a). *Embedded formative assessment.* Bloomington, IN: Solution Tree.

Wiliam, D. (2011b). What is assessment for learning? *Studies in Educational Evaluation, 37*(1), 2–14.

Wiliam, D., & Leahy, S. (2014). *Embedding formative assessment professional development pack.* West Palm Beach, FL: Learning Sciences International.

Wiliam, D., Lee, C., Harrison, C., & Black, P. J. (2004). Teachers developing assessment for learning: Impact on student achievement. *Assessment in Education: Principles Policy and Practice, 11*(1), 49–65.

Wiliam, D., & Thompson, M. (2008). Integrating assessment with instruction: What will it take to make it work? In C. A. Dwyer (Ed.), *The future of assessment: Shaping teaching and learning* (pp. 53–82). Mahwah, NJ: Erlbaum.

Willingham, D. T. (2009). *Why don't students like school: A cognitive scientist answers questions about how the mind works and what it means for your classroom.* San Francisco, CA: Jossey-Bass.

Wilson, G. (1999). The grammar school master. In G. Wilson (Ed.), *Mickey Braddock's works do and other stories* (pp. 89–100). Disley, UK: Millrace Books.

Wilson, S. M., & Berne, J. (1999). Teacher learning and the acquisition of professional knowledge: An examination of research on contemporary professional development. In A. Iran-Nejad & P. D. Pearson (Eds.), *Review of research in education* (Vol. 24, pp. 173–209). Washington, DC: American Educational Research Association.

Winner, E. (1996). The rage to master: The decisive case for talent in the visual arts. In K. A. Ericsson (Ed.), *The road to excellence: The acquisition of expert performance in the arts and sciences, sports and games* (pp. 271–301). Hillsdale, NJ: Erlbaum.

Wylie, E. C., Lyon, C. J., & Goe, L. (2009). *Teacher professional development focused on formative assessment: Changing teachers, changing schools* (Vol. RR-09-10). Princeton, NJ: Educational Testing Service.

Wylie, E. C., Lyon, C. J., & Mavronikolas, E. (2008). Effective and scalable teacher professional development: A report of the formative research and development (Vol. RR-08-65). Princeton, NJ: Educational Testing Service.

Yeager, D. S., Purdie-Vaughns, V., Garcia, J., Apfel, N., Brzustoski, P., Master, A., . . . Cohen, G. L. (2013). Breaking the cycle of mistrust: Wise interventions to provide critical feedback across the racial divide. *Journal of Experimental Psychology: General, 143*(2), 804–824. doi:10.1037/a0033906

Index

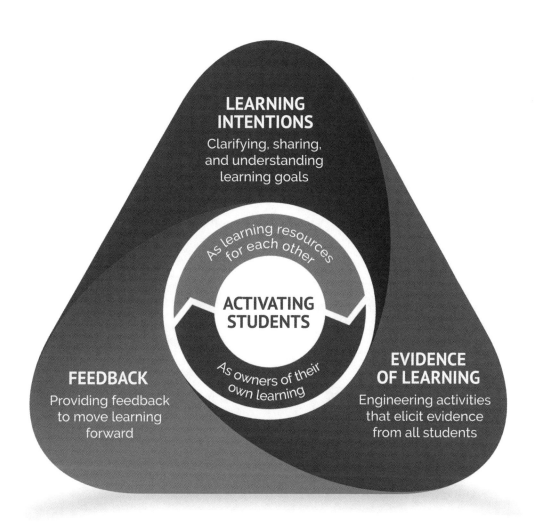

STRATEGIC
FORMATIVE|ASSESSMENT
Less Testing. **More Evidence. Better Learning.**

For more information, contact the Learning Sciences Dylan Wiliam Center
www.DylanWiliamCenter.com